LORD HERVEY AND HIS FRIENDS

Other Volumes Edited by The Earl of Ilchester

THE HOME OF THE HOLLANDS, 1605–1820

CHRONICLES OF HOLLAND HOUSE, 1820–1900

LADY ELIZABETH HOLLAND TO HER SON, 1821–1846

LETTERS OF LADY SARAH LENNOX
(with Mary, Countess of Ilchester)

HENRY FOX, FIRST LORD HOLLAND

FURTHER MEMOIRS OF THE WHIG PARTY

Ranelagh Barret, pinxit, after W. Hogarth, at Ickworth, circ. 1737.

LORD HERVEY AND HIS FRIENDS

Rev. P. Willemin	Stephen Fox, later Lord Ilchester	Henry Fox, later Lord Holland	John, Lord Hervey	Charles, 3rd D. of Marlborough	Thos. Winningto[n]

Frontispiece

LORD HERVEY AND HIS FRIENDS

1726–38

BASED ON LETTERS FROM
HOLLAND HOUSE, MELBURY, AND ICKWORTH

Edited by the
EARL OF ILCHESTER, G.B.E., D.Litt., F.S.A.

LONDON
JOHN MURRAY, ALBEMARLE STREET, W.

First Edition . . . 1950

Made and Printed in Great Britain by Butler & Tanner Ltd., Frome and London

CONTENTS

ILLUSTRATIONS

PREFACE

THE first mention of Lord Hervey's *Memoirs* occurs in Horace Walpole's *Catalogue of the Royal and Noble Authors of England*, 1758 (ii. 143): "Memoirs from his first coming to Court, to the death of the Queen". This embraces the years 1727 to 1737, a period almost exactly covered by his letters which I am printing in this volume. In 1788, Lord Hailes[1] published *The Opinions of Sarah, Dowager-Duchess of Marlborough*, in which he mentioned the *Memoirs*. "I have reason to believe they are written with great freedom. And here I must be permitted to observe, that they who suppress such memorials of modern times, do all that in them lies to leave the history of the eighteenth century in darkness. In the sixteenth century, it was the fashion to preserve original papers; during the eighteenth it is the fashion to destroy them. Hence we know more of the reign of Queen Elizabeth than we do of the reign of George I." In his preface, too, Lord Hailes had written on Duchess Sarah:—"In treating of George II, she spoke the language of her own times. There are who remember the early part of that reign, and they will not see anything new or singular in her animadversions and sarcasms. That which, in our more liberal age, would be considered as bare invective and scurrility, was the popular language of those times, re-echoed from the pampheteers and hawkers to disappointed and angry politicians."

At Lord Hervey's death in 1743, his papers—the Memoirs, and a great deal, if not all, of the other material now at Ickworth, passed to his eldest son, George William (1721–73), who became 2nd Earl of Bristol in January, 1750–1, and died unmarried. His brother, Augustus John (1724–79), 3rd Earl, the husband of the bigamous Duchess of Kingston, only left illegitimate children. He alienated all in his power from the family; and his son, Augustus Henry, by Kitty Hunter (Mrs. Clarke) received the manuscripts as well as an annuity. The 3rd Earl laid down in

[1] Sir David Dalrymple, Lord Hailes (1726–92), a Scottish Judge, whose publications on various subjects were voluminous and interesting.

his will that his father's Memoirs were not to be published in the lifetime of George III, a very praiseworthy proviso. He further appointed that, " they were not to be given, lent or loaned to his brother Frederic." [1] The manuscripts next passed back to the legitimate family, to another brother, General the Hon. William Hervey (b. 1732), and at his death they reverted to the Bishop's eldest son, Frederick William (1769–1859), 5th Earl and 1st Marquess.

There seems to be no doubt at all that the 1st Marquess was the person who was instrumental in the destruction or suppression of numerous passages in the original manuscript of the Memoirs, both short and long. At what date the excisions were made, it is impossible to say. Lord Bristol gave leave, seemingly about the year 1845, to John Wilson Croker, a well-known politician and writer on the Tory side, closely connected with the *Quarterly Review*, to edit the Memoirs, when all chance of offending the susceptibilities of anyone connected with those times had completely disappeared ; for all were long dead. Yet the conditions laid upon Croker to cut out everything which might be considered indecent or coarse, with alterations and omissions, " intended to remove every expression positively offensive to a delicate mind," were clearly of the utmost stringency ; for he attempted to minimise in his preface the importance of the excerpts, and never allowed himself to express any regret for the loss of missing material, with one exception only, a " chasm " in the Memoirs, which deprives the reader of information on a very important period covering more than two whole years, 1730–2.

Soon after Croker commenced work, he got wind of the fact that General Hervey had made a transcript of the Memoirs in the year 1781 ; and that at the General's death, this had been sent to King George IV. New hopes of fresh material were raised ; and with the consent of the family he wrote to the King's executor, the 1st Duke of Wellington, to ask if the whereabouts of the document was known. It could not be found ; although the Duke had all steps taken for a search to be made in the Royal Archives, at that time stored at Apsley House. Indeed, it was

[1] Frederick Augustus (1730–1803), later 4th Earl and Bishop of Derry.

not till the year 1931, that the papers were discovered, and were then sent to Windsor by the 4th Duke. Nearly a hundred pages of new matter thus came to light when the copy was thoroughly examined, including speeches, etc. which Croker had chosen to omit from his original edition in 1848. A three volume edition, unaltered, had seen light in 1884, long after Croker's death in 1857.

In 1931 Mr. Romney Sedgwick embarked on a new and largely unexpurgated edition. He had the assistance of the present Marquess of Bristol, and was allowed to read the manuscript. He saw the volume of copies of Lord Hervey's letters at Ickworth, to which I shall duly refer, and which have been of inestimable value to me in this volume. He had also access by my permission to Hervey's letters to Henry Fox, which were then at Holland House. But when he came to count up the advantages which had accrued from the discovery of the manuscripts at Apsley House, they proved disappointing. The portion which covered May 1730 to the late summer of 1732 was still missing; although there was every indication that it had been written. General Hervey made no allusion to this long gap, although he did mention the probable loss of a few sheets later on in the manuscript. From this, it would appear probable that it was intact in his day. The whole evidence, therefore, points to the fact that the first Marquess was responsible for the destruction of those precious pages, and that he had taken care that they should not survive in a copy. Mr. Sedgwick suggests that one of his reasons for such drastic action was a wish to hush up the scandal which led to the breach between Frederick, Prince of Wales and Lord Hervey.[1] To some extent this may have been the case; but after reading Hervey's rather pathetic lines[2] to Stephen Fox on December 25, 1731, I cannot agree with him that the chief cause of Hervey's anger "was being supplanted in Frederick's favours by Miss Vane", the former's late mistress. Whether or not the Prince had disregarded the elementary rules of good fellowship and good friendship, had knowingly gone out of his way to cut out Hervey in the lady's transient affections, and had taken her to his own bed and keeping seems

[1] *Egmont* and *Carlisle* (*Hist. MSS. Com.*). [2] *See* pp. 75, 128.

uncertain. But that clearly was Hervey's view. The stories of his struggles to remain in favour with Frederick are somewhat unconvincing, and come from tainted sources, Lady Irvine and Colonel Schutz—i.e. anti-Walpole.

So much for the *Memoirs*, a background which is necessary for the consideration of Hervey's letters, especially as the volume of Ickworth copies must have passed with all the other papers. I now come to those presented in this volume. They cover the same years; with the addition of a few in 1726, and a few in 1738 which refer to the Queen's death and to her epitaphs, one of which Hervey undertook to write at the King's request, and which have been largely overlooked. Hervey's handwriting is good, and therefore easy to read.

Lord Hervey's letters are drawn from four distinct and different sources. The original publication which I had in mind was a series of Lord Hervey's letters at Melbury to his adored friend, Stephen Fox, afterwards created Lord Ilchester; together with a larger collection in the Holland House papers, now also moved to Melbury, addressed to the youngest Fox brother, Henry, later 1st Lord Holland.

These sources, however, interesting as many of the letters are, proved to be of too scattered and disjointed a nature to constitute a satisfactory volume by themselves. I took upon myself, therefore, to approach Ickworth. I found that the present Lord Bristol, in the kindness of his heart, was again willing to cooperate: and he has allowed me the full use of the aforementioned and most important volume of copies of Lord Hervey's letters to various correspondents.

For the most part they too are written to the Fox brothers; but besides these there are a few to their sister Mrs. Charlotte Digby: as well as eight or ten of great interest, to Frederick, Prince of Wales, before the collapse of their friendship: a few to Dr. Middleton: to Bishop Hoadly: to the second Duke of Richmond: and to his mother, Lady Bristol. These copies are chiefly (the earlier ones entirely so) in the same handwriting, and are contained in ten small folios, now bound together. Amongst these copies are those of certain originals which are now at Melbury, Holland House and Goodwood; but the proportion is small. The greater number constitute fresh material, of which originals do not appear to remain in being. The most remarkable feature of the collection is that they are annotated by Lord Hervey with his own pen. Here and there he inserted dates, and the names of the recipients of the letters; he added explanations of names in cipher, and also made corrections and additions throughout. They commence, in 1726, with a number of letters to Henry Fox, a year earlier than the commencement of the Melbury series to his elder brother Stephen; an interesting proof that Hervey's first contact with the family was through the youngest brother. Very fortunately, this new influx of material dovetails into my own letters most conveniently; and a far more regular sequence is thus created. Further, *and this is of immense importance*, the number of letters is strongest in the years 1730 to 1732, when for reasons which we have already discussed, the *Memoirs* fail us.

I find it difficult to explain the reason for this volume of copies. We know that Lord Hervey wished his *Memoirs* to be published.[1] Were these replicas of his letters simply intended as an assistance in the work of writing the *Memoirs*, the commencement of which task Mr. Sedgwick places about 1733? This is a possible explanation; but is it not more probable that he intended that they also should be given to the public? He would hardly in the former case have gone to the trouble of explaining his own cipher names. I have noted these alterations in every case, as their significance seems of some importance.

Finally, a quite unexpected windfall was brought to my notice by Sir John Murray—a packet of Lord Hervey's letters to Count Algarotti, the friend of Voltaire and of Frederick the Great. These came to light in his own collection of manuscripts at 50 Albemarle Street; and he has very kindly allowed me to make use of them for this book. Unfortunately, the greater part are too late in date to be helpful, being after 1738; but several of the earlier ones fit very neatly into the general series, and are therefore of real value. My best thanks are due to him for the permission.

The reader will realise, when he comes to the later pages of

[1] *See Memoirs*, ed. Sedgwick, pp. 2, 363.

this volume, that a certain number of notes are referred to, as in the writing of Horace Walpole, who had by then succeeded as 4th Earl of Orford. The inclusion of these holograph comments requires some explanation. Apparently Henry Richard, 3rd Lord Holland, lent his packet of Hervey's letters to Lord Orford in the last few months of the latter's life. Horace made a few short entries on slips of paper, as he read ; and these were subsequently cut up by Lord Holland and pasted on to the appropriate letters when bound together. In letters to Anne, 2nd Countess of Upper Ossory,[1] Walpole had before this answered several questions which Lord Holland, then a young man of twenty-three, had asked her to put to him. He complained of a failing memory and preferred not to reply on paper. "I should be forming a *chronique scandaleuse*, and not a very delicate one, were I to answer all the queries which relate to the principle performer, Lord Hervey. Still *his* history (*with whom*, and with much of which I was well acquainted) was so curious, that I begged Lord Macartney,[2] to tell Lord Holland that, if he will honour me with his company for half an hour . . . I shall satisfy his curiosity as briefly as I can contrive to do, and without a tittle of invention, which at 79 I assure him I do not possess." In all probability the letters were handed to Walpole at that meeting ; though no actual record of it remains. Horace Walpole's handwriting in the notes is certainly that of the last years of his life.

A serious problem next arises, as to what passages in the letters should for various reasons be omitted from publication. There are certainly a number of no special interest in the early portion of the series, with which I part without regret. There are also a number of long declarations of friendship for the Fox brothers, and of even more sloppy sentiment, which may well be dispensed with, as they become boring from repetition. There are long dissertations to Dr. Middleton, some of which have seen light : and references to Roman history in his later correspondence with Henry Fox, which would be tedious for the reader. But as to

[1] Sept. 17, 30, 1796.

[2] George, 1st Earl Macartney (1737–1806), a close friend of the Fox family. Tutor and bear-leader to Stephen Fox (later 2nd Lord Holland for a few months) when abroad in early life.

the text generally, with the above exceptions, I must confess that my policy throughout has been to remove as little as possible. It is perfectly clear that in writing to his intimates, Hervey was accustomed to let himself go to any length. He spoke out his mind very freely, and did not care much what he said, or what language he used. He often wrote in a joking strain, and his ebullitions therefore must not always be taken too seriously or too literally! Consequently, he was often wont to express himself in the coarse vein which was so prevalent in his age, as we have seen in Lord Hailes's comments. To eliminate too much, therefore, would be to give an entirely false picture of the man and of his times. Nor do I think that we, in these days can afford to throw stones; considering the modern tendency in a certain class of our writings to immodesty and even lewdness.

Moreover, many of Hervey's letters are of special historical importance, for they give us one of the very few reliable accounts of the doings at King George II's Court, excluding the *Memoirs*, to which they can be taken as supplemental. The dearth of information of any kind regarding that decade is very marked. Few of Lady Mary Wortley-Montagu's letters survive. We have some of Lady Suffolk's correspondence it is true, and of Lady Sundon's, neither of them of great importance. In the *Hist. MSS. Com.* series, Lord Perceval's diary in the *Egmont Papers* gives some political debates, some account of current events, and some scattered social gossip; and there are also the *Carlisle Papers* on similar lines. We have Coxe's various *Lives* of the Walpoles, and Horace Walpole's *Recollections*, which were not at that period founded on personal observation. But on the whole, the early years of George II's reign are singularly devoid of episodical detail; and any additional information, especially from first hand, of the day to day life in country houses, and at St. James, Hampton Court, Windsor and elsewhere, as well as of Court gossip and intrigue, must be welcomed as a new light on that important era in English history, which preceded the foundation of the British Colonial Empire.

Naturally I have felt bound to eliminate some short passages which are definitely unpublishable, as well as one or two references which might upset private susceptibilities. Yet in reality they are but few ; and I have refrained from cutting out any more than what seems to me absolutely necessary. In the case of several passages relating to incidents or scandals at Foreign Courts, I have been guided by whether they have already appeared in print. Such is the story of the marriage of the Princess of Holstein (Countess Rosinska) : a lurid tale which has been fully detailed and documented by Thomas Carlyle, in his *Frederick the Great,* though under a different name, Orzelska. Of this Hervey gives an amusing, if a thoroughly amoral narrative.

To turn next to events nearer home, Pulteney's attacks on Hervey, which led up to their duel on a snowy morning in the Park, seem comparatively venial, when we come later on to consider Pope's onslaught on Hervey and Lady Mary Wortley-Montagu. The story of the duel finds no place in these letters ; but from contemporary accounts [1] we find that Hervey's reputation was greatly enhanced in public opinion by the fact that he issued the challenge. Henry Fox was his second.

But the subsequent recriminations with Pope, for which all parties were at fault, led up to such an unpleasant situation as to require unpleasing explanations. In fact, to ape the common expressions in that age, we find ourselves delving into positive manure heaps. For not content with leaving the victim to Pope, his followers the hackwriters of the *Craftsman* type, made full use of their patron's scurrilities, to continue the chase in the broadsheets which they took upon themselves to issue. In the opinion of the recognised authorities on Pope's works, Professor J. E. Butt, and the late Mr. Norman Ault, to whom I am deeply indebted for constant assistance on these subjects shortly before his recent and untimely death, he seldom repeated his malicious phrases. Three copies in manuscript of broadsheets, therefore, which I found lurking amongst Henry Fox's papers, sent to him by Hervey himself, cannot be ascribed to the poet. I have, however, placed them in the Appendices. One, " Lord Hervey's First Speech in the House of Lords " is apparently unique, whilst two others, " Horace to Barine," imitating Book ii, Od. 8, and " An apology for printing The Nobleman's Epistle ", are only repre-

[1] *Carlisle Papers. Hist. MSS. Com.* (Lady Irvine, to her father, 3rd Lord Carlisle, p. 80.)

sented by one printed copy of each in the Bodleian Library, and are therefore almost unknown. I cannot find them in the British Museum, but that is not to say that they are not there in some form ; and there may be copies at Ickworth. The better known *Tit for Tat*, in its reprint is not uncommon. But of its first edition, which was recalled owing to certain scurrilous lines on Queen Caroline and others (see p. 195), besides the Holland House version, only one printed sheet, and one copy in longhand, are in the British Museum, and as far as can be so far ascertained, there are none in the Bodleian. Far more valuable, however, than these, is a couplet on the same manuscript as the others, in Hervey's own handwriting, entitled "To Lord Hervey and Lady Mary Wortley, by Mr. Pope". These, according to the above-named authorities, can be definitely ascribed to Pope's own pen : and I have therefore included them in the main text as such.

Appendix A consists of the remainder of Hervey's long account to his wife of his return from Italy with Stephen Fox in 1729, part of which appears on p. 35.

In Appendix B, I have made use of two interesting letters, from Sarah, Duchess of Marlborough, which were at Holland House, to her great friend, my ancestress, Mrs. Strangways Horner : and a longer one to Henry Fox. They were written at the time of the old lady's quarrel with her grandson, Charles, 5th Earl of Sunderland (later 3rd Duke of Marlborough), when he announced his approaching marriage to Elizabeth Trevor (see p. 133). The subsequent crisis in the Spencer family made history ; and I feel that they may well be printed.

I have many acknowledgements of my deepest gratitude to make to those who have assisted me in this volume. First, as I have already stated, to Lord Bristol, without whose permission, indulgence and assistance it could not have been compiled. Also to Lady Bristol, for her great interest and help in the contents of the Ickworth papers of which her knowledge is far reaching ; as well as to her grandson the Hon. David Erskine, who has given much time and trouble in order to elucidate the problems of the Epitaphs which Lord Hervey wrote on Queen Caroline. Next to Sir John Murray, for allowing me to use his series of Hervey's letters to Count Algarotti. I have also to thank the late Mr. Norman Ault for much assistance regarding the Pope controversies; and also to Professor Butt for his judgments on the various documents submitted to him. Lord Bath also has allowed me to reproduce some lines from Pope's manuscript, "Six Maidens", which is at Longleat. My thanks are due to him, and to the Dukes of Richmond and Marlborough for leave to use the copyrights of letters. To Mr. Sedgwick for allowing me to quote from his edition of the *Memoirs*, and to Miss Dorothy Margaret Stuart for the use of her *Molly Lepell*. Also to Mr. Laurence Tanner, the Librarian of Westminster Abbey, and to Mr. C. J. Purnell and several members of the Staff of the London Library, for assistance in various problems which have arisen.

Finally, a word as to the arrangement of the text. The letters are printed chronologically, with connecting explanations, the elucidations of names and places being as far as possible reserved for the notes. Lord Hervey's special phraseology is retained for the most part; but spelling and punctuation has been revised. The location of individual letters is given in the notes—Holland House, Melbury, Ickworth, etc.; and Hervey's own alterations and corrections in the last-named series are noted. His explanations of names in cipher are given in square brackets.

ILCHESTER.

July 1950.

To whom can a history of such times be agreeable or entertaining, unless it be to such as look into Courts and Courtiers, Princes and Ministers with such curious eyes as virtuosos in microscopes examine flies and emmets, and are pleased with the dissected minute parts of animals, which in the gross herd they either do not regard, or observe with indifference and contempt?

(*Hervey's Memoirs*, ed. Sedgwick, p. 365.)

CHAPTER I

INTRODUCTORY

We have made it clear in the Preface that this volume has no pretensions to be considered as a biography of John, Lord Hervey. It consists of a series of letters brought together from three or four sources, chiefly addressed to the two brothers Stephen and Henry Fox, with the addition of a few others, to their sister Mrs. Digby, Frederick, Prince of Wales, Count Algarotti, etc. These introduce the reader to many incidents referring to the customs, life and manners of the Court of King George II, and to many individuals who were intimately associated with that régime. The letters should be read as supplemental to the *Memoirs*; for many small episodes are included, which are unnoticed in those pages: while many new references to politics, both at home and abroad, throw intimate side-lights on a period of English history which is singularly devoid of such records. The Ickworth copies are of especial importance in the years 1730–32, which, as we have already mentioned, are omitted from the *Memoirs*, whatever may be the explanation. The general period of our letters, running from 1728 to 1738, very closely corresponds with that of the *Memoirs*.

It is for the above reason that we do not propose to weary our readers with any detailed account of the Hervey family. Genealogical tables would be quite out of place in such a volume. But in any case, it is only to be expected that some preliminary remarks upon the parentage and family history of the principal actors on our stage should be inserted.

First and foremost amongst them we must deal with the writer of the letters. John, Lord Hervey was born in 1696. He was the eldest son of John, 1st Earl of Bristol, by his second wife. Lord Bristol himself was son of Sir Thomas Hervey, Kt., M.P. for Bury St. Edmunds, who died in 1694, having succeeded to the Ickworth and other Hervey properties from his elder brother, John Hervey. The future Earl of Bristol sat in the House of Commons for nine years, before he was raised to the peerage in 1703, as Baron Hervey, of Ickworth. He was promoted to the Earldom in 1719, for his services at the Hanoverian succession. Although steeped in the Whig tradition, Bristol took little active part in public life, from the fact that his interests lay more in the field of scholarship. Besides, he was by no means enamoured of Sir Robert Walpole's policy, both foreign and internal, and usually sided in private against him. His long life terminated in 1751, in his eighty-sixth year. His first wife was Isabella, daughter of Sir Robert Carr, of Sleaford, Lincolnshire. She died in 1693, after little more than four years of married life, leaving a son, Carr, and two daughters. In 1695 Hervey married again, this time Elizabeth, daughter of Sir Thomas Felton, of Playford, Suffolk; and ten sons and six daughters were born of their union. Lady Bristol died in 1741, at the age of sixty-four.

Carr Hervey, the son of the first marriage, born in 1691, sat in the House of Commons, 1713–22. He has been mentioned as the reputed father of the celebrated Horace Walpole. At his death a year later, his half-brother, the writer of these letters, succeeded to the courtesy title of Lord Hervey. Of his early life we have few details, beyond that he was educated at Westminster, and at Clare College, Cambridge. He was elected as Member for Bury St. Edmunds, in 1725, at a by-election, and followed Pulteney's banner as an opponent of Walpole. At King George I's death in 1727, however, when the new King turned definitely to Sir Robert, and the would-be First Minister, Sir Spencer Compton, proved his complete inefficiency for such a post, Hervey turned his coat, and was rewarded by a pension of £1,000 a year. His growing devotion to Queen Caroline dated from about the same period. Three years later, after a final break with Pulteney, which both his wife and father strove to prevent, he was appointed to a Vice-Chamberlainship. This threw him more than ever into close and confidential relations with the Queen; whilst his increasing intimacy with Walpole made him the connecting link in a combination of Queen and Minister, who were setting themselves to administer the affairs of State. The existence of this coalition was quite unknown to the King, who imagined that he was running everything for himself.

Queen Caroline remained Hervey's lodestar until the day of

her untimely and unnecessary death late in 1737. She was a woman of great character, true and straightforward, but imbued throughout with the feeling that England was in her keeping, and that the whole object in life was to secure the country's welfare and that of its inhabitants. Her association with Hervey therefore was a fortunate chance for both; and the fact that she trusted him implicitly and believed in his good judgment and advice was one of the longest feathers in his cap. Hervey's relations with King George were never on the footing of any profound attachment. They went little deeper than lip-services, and courtierlike flattery. From the day of the Queen's death his allegiance to King and patron wavered. He had long been dissatisfied that nothing better than a Court appointment had been found for him, but he had accepted the situation owing to his love for his Mistress. In 1740, however, he had his reward; for Walpole was persuaded to appoint him Lord Privy Seal, notwithstanding all the efforts of the Duke of Newcastle, with whom he had always been on terms of mutual dislike or something worse.

When Lord Hervey was to be made Privy Seal [wrote the third Lord Holland to John Murray in 1821], the Duke of Newcastle, to prevent it, got Ld Carteret to consent to accept it, and moved for his having it at Council. Sir R. W. said he did not know whether Ld Carteret would accept it. The Duke said he would answer for him. Sr R. W. replied, "I always suspected you had been dabbling there. Now I know it; but if you make such bargains, I don't think myself obliged to keep them." And Ld Hervey was made Privy Seal.

But promotion came all too late; and Hervey's intrigues to maintain himself in office at the time of Walpole's fall in 1742, were hardly to his credit. He lost his post under the new Ministry; and in the following year death terminated many long months of failing health.

Throughout his life Hervey had been tormented with a weakly constitution, which doubtless had not been improved by excess in early life. He spoke in one of the letters of his "odd mind and odder body." His pictures certainly do not give the impression of a man who was likely to make old bones; while the delicate and effeminate features which they portray do lend themselves to the taunts of his detractors. But much of the ill-health from which he suffered throughout his life seems attributable to congenital sources, and was apparently inherited largely from his mother's family, the Feltons. He spoke of Lady Bristol as the " vehicle of all ills I ever complained of ! " The medical history of his three eldest sisters, which he traced, in 1731, in notes on his own constitution, ailments, and methods for alleviating them (*Memoirs*, ed. Sedgwick, p. 961), is exceedingly illuminating. All three were subject to similar disabilities, and none of them were free from the fits, probably of an epileptic nature, which on more than one occasion laid him low in public. He mentioned, too, that one of his brothers was very subject to them. It is amusing to read of his father's belief that his ill-health was largely due to, " that detestable and poisonous plant ", tea !

Early in life he had put himself in the hands of reputable physicians. But neither Dr. Freind, nor the more distinguished Dr. John Arbuthnot, were successful with their prescriptions. Next he tried the celebrated Dr. George Cheyne, by then established at Bath. The new treatment gave instant, if temporary, relief. Early in 1728, however, he again became seriously ill. Cheyne advised a course of foreign waters and a complete change of scene. So in July of that year, he set out for Spa, attended by a new companion, Stephen Fox, whose intimate friendship with him will be discussed in due course. Fox was to be his constant attendant during the many months which were to elapse, chiefly spent in Italy and France, before they regained the shores of England towards the end of 1729. Hervey, after many physical variations, finally returned a different man, and henceforward was able to minimise his sufferings—for sufferings they must have been, tied to the musty atmosphere of the Hanoverian Court, performing various duties, and attending on his Sovereigns during long hours which would have tried the most robust. Beside his epileptic tendency, he may have suffered from gall-bladder trouble, or even from gall-stones ; for surgery as practised in those days was unable to deal with such problems. Pyorrhea too may well have accounted for his loss of teeth, aggravated by the mercury prescribed by his doctors. (See Sir W. Head's note, *Memoirs*, p. 987.)

In 1720, he married that radiant beauty, Mary, best known in her young days as Molly, Lepell, daughter of Brigadier-General Nicholas Lepell, a German Protestant, naturalised in 1699. She was a Maid of Honour to Caroline, then Princess of Wales. She presented him in due course with eight children ; but as we hear little or nothing of her in these letters, her good qualities hardly come within the scope of this volume. It is remarkable, however, that the Fox brothers were counted among her most devoted friends later in life. Privately and publicly, the relations between the Herveys were always of a friendly nature, at any rate up to the birth of their last child in 1736, notwithstanding Hervey's many deviations from the paths of virtue. Lady Louisa Stuart, in her *Introductory Anecdotes* to Lord Wharncliffe's edition of *Lady Mary Wortley-Montagu's Life and Letters*, i, 66, wrote "That *dessons des cartes*, which Madame de Sévigné advises us to peep at, would here have betrayed that Lord and Lady Hervey had lived together upon very amicable terms, as well-bred as if not married at all, according to the demands of Mrs. Millamant in the play[1] ; but without any strong sympathies, and more like a French couple than an English one."

With his father, Hervey was always on excellent terms ; although they usually took opposite sides in the rival sections of the Whig party, especially in the last ten years of the latter's life. "He is safe, affectionate and sincere," he confided on one occasion to Queen Caroline, "and I live with him, just as your daughter Caroline does with you." Indeed, Croker's remarks do not ring true (*Memoirs*, i, xxx) when he states that Hervey never willingly visited Ickworth again, after his return from foreign parts in 1729. His letters tell a different story, although he does expatiate upon one occasion on how much happier he could be, if his mother was not there. For with Lady Bristol he was never on comfortable terms. Her flighty and ephemeral nature was never congenial to him and was actually antipathetic. Filial affection for her seems to have been largely lacking. But at least he had to thank her for one thing, which doubtless proved of great use to him in his life in Court circles. We refer to her tuition in all the wiles of the gaming tables ; for the lords and

[1] Congreve's *Way of the World*, 1700.

ladies who played high at the Palaces were easy pigeons to pluck. To this may be added a remark of Queen Caroline's, that she saw that Lord Hervey had derived his talent at repartee from his mother—a quotation from one of Lady Bristol's own letters to her husband (*Memoirs*, i, xxii). Later, Lady Bristol's support of the Prince of Wales, notwithstanding her position in the Queen's household, infuriated her son, after the intimate relations which he had willingly established at one time with the heir-apparent had turned to hatred and enmity.

Hervey was definitely an opportunist. No one knew better how to flatter, to toady and to strive for the winning side. The life at Court was to him the breath of Heaven ; notwithstanding its artificiality, of which he was fully aware, and strove in his writings to emphasise its boredom, dissociating himself from the Courtiers with whom he was thrown in daily contact. He had little respect for religion, and his disbelief in the teachings of the Church were closely in keeping with a lack of moral sense, which often intrudes itself on our notice, with little attempt on his part to disguise it. He wrote as he thought, and his expressions were in close keeping with the coarseness of that outspoken age. To soften or omit such utterances, which have already their counterpart in the *Memoirs*, would be to give a false impression of him and of the times in which he lived. The *Memoirs* too were clearly written for publication ; [1] and the existence at Ickworth of the copies of his letters, annotated in his own hand, seem to indicate some desire that they also should not be lost to posterity. We have discussed this point at some length in the Preface. Naturally it is with these that we are chiefly concerned ; and in them, for the most part addressed to his most intimate friends, he allowed his astonishing agility of mind and his surprising methods of expression to run riot : and then employed a pretty wit to leaven the whole. He loved receiving letters, and revelled in giving " first intelligence of extraordinary news to curious people." Indeed, his letters might have been even more interesting, but for the fact that they were being for ever opened, a constant source of complaint, which naturally made him very careful as to what he wrote. His likes and dis-

[1] See *Memoirs*, ed. Sedgwick, pp. 2, 363.

likes were most marked. He unhesitatingly called a spade a spade; and where his enemies are concerned he did not spare them. On the other side of the picture, his affection for those whom he took under his wing and believed in as his friends, effervesced to such a degree that sentiment was apt to run away with his judgment, while constant repetition led to overstatement. But the kindliness remained; and to be a beloved friend of Lord Hervey was to be beloved indeed.

His style, as in his *Memoirs*, seems set in a somewhat stilted mould; and his constant use of antithesis in the letters at times becomes boring. But these faults have produced the criticism that his writings were prepared with care, and that his phraseology was studied; while even the third Lord Holland in a note in one of the volumes of mixed letters in the Holland House collection, wrote: " *Lord Hervey's Letters.* Full of news, literature, tittle tattle, wit and amusement, but very affected." But if " studied " or " affected " are the right words, he must have had the gift of natural spontaneity. We read constantly in the letters, that he rarely had sufficient time on his hands, in the day-time at any rate, to sit down and seriously think out what he was putting down on paper. His scraps to the Foxes were often written after a long and probably tedious visit to the Opera or theatre: they were often written at Court, with people at his elbow or talking all round him. It is hardly likely, therefore, that the highest form of composition could be expected; and his letters can certainly never lay claim to be great literary productions. Indeed, they bear all the signs of hurry and hasty writing, from which even grammar suffered. But there is in them an astonishing brilliance, a marvellous sense of humour, a pungency, an originality of thought, and a subtle vein of sarcasm and cynicism, which cannot but place them among the brightest and most amusing creations of that age.

As a versifier, for poet he can hardly be called, he was not so successful, though he flattered himself that he could more than hold his own. He mentioned on more than one occasion that rhyme flowed as easily from his pen as prose, and that " it is ridiculous to say one writes in a hurry when one writes in rhyme, but 'tis true ". But it was a fatal delusion to class himself highly enough as to believe that he could cross swords on equal terms with such as Pope ; and, after burning his boats, he realised all too sadly that he had gone much too far.

It has been the custom amongst Hervey's critics to decry the scope of his general learning, and to say that his knowledge of literature was scanty and superficial. He may not have been a great classical scholar ; and speaking of his Latin epitaph for Queen Caroline he confessed that the Latin cost him great pains. But, as Croker says, " few men retained more of, at least, Latinity ". In the history of the Roman Empire he certainly took an absorbing interest. No doubt his lengthy correspondence with Dr. Middleton was founded on a mutual feeling of scepticism ; but he kept up his end well in those technical dissertations.[1] This class of discussion delighted him, as is also shown by his correspondence with Henry Fox on Montesquieu's work on the Roman Empire (which is mostly omitted from these pages), and by his long letters to Count Algarotti in 1736–42. The quotations of which he made use from contemporary and early works, are another proof of his wide reading on the subjects which interested him. These quips are amusing and always to the point. But their origin is often difficult to trace, especially those from French sources ; and we must frankly confess to our inability on several occasions to solve the problems involved.

Finally, we must very shortly refer to the uncomplimentary " portraits " of Lord and Lady Hervey written by Charles Hanbury-Williams (Holland House MSS.)[2] ; though we do not ourselves feel that these need to be taken too seriously, although they make good reading. In the account of Hervey's career, Williams does not wander too far from the truth, although he seems determined to make the worst of all he was saying, a habit in which the writer was a past-master when he so wished. But when we come to the paragraph describing Hervey's character, the remarks are definitely spiteful and often unreliable.

[1] *Letters between Lord Hervey and Dr. Middleton concerning the Roman Empire*, ed. Knowles, 1778.

[2] Hervey's " portrait " is printed in the editor's *Life of Sir Charles Hanbury-Williams*, p. 63 ; and *Memoirs*, ed. Sedgwick, xlviii.

We believe that these "portraits" were written long after Hervey's death, at a time when Hanbury-Williams was writing to while away dull hours in one of his foreign diplomatic posts. We suspect, judging from the scanty references to one another in the correspondence of both individuals, that there had never been much intimacy between them. And we must remember that Hervey in those later years of his life, notwithstanding the fact that he had been made Lord Privy Seal, and that the brothers Fox had at long last received the advancement which he had coveted for them, had struck trouble with the Walpole Whigs. He had won for himself the unenviable reputation of being inclined to desert his patron at the time when the latter's long Administration was tottering to its fall. Consequently it seems hardly surprising to find Hervey an object of suspicion amongst the true supporters of their revered leader. Hanbury-Williams had always been Walpole's devoted servant, and may well have resented Hervey's unmistakable efforts in 1742 to retain office. The latter's correspondence, too, from one reason and another, had notably slackened with the Fox family after about 1737, and the few letters which remain have a rather querulous note. Perhaps he was himself feeling the qualms of conscience, engendered by a change of spirit after his beloved Queen's death.

We must now turn to the two brothers Fox, the recipients of the bulk of the letters from Lord Hervey which are included in this volume. The difference of age between Stephen and Henry was little over a year, the former being born in September 1704, the latter in the same month in 1705. They were the sons of Sir Stephen Fox, the offspring of his second marriage. Sir Stephen Fox emanated from the village of Farley, on the southern confines of Salisbury Plain, about six miles from the cathedral town of Salisbury. Born in 1627 of good middle-class, country stock, he obtained an introduction to the Court of Charles I through his elder brother John, who held a minor post there under Lord Percy: and, following Prince Charles into exile after the execution of the King, became largely responsible for the solution of the difficult financial problems which enabled the rightful owner of the Crown to keep up a reasonable degree of state at the Courts of Western Europe. After the Restoration he became Paymaster, a very different office to what it became later on; for at that time the land forces were paid directly by the King, for whom the Paymaster had to find the money. He sat in Parliament in five reigns, and held various offices in three. The initiation of the scheme for the building of Chelsea Hospital was largely due to his advice and activities; and he himself was a very liberal contributor to the funds raised to carry out the project.

By Fox's first marriage to Elizabeth Whittle in 1650, he had ten children, three only of whom grew to maturity. Lady Fox died in 1696; and seven years later, at the age of seventy-six, he married Miss Christian Hopes, the companion for a number of years to one of his daughters. Four children were born of this alliance, two boys and two girls, of whom one daughter, the youngest, a twin with Henry, died from an accident; while the other, Charlotte, married Hon. Edward Digby in 1729. The second Lady Fox only outlived by three years her aged spouse, who died in 1716. The three children, therefore, were thrown parentless on the world, for their step-brother was dead. Their future, however, had been carefully provided for; and they were brought up by the executors of their father's will.

Stephen had succeeded to the Redlynch property in Somerset, where Sir Stephen had built himself a house about two miles from the small town of Bruton; and there the orphans were established. A small house in London also was taken for them. In 1715 both boys went to Eton, and early in 1721 to Christ Church, Oxford. Henry certainly remained until the end of 1724. Stephen left a year earlier, and went abroad with Dr. John Wigan, the brother of their University tutor, George Wigan, and stayed there until late in 1725. From that time onward his brother and sister took up their abode with him in Somerset: and at the end of May, 1726, he was elected to Parliament for the Borough of Shaftesbury, in Dorset.

Henry joined his brother and Wigan in Paris in October in 1725, and came home with them. He was of a far more ambitious and progressive temperament than Stephen. "I must say," wrote John Wigan to him in 1725, "he [Stephen] is very sober and vertuous, which I hope rather than believe you are to perfection, if you will let me form my judgment from your own designs and schemes of life." Bath, the hub of provincial Society in those days, was but a step from Redlynch ; and what is more likely than that young Harry should have drifted over there to the fascinations of fine ladies and of the gaming tables. Lord Hervey's miserable health, as we shall see later, had already driven him to seek the alleviation of the waters. Here, no doubt, he and Henry Fox first met ; and we have included Hervey's first letter addressed to him in November, as it proves from the last lines that the acquaintance was still in its early stages. Clearly Stephen did not come into his life till some months later ; as the Ickworth series are earlier than the Melbury letters, and all the early ones are addressed to Henry. It may be interesting to note the resemblance to those which we find him addressing to Stephen later. In the letter above mentioned and the next, we find the same sentimental reasonings on the value of friendship, which Hervey later put forward so strongly in an even more extravagant form to the elder brother. Here he cried out for immediate replies to his letters, in the same way as a few years afterwards he cavilled at Stephen's failure to write to him every day. Indeed, but for Hervey's notes in his own hand-writing on the Ickworth copies, it would be often difficult to decide which brother was being addressed.

Before leaving the Fox family, we may add a few words on the sister, Charlotte, as we find in the Ickworth series several letters addressed to her by Hervey. She was Sir Stephen's youngest child, born on April 19, 1708. She married, in July 1729, the Hon. Edward Digby, and by him had many children. Her husband predeceased his father, and never succeeded to the titles. She is often referred to early in life as " Miss ". Hervey seems to have favoured her as much as he did her brothers, and always spoke of her in terms of the highest admiration and with great regard.

CHAPTER II

1726–1728

TO HENRY FOX *Bath, November 23rd, 1726*[1]

Though the loss of you, and the want of a certain resource I used to have in very low spirits, have made me very unfit for writing, yet the pleasures of conversing with you are so fresh upon my remembrance, that I can't help doing the thing that seems most like repeating them. I know by this confession, I destroy the merit I might plead from this early obedience to your commands. But 'tis doing oneself no great violence to renounce a false merit in order to lay claim to a true one (especially of greater value); and whatever I take from my complaisance on this occasion I design you should place to my inclination. How well that stands affected towards you, I believe you too clear-sighted to doubt, which is some consolation for my being unable to tell it. The best way I could go about it would be to give you a faithful journal of my manner of passing these last four-and-twenty hours since you went; but if you can be unjust enough to me not to guess, you don't deserve to be informed. I insist on being told what you do from morning to night in the country, and if it would not be making you deviate too much from stated rules you may have laid down to yourself, I would now and then be glad to be told what you think. I have an unbounded curiosity with regard to those I love; but your reservedness, I fear, will make it live upon as slender a diet as a patient of Dr. Cheyne's.[2] I should be glad to have your pen go halves with your gun, and for my good will never have you shoot of a post-day. But 'tis something unfair to be asking new favours without having said one word in acknowledgment of old ones; though if you knew my reason for being silent on that chapter, you would not think you had any to reproach me

[1] Ickworth, "To H. F." in Hervey's writing.

[2] Dr. George Cheyne (1691–1743), established at Bath. Consulted by Hervey. He was a great upholder of vegetarianism.

with it . . . I think with pleasure on everything you have ever said to me, but never find so much satisfaction in reflecting on our short past acquaintance, as when I think it an earnest of a long future friendship. Adieu.

The next letter follows ten days later:

TO HENRY FOX *London, December 3rd, 1726*[1]

Dear Comes![2]

You are too fond of your Godfather not to be so of this name; therefore I'll make no apology for beginning my letter with it, but proceed to telling you that I had yesterday the pleasure of your's, and, great as it was, I am so used to be pleased with everything that comes from you that I can't say it was more than I expected the moment I saw your hand. How happy should I be, if I could believe you thought of me as kindly as you speak to me, and that I had merit enough to make you feel what you have at least good-nature and civility enough to say. What you tell me of that flight of woodcocks that has postponed your journey hither is enough to make me wish the whole race of them exterminated out of the Creation; and as to Fortune (on whom you lay the blame, partially, as I think, to excuse your brother), she has never been enough my friend for me to take her part, since you will allow her to have had[3] no hand[3] in our acquaintance. Therefore let her bear the blame with all my heart. It is indifferent to me where the fault lies, since the punishment must still fall on me. You say your thoughts are divided between me and your losses at Bath. If that acquisition is the only counterpoise to those losses, I shan't be surprised to hear you long feel the weight of them; and if your diet and the weather determine which shall prevail, I suppose by the help of beef and easterly winds, my poor scale by this time is mounted quite out of sight. However I shall renew my attack when you

[1] Ickworth. "To H. F." in Hervey's writing.

[2] This seems to be the first reference to the nickname, "Count", by which in those early days Henry Fox was always known to his friends and associates. We have no clue, however, to its significance. We do not know the names of his godfathers.

[3-3] In Hervey's writing.

come to town, for the pleasure of being loved by one so amiable is one I can't part with without some struggle. In the meantime, I shall ply you frequently with letters to keep a place in your remembrance, though I lose ground in your heart, an exchange nothing could induce me to make but the fear of losing you all. . . .

"I am quite provoked at your saying nothing of coming to town," Hervey wrote on December 27, 1726.[1] "I suppose the Somersetshire roads are in such a plight that a land carriage is impracticable. But why don't you come by water? I shall watch for a westerly wind, and hope you'll embark the first fair gale. What amusement you find now in the country I cannot conceive. I take the season to be rather too cold for the diversion of swimming. I'm sure 'tis too wet for any other without doors. The floods must have confined you to your Ark; and if your brother still shoots, it must be out of his window."

Early in January Hervey complained that, from the scarcity of replies, his letters did not seem to be reaching their destinations. "But perhaps pens and paper are not the growth of Devonshire, and the occasion of your silence was not the want of will to converse with me, but the want of means to gratify it. If I am to suppose this too, let me know, and you shall find my supposing faculty as extensive as you can wish it, for

'tis equally unwise,
To see the injuries we won't resent,
Or weep misfortunes which we can't prevent."[1]

In a letter of January 19, 1726/27, comes clear proof that Hervey and Stephen Fox had not yet met. "I hate your brother without knowing him (which perhaps is the only way one can hate him), for postponing another week a pleasure I have waited for so long, and expected with so much impatience."

Yet both were members of the House of Commons, for Hervey had been elected for Bury St. Edmunds at a by-election in 1725, before Stephen had become Member for Shaftesbury in May 1726. The leanings of the Foxes in a preceding generation had been to the Tory party; and it may have been due to the influence of their friend, Thomas Winnington, also originally a Tory, but later a close adherent of Walpole, that he selected allegiance to that party. And this may be the explanation—Hervey was at that time enrolled under Pulteney's banner, and therefore belonged to the dissident section of the Whigs.

[1] Ickworth.

But by the end of May the introduction had taken place, and appears to have been an instantaneous success on both sides.

By that time it seems clear that Hervey's impassioned friendship for the younger brother was wearing a little threadbare. Two letters about this time are significative : [1] " I am so sorry for both our sakes that you are sometimes so difficult, often so unintelligible, and always so impracticable. I wish I was more master of my time, and you of your temper : those two things might contribute to make us both much happier." And again, after recounting certain recently formed impressions, he wrote. " These are the consolatory reflections I have recourse to upon every repulse, and the plea my inclination makes use of, [2] to induce me to continue [2] what my judgment perhaps would counsel me to give over." Hervey therefore turned rapidly to the elder brother for the friendship for which his soul yearned, the reasons for which we shall discuss on a later page. But in no way did he cast off his first love ; and correspondence between him and Henry Fox continued as before, but on a more equable footing.

But even in the first few weeks of his new friendship Hervey's acute brain soon began to realise that it would be far more difficult to decoy Stephen from the country than he had found it with his brother. Stephen by nature was perfectly content to stay at home, and to devote himself to country pursuits and field sports. He would be happy to remain for months on end in the West ; while Henry was far too active in mind and in ambitious projects to stay in one place more than a few weeks. It took Hervey a very short time to realise the true position ; and he expressed his thoughts fully in the first letter of that new series which comes to hand. But friendship he must have : and in this case he would not be denied.

TO STEPHEN FOX *June 1st, 1727* [3]

I can't help taking a malicious pleasure to hear the country affords you so few of any kind, and that your joys there are at so low an ebb that a sound horse and a big-bellied pheasant are the only ones you have yet experienced. You will easily believe me, when I tell you these are such as I shall never envy you ; but you will not find it quite so easy to make me believe you, when you say you wish yourself in town again. If your wishes were very strong (since your horses are so very sound), what hinders the gratification of them ? It is possible the same strain of sincerity may run through your whole letter, and that a pen

[1] Ickworth. [2–2] In Hervey's writing. [3] Ickworth.

and ink may be as obedient instruments of your *gamming* disposition as the muscles of your face ; if so, I should not be left your dupe in giving credit to the things you write than I have often been for believing the things you say. But don't be too vain upon your success in either. For in things one wishes to think true, the deceit oftener prevails from the weakness of one's own heart than from the strength of another's head ; and the deceiver with great vain-glory falsely imputes that to the effects of his art which in reality is only the natural consequence of the other's credulity.

I won't tell you how I feel every time I go through St. James's Street, because I don't love writing unintelligibly ; and the more faithful the description was, the farther one of your temper and way of thinking would be from comprehending what it meant : I might as well talk to a blind man of colours, an atheist of devotion, or an eunuch of . . . That regret for the loss of anybody one loves and likes is a sort of sensation you have merit enough to teach, though I believe you'll never have merit enough to learn it. You have left some [1] such remembrances behind you, that I assure you (if 'tis any satisfaction to you to know it) you are not in the least danger of being forgotten. . . .

I would fain have picked up a little news for you, but there is no such thing stirring. Books, I would send you too, if there were any new ones, or if I knew what old ones would suit your taste. If your studies are to be of a piece with your other occupations, I should think Switzer's [2] *Complete Gardener*, Hubbard upon Agriculture, and Hales [3] upon Vegetation would not be unwelcome. In case this is the sort of reading you intend to take to, you will let me know, and you shall be sure to have a cargo out of this class by the first opportunity. Adieu. My compliments to all at Redlynch.

Hervey had written to Henry Fox, on May 30, 1727,[4] two days before the preceding letter to Stephen Fox :

There has nothing happened in town, since you left it, worth transmitting to you. The occurrences of all the Birthdays are

[1] In Hervey's writing. [2] Stephen Switzer (1682?–1745). Agricultural writer.
[3] Stephen Hales (1677–1761) wrote *Vegetable Statistics*, 1727.
[4] Holland House.

alike. There was a great crowd, bad music, trite compliments upon new garments and old faces in the morning ; feasting and drinking all day ; and a ball with execrable dancers at night. The day for the King's going [1] is yet unfixed. Mine to Lord Bateman is again put off. I cannot persuade myself to leave this town whilst any body will stay in it with me; which I fear will not be longer than this week. If you would know how I pass my time, 'tis more than I can tell you ; all I know is that it does not lie upon my hands. 'Tis a merchandise for which I still find a vent, though the Redlynch coterie has robbed me of my best customers.

The next letter of June 13, gives a vivid description of the constantly recurring troubles at the Royal Academy of Music, where Opera was given from 1720 to 1728. The two Prima-Donnas, Cuzzoni and Faustina (later the wife of Hasse, the composer), had made their debut together in 1719 in Venice, and were in continuous rivalry, though in entirely different styles. The former opened in London in Handel's *Ottone* in 1723 ; while the latter only came over for two years. Their final quarrel, which is here related, took place on the last night of Buononincini's *Astyanax* in June.[2]

Senesino, a noted male contralto (" modo vir, modo fœmina "),[3] came to blows some years later, in 1733, with Handel, who had the support of the King and the Court at the King's Theatre. Many of the nobility then joined together to establish a second theatre in Lincoln's Inn Fields, to which Senesino attached himself in due course, as well as Farinelli and most of the best singers. Indeed society was split asunder by these quarrels. The Duchess of Queensberry, early in 1729, was forbidden to appear at Court, for her support of the poet Gay, who was said to have satirised Walpole in the *Beggars' Opera*.

TO STEPHEN FOX *June 13th* [4] [*1727*]

. . . I hope you will never again pretend to be an advocate for the country, after putting its recreations in so low a form. You

[1] George I was in Hanover.

[2] A notice in the *London Journal* of June 10, 1727, stated : " The contention at first was only carried on by hissing on one side, and clapping on the other ; but proceeded at length to the melodious use of cat-calls and other accompaniments, which manifested the zeal and politeness of the illustrious assembly."

[3] Clement XIV (Pope, 1769–74) was the first to allow female singers in Roman Churches : and at the same time advised the theatres to accept them. Before that all female parts were taken by men (*Edwards's History of Opera*).

[4] Ickworth.

will not place ours in town in a much higher rank I believe, when I tell you we have talked of nothing but Opera disputes, and Ruffs since you left us . . . The revivers of the latter I take to be very adroit ladies. Nature never put them in their youth in any eminent light. Time had still deepened the shadows; and this scheme has not once drawn them from an obscurity, whose clouds without it they could never again have broke through. One of them was the other night in the Park, knotting as she walked, which fashion I am in great hopes will obtain, since naturally the next they will introduce, must be to *stitch* there. I have inclosed a ballad, which perhaps you have already seen. I shall be sorry if you have, for it has nothing but it's being new to recommend it. There have been several more jokes on the ruffed ladies, but none of them worth repeating. They are all as obvious as their artificial ruffs, and as stale as their natural ones.

As to Opera feuds, they are hotter than ever. I suppose you have heard already that both Cuzzoni and Faustina were so hissed and cat-called last Tuesday that the Opera was not finished that night: nor have the Directors dared to venture the representation of another since. They both threaten to go, but after a little bullying will infallibly stay. 1500 guineas are mediators whose interposition they'll never be able to resist . . . The Directors have but to throw out these lures, as Hippomenes did the golden apples; and these Atalantas, like his, I'll engage will stay to gather them, though their minds are never so much set upon running. Senesino thinks it sounds so inglorious for him to have no share in these commotions in the State of Music, that he's resolved to make himself a party concerned, whether they will or no. I believe he takes it for a mark of contempt that he was not distinguished with a cat-call, which puts me in mind of a passage in the *Persian Letters*,[1] where a woman quarrels with her husband, that he does not think her worth beating, and complains of it to her mother as very injurious usage.

Whatever his real reason may be for asking his dismission, his pretended one is this. He says, though the affront was not

[1] *Lettres Persanes*, by Montesquieu.

particular to him, yet it was such an indignity offered to the profession in general, that he thinks it inconsistent with his honour to entertain a people who pay so little deference to the merit of his society. In short, the whole world is gone mad upon this dispute. No Cuzzonist will go to a tavern with a Faustinian; and the ladies of one party have scratched those of the other out of their list of visits. I was t'other night upon the water, and heard nothing till three a clock in the morning but invocations of one and execrations upon the other. The next night I went again, and heard the same ceremony performed by another company, with the names reversed; so that these transient deities, like the Egyptian ones, are alternately sacrificed to one another. I can't applaud the taste of my countrymen, who stop the mouths of these women upon the stage, give them £3000 a year to come there to have the pleasure of hissing them off when they are there, and prefer their conversation in a barge to their voices in a theatre. . . .

. . . Had I not feared your own way of thinking might induce you to imagine absence had changed mine, I would have deferred writing till Thursday, being quite stupified to day with setting up till four oclock this morning upon the water. Once more, Adieu. I want to know, when you are not swallow-shooting, how you pass your time at Redlynch; whether you have done wishing for me there yet or not, and if you are still enough acquainted with me, for me to venture thither without an invitation.

Before the next letter on June 15, the unexpected had happened. King George I died on his return journey from Hanover, where he had spent several months.

TO HENRY FOX *June 15, 1727*[1]

Though I doubt not but the news of the King's death will reach you long before this letter, yet I cannot let so remarkable an occurrence pass by unmentioned. I suppose you will not be very curious about the particulars; all that are known in England as yet are, that he swooned in his coach with fatigue

[1] Ickworth.

and fasting about forty miles on this side of Osenbrugh [1] (his brother's residence), upon which he was immediately blooded, but could not be persuaded to stay any time where he was taken ill. He arrived at Osenbrugh about nine at night. The news came hither at three yesterday. The King (who was not [2] proclaimed till this morning) and the Queen were in town by five. All the men in London of all parties went immediately to Leicester House, and kissed both their hands. The ladies were not admitted till this morning. The Council sat till twelve last night; and this day all the members of both Houses who were in town went to Westminster to take the oaths.

I conclude your brother will not be the only Member of Parliament in England that will not come up on the 27th,[3] and that I shall be an early gainer of one pleasure at least by the new reign, and one which I can with great truth assure you I prefer to most others.

Hervey's letter to Stephen of June 27, 1727, of which we below print a short extract, shows that Henry's political aspirations had been recently getting him into trouble. He won a by-election in Wiltshire that year, at Hindon, and was displaced on petition by his opponent, Mr. Townshend Andrews. Nor did he fare any better, when he fought the seat again a few months later at the General Election. It also introduces us to a bosom friend of the Fox family, Thomas Winnington.

Thomas Winnington appears on the right of the group which forms the frontispiece of this volume; the others being the Fox brothers, Hervey, Charles Spencer, 5th Earl of Sunderland and 3rd Duke of Marlborough, and Parson Peter Willemin, a friend of the Foxes, and vicar of Isey, near Cricklade. The original picture, painted by Hogarth in 1736, is at Ickworth; but a very fine contemporary copy, by Ranelagh Barrett (Barrit, or Barwick as George Vertue sometimes calls him), hangs at Melbury, and is here reproduced. Winnington was born in 1696, the same year as Lord Hervey. He was the son of Sir Francis Winnington, who represented Worcester City in Parliament for many years. Thomas entered Parliament in 1725/26 as Member for Droitwich, and sat for it until 1741. Originally a Tory, he became a strenuous supporter of Walpole in the Whig

[1] Osnaburg.

[2] In Hervey's writing.

[3] Parliament was called to meet on that date; and was dissolved as soon as the Civil List had been voted. The new elections took place during the autumn.

interest. It seems clear that by his influence the Fox brothers, who had also been brought up in the old Tory school, changed their allegiance, and were enrolled under Sir Robert's banner. But Winnington himself suffered from a looseness of morals, and by instability in his political outlook; and these clouded his chances of advancement. Sir Robert never knew quite how far to trust him, and the King and Queen disliked him. He never therefore rose, though very able, to high office; but was for some years a Lord of the Admiralty, and a Lord of the Treasury. Later, after the period of these letters, he held the Paymastership and other posts, before his untimely death in 1746.

TO STEPHEN FOX [1]*June 27, 1727*[1]

I have seen Winnington every day and night since you left us. We dined together yesterday with Sir Robt. at Chelsea. . . .

The political world rolls on just as it did. The Parliament rises on Monday, and the writ for a new one will be out the beginning of August.[2] Winnington said he would write you word what a noise your brother's corruption at Hindon had made, so I shall not enter upon it.[3] Pray my compliments to the seducer, and let him know, if I could make him the thousandth part of a vote by writing a ream of paper, I would; but as votes are all he thinks of at present, I shall send him no letters till he is enough at leisure to remember his friends and endure their impertinence.

Hervey wrote again:

TO STEPHEN FOX *July 3, 1727*[4]

Though I have lived ever since I saw you, in a constant hurry and a perpetual succession of different company, I don't find

[1—1] In Hervey's writing. Ickworth.

[2] Hervey wrote in the *Memoirs*: "As soon as the King had put an end to this session of Parliament, he went to Richmond, as he said, because it was an old acquaintance. He went afterwards to Hampton Court and Windsor, as others said, because they were new acquaintances."

[3] *The Life of Lord Shelburne* (by Lord Fitzmaurice, i, 130) gives a passage from his *Autobiography*, from whence it appears that Henry all but won the day in the House of Commons against the Government, who supported the petition: and actually carried the first two questions. His activity had gained him much support among the young men of fashion.

George Heathcote took the seat, which was a two-member borough, Townshend Andrews being the other member. (*See* p. 47, and Lord Perceval's *Diary* (*Egmont*, i, 27).)

[4] Melbury.

any change can produce so great a one in me as to make me less regret the loss of you. I have made a visit of a day and a half to some friends at Tunbridge, and set out to-morrow for Suffolk ; from whence you may imagine I cant have much time to spare to-night : but as I hope an empressement [1] to thank you for your letter will convince you of the pleasure it gave me, there is nothing I had not rather neglect than this opportunity of answering it. I am so used to be pleased with everything you say to me, but more particularly with any assurances of your friendship, that 'tis needless to tell you the satisfaction I tasted in so warm a repetition of them. Preserve the same sentiments towards me ever, and believe 'tis impossible for me to forfeit the only merit I can plead as a title to such a distinction, which is the sense I have of all the agreeable qualities you are master of, and the value I have for all the good ones. I would not *say* this to you, for fear you should think it proceeded from my civility more than my affection ; and that I imagined myself warranted by custom for making professions of what I neither felt nor expected should be believed. But what one writes, I hold to be as sacred as what one swears ; and I should not have a worse opinion of anybody who gave a lie in evidence in a Court of Justice, than I should of him who gave one under his hand in a letter to his friend. I insist, therefore, on your never doubting what I convey to you that way, that you take it all for gospel, and never send me any thing apocryphal in return.

You will see by the King's Speech this post what an amicable dismission he gave yesterday to us, his zealous, generous and faithful Commons ; and I dare say he would be very glad to make the same compliment to their successors, which he received himself from these—which was that he inherited all the virtues of his predecessors. The Speaker [2] made a harangue with the

[1] In the copy at Ickworth of this letter, Hervey has changed the word *empressement* to *impatience*.

[2] Sir Spencer Compton (1673–1743), who had also held the post of Paymaster since 1722. The new King, out of dislike for Sir Robert Walpole, had had every intention of making Compton Chief Minister, but the latter showed himself quite unfit even to draft the King's Speech, and was obliged to ask his opponent to do the task for him ! He was shortly afterwards raised to the peerage, as Earl of Wilmington.

usual solemnity on the delivery of the Money Bills, which I had the good luck to hear: a piece of good fortune I am the more sensible of, as it is not to have the justice of being committed to the press.

I suppose the prints have informed you that the D. of Rutland is declared successor to Lord Lechmere in the Chancellorship of the Duchy of Lancaster; and when I tell you that Lord Chesterfield [1] is to go Ambassador to France, I am at the end of my news as well as my paper, and a great deal beyond my time. Adieu.

Continue to write to me in Burlington Street. Write to me frequently, and wish mightily to see me.

Hervey had been for some years in the other camp of the Whig party, and since the new King's accession, had been awaiting the course of events; but he had to some extent foreseen what was likely to happen, and embarked on an anonymous letter to Sir Robert Walpole, printed in the *Memoirs* (p. 32), giving some advice on the situation.

Walpole's action in securing a great advance of income for both King and Queen in the Civil List, soon had its effect. Compton's idiotic tactics too, if tactics they could be called, tended to secure his certain downfall. For the future Hervey was Walpole's devoted servant; although the final break with Pulteney was postponed, probably by his long sojourn on the Continent in search of health.

The next letter is in French, and is printed in the original spelling. Punctuation is altered. As it is in the Melbury series, it is doubtless addressed to Stephen Fox, but might be to either brother. Hervey spoke and wrote French constantly, it being the usual language of the Court.

Houghton, le 14 Août, 1727.

Vous serez sans doûte surpris de la datte de cette lettre. S^{r}. Robt. Walpole qui vient d'arriver aussi bien que moi, envoïa chez moi par avance pour me prier de le rencontrer içi. Des ordres si obligeans ne laissent aucune merite à ceux qui les obeïssent. J'envoyai mes relais d'abord que je les reçus; et malgré la distance et les affaires qui me demandent à Bury, je me trouve aujourduy, à quarante miles de chez moi. Votre lettre m'est venu le moment avant que je partis d'Ickworth: mais je n'y ai rien reçonnû de vous que le caractere. Par le stile et les

[1] Philip Dormer, 4th Earl (1694–1773), writer of the well-known series of letters to his son.

sentimens, je ne l'aurois jamais crû de vous. Qu'est devenûe vôtre enjouëment ? Qu'est devenûe votre amitié ? Vous aurez écri justement comme ça à Monsieur Guise. La froideur de cette lettre m'a glacé même dans la canicule ; c'est ce qui s'appelle proprement de citrouïl friccassé à la niege. Cette opposition dont vous me parlez ne vous a pas seulement ôté cette humeur badine et folâtre qui dominoit autrefois en tout ce qui venoit de vous, mais elle a rendurci aussi *quel petto adamintino* que je vous ai si souvent reproché. Pourquoi à moi cette tiedeur ? Je vous jure que ce n'est pas moi qui vous ai sçussité [? resuscité] ce concurrent à Shaftsbury, que je ne l'assiste pas, que je ne l'aime pas et, même que je ne le connois pas. Si vôtre esprit continue dans ce derangement, je n'aurois pas beaucoup à regretter, en cas que je ne puisse pas me trouver à Redlinch. Mais rentrez au nom de Dieu dans vôtre naturel ; soyez vousmême, et sachez que plus vous le soyez, plus vous serez toujours aimable. Voilà assez vous gronder. Un petit mot à cette heure de l'endroit où je suis. Le pays n'est pas beau, célà est sûr ; il a fait pourtant un parc planté d'un bon gout. Pour la maison, elle est magnifique ; on ne peut rien voir de plus beau. Elle a toute la beauté de celles qui sont élevées dans les regles et toute la com̃odité de celles qui ne le sont pas. Il n'y manque rien que la depense peut fournir ou le gout peut inventer, pour la rendre et par dehors et en dedans une pièce achevée. Je suis faché, pour l'amour de Winnington qu'il n'est pas içi. Qu'il seroit heureux de se trouver aupres de my Lady Walpole [1] dans toute cet éclat de beauté que lui donnent à present la jeunesse, la santé, et la fraicheur de la campagne. Pour moi je suis içi tout à fait a mon gré. Nous trouvons la journé courte, nous ne politiquons point, nous causons beaucoup, nous sommes tous de bonne humeur. Je me porte mal pourtant : j'ai le visage toute enflé, et des douleurs quelque fois pour une demi heure de suite effroïables. Tout le monde est allé coucher ; et moi, je me suis retiré pour vous faire cet détail. Remarquez, s'il vous plait, la difference entre nous deux, et avouez nettement que voilà une distinction que vous auriez été incapable de me payer. J'ai lû en quelque part,

[1] Sir Robert's first wife, Catherine Shorter, daughter of John Shorter, of Bybrook, Kent. She had married in 1700, and died in 1737.

qu'il y a des gens dont les cœurs ressemblent à un miroir. Ils prendent vivement l'impression de tout ce que leur est proche, mais on n'en est pas plûtot éloigné un peu, que l'image n'en est effacé comme si il n'y avoit jamais été. N'êtes-vous pas de ce nombre ?

Mandez moi au plûtôt quand votre election se faira,[1] et si vous voulez me rencontrer en quelque part pour me mener dans vôtre chaise à Redlinch, en cas je pourrais y aller. Je serai à Londres la semaine qui vient. Adieu. Je dors ; mais il faut que ce soit bien profondement quand je ne me souviens plus de vous. Adieu.

About the commencement of the year 1727/28, follows a small spate of letters to Stephen, of no special interest, but full of allusions to their growing friendship. Hervey besought him in honied words to tear himself from rural pursuits, and to come to town. One success at least he achieved. Stephen began to think of taking a house there.[2] "I went with your brother to see the house in Grosvenor Square. There are four rooms in it as good as any in houses of £400 a year rent. The stables to both that and Sir Robert's, Mr. ——, the Surveyor says, are but slight ; and that the new one, before you can fit it even ready for *furniture*, will cost you three or four hundred pounds more than the purchase money. How he makes this out, the Lord knows. He seems no conjurer and Sir Robt.'s friend."

We hear of this house again in the next letter.

TO STEPHEN FOX *January the 9th, 1727/8*[3]

'Twas impossible for me to write to you on Saturday ; and I insist on your believing it, without my expatiating farther on the reasons why it was so. Had it been otherwise, my impatience to acknowledge the kindness in some parts of your letter, and my eagerness to correct you for the impertinence in others, would infallibly have made me seize the first opportunity to vent both my gratitude and resentment. But as one is always readier to resent injuries than acknowledge obligations, I shall begin with your faults. And in the first place, as to your criticisms upon my account of your house, I take 'em to be

[1] At the General Election.
[2] Ickworth, *December 30, 1727.*
[3] Melbury and Ickworth.

as false as Voltaire's upon the "Intrigue between Sin and Death," and perhaps for the same reason, which is for want of understanding your author. But the alacrity of such bright parts is apt now and then to hurry men of your fire into some little mistakes; and one may say on that occasion, as Prior does on another, "A bad effect, but from a noble cause". 'Tis certain you great geniuses, who from excessive spirit will always be jumping on without examining the road you travel or having any regard to the soil, will have the misfortune now and then to s'embourber a little; and as I take it in this instance, you are at least knee-deep, and as dirty as *Godminster Wood*[1] or the *springiest gully* in Somersetshire can make you at Christmas. When I said there were four good rooms in the house in Grosvenor Square, why you were to presume a subintelligitur of, *on a floor*, I don't comprehend. What I meant, and all that the words import, was, that in that dwelling there were four good rooms, without the least allusion to garrets, kitchens, cellars, stables, etc. So that the inaccuracy was not in my text but your comment, where pour la justesse il n'y en avoit point, and pour de l'esprit—pas beaucoup. Vous voilà à terre—and since by this time you must be ashamed of your paltry cavil, I'll spare you. *Parlons d'autre chose.*

I wont make you any apology for my last letter; for, without affectation, 'tis some days so much more natural to me to write in verse than prose, that I did for my ease; and 'twas only want of time that hindered me putting it into a common epistolary form. As to your reproaching me with the love of London, I am ready to plead guilty to that charge; but you know it was not that which hindered me accompanying you to Redlynch . . . .

I forgot to tell you, that upon a second reading of the ballad I spoke to you of, I thought it too stupid to deserve transcribing or sending. There is an ode come out upon your Somersetshire antagonist, D—n[2] and some of his ladies, in imitation of "Donec

[1] A wood at Redlynch.

[2] No doubt George Bubb Dodington, a member of an old Somerset family, and Lord-Lieutenant of that county 1721–44. M.P. for Bridgwater 1722–54. He was later in life created Baron Melcombe. His *Diary* was published in 1784. Of it, wrote Horace Walpole: "Never was such a composition of vanity, versatility and servility! In short there is but one feature wanting—

gratus eram tibi ", scurrilous, unfair, and dull. Every day produces some heavy, unspirited venom in verse or prose in the same style. Men and women promiscuously, in their political and moral capacity, in their public and domestic characters, in their own persons and those of their whole family, friends or acquaintance, are one and all brought upon the stage, and forced alternately to represent the vile parts given them by their enemies in every low farce they think fit to publish.

Your brother and Winnington do nothing but politiquer from morning to night. I hear of nothing but petitions, journals, treaties, alliances, etc., whenever I see them ; and as for Winnington (without any sort of joke) unless he will bleed, purge, and keep to a very low diet, I am sure when the Parliament meets, too much business will produce the same effects in him which Felix apprehended too much learning had in St. Paul. Your brother and I are to play to night after the Opera at Mr. Pulteney's[1] . . . I have a little scheme on foot that concerns you which I am to put in execution to day where I dine. If it succeeds, I shall be very happy, if it miscarries you will be very peevish, for I shall never let you know what it was. I know this is provoking, but so it will be.

Pray make my compliments to " Miss."[2] I envy you both. The serenity, the uninterrupted, unalloyed, full satisfaction that two agreeable people have in a country life is to be equalled or rivalled by no other. Yet, as well as I wish you both, the interestedness or envy of my own temper makes me grudge you every hour you have to come there.

Perhaps you expect an account of the transactions at Court last night. There was dice, dancing, crowding, sweating and stinking in abundance as usual ; but I had the prudence or stupidity, which you'll please to call it, to absent myself. And, after dining at a feast, where there were about ten or a dozen men and women, who neither were nor desired to be acquainted,

his wit, of which in his whole book there are not three sallies. I often said of Lord Hervey and Dodington, that they were the only two I ever knew who were always aiming at wit, and yet generally found it." (*Letters*, ed. Toynbee, xiii, 157.)

[1] William Pulteney, M.P. (1684–1764), created Earl of Bath in 1742.

[2] Mrs. Digby.

I went to supper with a little coterie which you only could have improved, and where we entertained ourselves with clubbing our accounts of all the impertinencies we had gone through in the day, and, despising those we had avoided, appropriated for the evening.

In the sequel, the Grosvenor Square house proved unacceptable to Stephen Fox; and as nothing else suitable seems to have turned up, we find Hervey selling to him his own residence in Burlington Street (now 31 Old Burlington Street) in 1730,[1] after their return from their travels on the Continent. We have no evidence as to the terms upon which it changed hands. The staircase and the decoration of the two lower rooms are most dignified and of the highest merit, in the style of William Kent. The latter worked largely at this time under the auspices of Richard, 3rd Earl of Burlington, who had leased a large piece of ground, known as Burlington Gardens, and sublet it shortly afterwards in small building plots. Lord Hervey appears to have built the house about 1722, for it does not appear in the Rate-books for that year in the street which by 1727 was called Burlington Street.[2] Formerly it had been called Nowell Street, perhaps from Lady Burlington's maiden name (née Noel).

[1] *Reid's Weekly Journal*, October 1730.

[2] The freehold of the house, the staircase, and the internal decorations of the lower rooms, still remain the property of the Ilchester family, although the whole is let on a long lease to Messrs. Lenygon. According to *Reid's Journal*, Lord Hervey moved to an apartment in St. James's House.

CHAPTER III

1728–1729

The letters make no mention of the Coronation in October, 1727; nor of the opening of Parliament on January 23, 1727/28. Sir Spencer Compton was succeeded as Speaker by Arthur Onslow, who held the post for the next thirty-three years. Hervey criticised the King's Speech as being in hereditary form, for it was just in the same strain as the last half-dozen of his father's; and any comment which he reserved for it in the *Memoirs* was inclined to be derogatory—a curious line to take, as he himself moved the Address to the King. Probably he was expecting office, and was disappointed; and would have preferred it to the pension of £1,000 p.a., which he obtained as a sop. He tells us in the *Memoirs* that the proceedings of the Session were uninteresting, being largely confined to the subjects of the current services for the year, and to the hearing of Election petitions.

All this time Hervey's health seems to have been consistently deteriorating; so much so that Stephen Fox finally offered to take him abroad, as we have seen. Exactly what the arrangements were, or when they were made, does not transpire. No mention of these plans is made in the four or five letters to Stephen Fox in June.

He wrote:

June 18th, 1728[1]

I am this moment come from Richmond, but late as it is, your absence allows me too few pleasures for me to neglect any opportunity of taking so sensible a one as that of writing to you. You are by this time at Redlynch, and finding your park wall advanced, the foundations of your new building laid, your slopes improving, your puddles filling, and your plantations thriving. 'Tis possible your joy for these changes without doors may banish all the pain I flattered myself you would feel for one you will find within. If I should guess right, at least have the charitable dissimulation to swear I do not, and sacrifice your sincerity to my vanity; rather than give me the mortification of thinking you did not sacrifice your inclination to your business, when you left the place where I was, for any

[1] Ickworth.

other. Walk often through "Hervey Grove", and now and then visit the ash by the *pas-glissant*. . . .

TO STEPHEN FOX *June 22, 1728*[1]

I find I can no more help sending you a letter every time the post goes out than I can help wishing for one every time it comes in; and only desire the consequences of the one may be as agreeable to you as you have made the effects of the other to me. I am extremely glad to hear the charms of Redlynch are in so languishing a condition. The place where you are and I am not, can never have too few. I dined to day at Cranford with Lord Berkeley,[2] Lady Bolingbroke,[3] and Lord Carteret.[4] The first insulted me in your style, with making every bit he eat of a fat sturgeon pass across my nose to his mouth. . . . The Lady was not at all in spirits; the other was both in spirits and in words, all in the narrative, the marvellous, and the frivolous: a man that almost every body commends and no body is a friend to: that has many admirers and not one adherent: that is in a high station without being envied: that is servile to those who rebuke him and shy to those who would caress him. Such a man's character makes a riddle to which his name only can serve for a solution. I spoke to Lord Bristol about Patch,[5] and he will be sure to take care of him; he goes to morrow to Ickworth, but I could not prevail with myself to accompany him. The Count is much as he was, and your humble servant grown a great rake. I sup and sit up; and in a little time I believe you will hear of my getting drunk, breaking windows, beating the watch, being knock'd down by a constable, and lying all night in the round-house. Adieu.

[1] Melbury and Ickworth.

[2] James, 3rd Earl (1680–1736), dismissed by Walpole from the Government a few months before.

[3] Marie Claire de Mercilly, 2nd wife of Henry St. John, Viscount Bolingbroke, was connected by marriage with Madame de Maintenon, and was widow of the Marquis de Villette.

[4] John, Lord Carteret (1690–1763), the future Chief Minister, was later created Earl Granville.

[5] Probably Thomas Patch, painter of caricatures in oil, and in etching. He lived mostly in Florence.

TO STEPHEN FOX *June 27th, 1728*[1]

The little time other people allow me to write to you in, and the little time you allow me to think of other people, makes me perpetually absent from the thing I am doing, and often constrains me in the thing I would do. They have no good of me, nor I of myself. I am absent from them without being present to you ; and very naturally (and consequently very simply) because I can't enjoy what I would, I don't enjoy what I might ; which is just as reasonable and as prudent a way of acting, as if I should cut off my legs because I have not wings : or should resolve never to eat, when the thing I loved best was not in season. Yet so we are made, and so we act : at least the generality of mankind. But among many other peculiar blessings bestowed by Heaven upon you, you enjoy that negative one of this troublesome ingredient being left quite out of your composition. You have a proneness to be pleased, and are not only exempt from the pain of ever wishing for anything you do not possess, but have a capacity given you of extracting a joy out of everything you do, and to put your pleasures in the strongest light, are not capable of giving greater than you take. You are to your company, just what you are to your food : you can sit down to what I am sure you could never hunger after : can swallow what does not please your taste : and digest what one would imagine must have made anybody sick. Don't imagine I am modest enough to think myself such a sort of dish, for 'tis the least of my thoughts ; and if I could, would certainly persuade you not only to have me always at your table, but to eat of no other. Adieu. . . .

The date upon which Hervey and Stephen set out upon their travels remains unrecorded ; but it was definitely sometime in July 1728. It appears rather remarkable, as Croker points out, that Lady Hervey was not in charge of the party, for her husband was seemingly so ill. But we must bear in mind that she had four young children to look after, and that her time therefore was not her own. Spa was their first objective, so that the invalid might try the effect of the waters. A letter from Lady Hervey to Stephen Fox, of September 20,[2] gives the first news of how things were going—by no means well, it

[1] Ickworth.

[2] Melbury.

would appear. Apparently she was afraid that her husband's health was worse than he was making out to her, and spoke of hearing that he had been very ill shortly before they had left Spa. She asked for the truth, " I hope he was not so ill as he was last spring in town, nor worse than he was last winter." Hervey was not to know of her letter.

Apparently, the travellers had started southward on their journey, for Winnington writing to Hervey said that he had had communications from both in Paris. Hervey seemed " neither better nor worse than when he left England ".[1] They were still there early in November, and went on to Italy by slow stages later in the month. Rome was their first halt, after which they moved on to Naples in January, where Hervey became worse again.

[2] " Mr. Fox never left me night or day. I saw no body but him and the servants. He went out with me when I was able to go out, read to me at home when I had no spirits to talk, and constantly lay in my room. I looked so dreadfully, that he has sometimes come to my bedside, and doubted if I was only sleeping or dead. . . . His good sense made his company a constant amusement and his care never a trouble. His spirits enlivened and comforted, but never overcame or oppressed me. He showed an incessant, reasonable and tender concern for me, without all the fiddle-faddle impertinence of official attention, which is often affectation, often teazing and never useful."

Two letters from Stephen to his brother Henry give an account of a series of earthquakes, which happened during their stay in Florence at the end of June 5, 1729. They also speak of a great change for the better in the invalid.

STEPHEN FOX TO HENRY FOX *June 24, 1729*[3]

At a quarter after three I was waked by a violent earthquake (which is a much more terrible thing than I imagined). The first shock lasted a long minute and a half. We got up, and in a moment all the house was assembled in our land-lady's chamber, who was in such an agony occasioned by fear, that I thought she would have died of the fright, as one of her neighbours has since. While we were there, giving her cold water and drops, there was

[1] Holland House, *September 29, 1728*. [2] *Memoirs*, pp. 97–8.
[3] Holland House.

a second shock pretty violent, but not near so long as the first. . . . Within an hour after that of yesterday morning, all the squares and streets were full of people confessing themselves in their shirts and smocks. The motion was so disagreeable and unnatural that it made everybody sick; and I believe the dogs, for they howled in a most terrible manner. The birds, especially the pigeons, were extremely frightened; but nobody nor nothing more so than the Great Duke,[1] who ran into his garden, and had mass begun as soon as the first priest could be found. . . . Ld Hervey's servant ran out upon the terrace, and says the mountains skipped like rams and the little hills like young sheep. They say they have never felt a more violent terra mota; but notwithstanding its violence, it has done but little mischief. It threw down some chimneys of the adjoining house, which made the most damnable noise; but the chief harm it has done in Florence is the throwing down one end of a large Church. . . .

. . . I am better every day, my spirits revive, and my embonpoint returns. We don't talk of leaving this place till the end of August; but if you will have my private opinion on that head, it is that we shall be very near England by that time, for la maladie des Suisses, and la maladie of a fine English gentleman (c'est à dire l'ennui), are so prevalent at present in our constitutions, that I am apt to think we shall never hold it till then in Florence. Adieu, dear Count.

STEPHEN FOX TO HENRY FOX *July 2, 1729*

. . . Everybody endeavours to give a reason for these earthquakes. The clergy say that they have happened because there is not that respect paid to the Church as formerly. The laity say they have been occasioned by the extraordinary wickedness of the clergy; and give for instance a chaplain belonging to the Court, who not only made the Opera, but sits in orchestre publicly playing upon the harpsichord. This last instance of impiety takes much with the vulgar, and is at present generally

[1] Gian Gastone, 7th and last Grand-Duke of the Medici family. He died in 1737.

believed to be the occasion of the earthquakes, which have done a good deal of damage about ten miles away. . . .

'Tis surprising to see how well my Ld Hervey is grown within these three weeks. I think he is at present as well as I ever knew him. He has translated a new prayer against earthquakes and lightning into English verse very humorously for Mrs. Lepell's use. . . .

During the travellers' stay in Florence, the oft-quoted *Epistle to Stephen Fox* was written by Hervey, in imitation of *Horace*, Ode VI, Bk. 2, claiming that his recovery was largely the result of Stephen's care and attention.

Thou dearest youth, who taught me first to know,
What pleasures from a real friendship flow ; . . .

* * * * *

When wasting sickness and afflictive pains,
By Æsculapius's sons opposed in vain,
Forced me reluctant, desperate to explore
A warmer sun, and seek a milder shore ;
Thy steady love, with unexampled truth,
Forsook each gay companion of thy youth,
Whate'er the prosperous or the great employ,
Business and interest, and love's softer joys,
The weary steps of misery to attend,
To share distress, and make a wretch thy friend.[1]

The travellers remained in Florence during the hot summer months, when the above lines were doubtless written. Hervey had a " long and dangerous " operation whilst there. As soon as his wound was healed, he and Fox set out for England ; and amongst the Fox papers at Melbury, we find an envelope of later date, entitled, " Lord Hervey and Lord Ilchester were in Italy together, when the enclosed was wrote by the former to Lady Hervey, then in England." It contains a long letter in jingling verse, describing the travellers' adventures on their way home as far as Lyons in 1729. It is unpublished : but it is too long to print here, and we shall relegate that portion of it which deals with the episodes of their journey to Appendix A (p. 283),

[1] To this Lady Mary Wortley-Montagu wrote a " Continuation ". Here are the first two lines :

" So sung the poet in a humble strain,
With empty pockets, and a head in pain. . ."

giving only a few excerpts which touch on the writer's relations with his wife, and with his self-suggested facility for writing in verse.

Tho' by this post (my Dear), I chose
To write in verse, pray don't suppose,
With tropes and flights that I design
To raise my style, and swell each line.
Those fustian trappings of a poet,
Are what I never wear ; you know it.
Such bards like strolling players shine,
Who with black gems and tinsel fine,
Strut on some little country stage,
And, tho' profaning Shakespear's page,
Think they're the Oldfields of the age.
I hate the pedantry of schools,
Nor write, nor speak, nor act by rules.
No invocation of a Muse
By way of Preface I produce,
No allegory dark will sing,
Nor unlike similes will bring,
That lead astray the reader's brain,
And puzzle what they ought t'explain.
The little scheme that I lay down,
Is barely telling how we've gone,
From Arno's banks to those of Rhône.
If then my numbers seem uncouth,
Think, to atone, they're fraught with truth.
And when I would say something kind,
Why should a Muse inspire my mind,
Or nature borrow ought from Art ?
Since love and you inspire my heart.

* * * * *

But all our frights and dangers past,
To Lyons safe we came at last.
Witness my hand. For there I'm writing
What truth and kindness are inditing.
Yet dont imagine that I think
This casual child of pen and ink

Deserving to be sent so far.
But that ev'n trifles, light as air,
(As from Otello I can prove),
Cease to be such to those who love.
I send it for this cause alone ;
And for the rest I freely own,
'Tis the poor offspring of a day,
Just to be read and thrown away.

According to the *Memoirs*, Lord Hervey was back in England late in September 1729. Our letters in November made mention of the problems which confronted him on his return. We refer especially to his relations with Pulteney, which are important in view of their future status. He wrote of himself in the *Memoirs* :[1]

" He loved Mr. Pulteney, and had obligations to Sir Robert Walpole ; he had lived in long intimacy and personal friendship with the former, and in his public and political conduct he always attached himself to the latter. But as the dissentions of these two men were now grown to such a height that it was impossible for anybody to live with both, Lord Hervey at his return found he should be brought to the long-feared disagreeable necessity of quitting one or the other."

He continued that Lady Hervey was a friend of Pulteney, and disliked Sir Robert, to put it mildly, having rebuffed some former attempts to make love to her.[2] Consequently she and Pulteney plotted to detach her husband from Walpole, by extracting a promise from Lord Bristol (who was on their side) to make up any financial loss which might accrue to his son, if his pension was taken from him. Sarah, Duchess of Marlborough also took a hand in the intrigue. They succeeded to a point ; as Hervey actually wrote a letter to Sir Robert. But this pleased neither the recipient nor Pulteney ; and further than this he would not go.

On November 15, however, we get some closer insight into Hervey's position as regards Sir Robert ; for clearly the letter to which Hervey referred as shown to his correspondent, was that, mentioned above, which is published in the *Memoirs*. But notwithstanding the fact that he was " not at all pleased " with his subsequent interview with the great man, as recounted in the next letter three days later, Hervey " assured him that he would take the first opportunity on the

[1] p. 103. Hervey always wrote of himself in the *Memoirs* in the third person.

[2] Lady Hervey wrote many years later, " I had no partiality for the man ; he was to me disagreeable in many articles." By that time, she had changed her mind so far anyhow as to believe in Sir Robert's ability and supreme importance to his country.

Enoch Seeman, pinxit

MARY (MOLLY LEPELL), LADY HERVEY

meeting of Parliament publicly to demonstrate himself as much attached to his interest as ever."

TO STEPHEN FOX *November 15th* [*1729*] [1]

. . . I began the day by a tête à tête with the man to whom I showed you a letter. Caresses, fine words and professions were not spared; but you know Ministers promise, as Lady Bolingbroke commends, assez volontiers. In short, I was, what perhaps your opinion of my vanities will make you think impossible, mightily flattered and not at all pleased. They are heartily out of humour: things go certainly ill at home, and very doubtfully abroad. This made me make great allowances; and when I consult my heart I feel I wish them well. Piques and quarrels are as busy in the polite as the political world, and as little to be accounted for. Lord Chesterfield [2] and our Duchess [3] dined here yesterday, without exchanging a single syllable. Whenever either of them said any thing that looked like an answer to the other, 'twas always addressed to some third person. Does not this astonish you? It did me; but I am determined to know the meaning of it, and of course then you will hardly be ignorant of it. . . .

A further letter on November 18 [4] tells us something of Hervey's personal plans. He spoke also of the news of the Treaty of Seville,[5] with a little gossip on home politics. It is interesting, after reading

[1] Ickworth.

[2] Lord Chesterfield was still Ambassador in Holland; but in 1730 received a Court appointment as Lord Steward, much to his disappointment, as he aspired to the Foreign Secretaryship to replace Lord Townshend.

[3] No doubt the Duchess of Richmond, one of the Queen's ladies. How this coolness came about does not transpire. She was Sarah, daughter of William, Earl Cadogan, and married Charles, 2nd Duke, in 1719.

[4] Ickworth.

[5] The Treaty of Seville was signed on November 9. It was definitely advantageous to England, for Elizabeth Farnese, the Spanish Queen, wife of Philip V, was greatly annoyed by the disinclination of the Emperor to guarantee to Spain the possession of the Italian Duchies and turned in consequence to England and France. In the Treaty no further mention occurred of the surrender, strongly pressed for in 1728, and Spanish garrisons were to be introduced into Parma and Tuscany. By a secret article armed opposition to the Emperor was foreshadowed, should he resist the powers.

the letter of three days' earlier, to find Hervey entertaining the Pulteneys!

. . . I am going with Mr. Mansel to-morrow for two or three days to The Grove,[1] and at my return hope to hear you are at Redlynch, which is all I wait for to fix my own journey thither. The Duke of Richmond who goes into Sussex to-morrow, has invited me thither to hunt, but I shall *Fox*-hunt only towards the West. 'Tis the chase I am most eager after. You will have me in great contempt as a newsmonger, for telling you news was doubtfully good from abroad, in the same moment that an express arrived at St. James's with an account of the Peace with Spain being quite concluded. Mais peutêtre n'était-il pas dit fort mal à propos ? though I don't pretend 'twas by way of refinement, but in mere chance and ignorance. They say the conclusion of this Treaty has not secured Don Carlos's succession in Tuscany more effectually than it has defeated the hopes of Lord Chest[er-fiel]d's in the Cockpit, though 'tis thought Lord Townshend's demise is as near at hand as the Great-Duke's. But if his fall is foreseen with no more certainty than the rise of the stocks upon this occasion, the cunning men at the Backstairs may chance to be bit as much as those of Exchange Alley, and wish like them that they had stuck to their *Bear*. I am grown already quite an English fine gentleman. I do a hundred different things a day and like none of them : yawn in the faces of women I talk to : eat and drink with men I have no friendship for : play despising the Court, and live in the Drawing Room : rail at quid-nuncs, and go hawking about for news : throw the faults of my constitution upon the climate : flatter awkwardly, rally worse ; and in short make none of my actions conducive to the pleasure or profit either of myself or anybody else.

You are in part responsible for this. If I regretted less what I have lost, I should be less indifferent to what I possess : and if I had a worse opinion of you, perhaps I might have a better

[1] Near Watford. This property had been sold to the Trustees of Fulke Greville in 1728. The owner being a minor, the house was doubtless let at this time. It was resold in 1743 ; and again in 1763 to Hon. Thomas Villiers, 2nd son of Earl of Jersey, who was created Earl of Clarendon. It remained in that family until recently.

of other people : consequently, should be better pleased myself, and of course more industrious to please them. But as things now stand, I look upon you as my dwelling : and feel the inconveniences of these other animals as I did those of Italian inns, hate all their filth, and would no more make friends of the one, than I would my home of the other.

Pray make my compliments to Miss. You are an unjust, base creature, if she is not sensible how few people I think better to be liked. Adieu. 'Tis three a clock. I am quite undressed, and expect Mr. and Mrs. Pulteney every moment to dinner. The Dr. is already here, and says, " Oh ! you have writ enough." I should be of his mind, if I thought anything I have said had explained to you how affectionately, entirely and unalterably, my dear, dear creature, I am your's.

Four days later Hervey wrote, " Your letter had been opened, as everyone I have written or received since I came to England has been ; so take care what you say. This makes me postpone the *suite* of the Sunday dinner story,[1] which I am thoroughly informed of by the party concerned."

TO STEPHEN FOX *November 25, 1729*[2]

I left the country yesterday, when the good weather left us ; for I was wet to the skin in coming from Cassiobury[3] where I breakfasted. That neighbourhood made The Grove very agreeable. When I was with you I used to think the fewer neighbours the better ; but I find variety very necessary to chasser the ennui of your absence, though 'tis the thing in the world your presence makes me least covet. I think Lord Essex is in his understanding, just what he is in person. He is ill-made, has a face without one good feature, yet is altogether a pretty figure : and without wit, knowledge, judgment or good breeding, is an amusing, cheerful companion. If I was to define the *je ne sçais quoi*, it should be by giving him for a sample. . . .

[1] No doubt the coolness referred to above.

[2] Ickworth.

[3] Lord Essex's. William, 3rd Earl (d. 1743). In earlier days Essex was always anti-Walpole, and his affairs were largely in Lord Bolingbroke's hands. He therefore cultivated the Prince of Wales on his arrival in England ; but obtaining nothing which he wanted, he renewed his allegiance to the King's party. (*Memoirs.*)

I am just come from Court, where I saw nothing but blue noses, pale faces, gauze heads and toupets among the younger gentry: and lying smiles, forced compliments, careful brows, and made laughs amongst the elders. People talk of nothing but foreign peace, and think of nothing but domestic war. For my own part, I am quite sick of hearing the same things over and over again from morning till night. Quid-nuncing is more my abhorrence than ever. I despise the actors, hate the piece and dislike the theatre so much, that 'tis making you no great compliment to say I long to get into the easy commerce of such a conversation as yours, when at the same time I am to get rid of the unentertaining, unprofitable galimatias, which folly, [1]ignorance and hypocrisy[1] pour into one's ears here all day long.

I need not tell you the inclosed is written by Swift.[2] It bears too strong a stamp of the distinguishing qualities of all his writings for you to want that information. Wit, humour, wildness, nastiness and rancour, make it easy for one to know his pen, and as little desirable to know his person. I am pleased with as much reluctance by such a man's writings, as I used to be by Don Galoppo's jokes. Whatever one may think or venture to say in private company, sure no man ought to be suffered to write and print a ridicule upon the established religion or an invective against the established Government of any society of which he is a member, and under whose protection he lives in ease, affluence and liberty. The inclosed, and the *Tale of a Tub* are indisputably written with a vast deal of spirit and vivacity; but I think he deserves to be hanged for one, and to have his gown pulled over his ears for t'other. Adieu,

> My heart's delight, in whom alone I find
> All that at once improves and charms the mind.

Trouble with the posts did not end there!

What the meaning can be of your having received no letter from me by Monday's post I can not conceive. You ought to

[1–1] Corrected in Hervey's writing.

[2] "The inclosed" must have been a pamphlet, from the reference in letter of December 2, but it is difficult to identify.

have had two, one for yourself, and another for your sister enclosed to you. Whoever has had curiosity enough to keep them, has robbed you of nothing very valuable. . . . This conveyance is become so little private, that I have some thoughts of saving the expense of wax for the future, myself the trouble of sealing, and the postmaster that of opening my letters. . . .

Early in December, on the 2nd, Hervey wrote again. In this we find another blood feud amongst the operatic stars, in the persons of Signora Stradina (no doubt Strada, a very fine "treble") and Signora Merighi, who were engaged by John James Heidegger, the Swiss impresario, at the time working with Handel at the King's Theatre, to which they had moved after the Academy of Music had failed to open its doors.[1] Heidegger was still running masquerades at the King's Theatre, Haymarket, in a large adjoining room. These commenced during George I's reign. Merighi was a woman of very fine presence, and an excellent actress.

TO STEPHEN FOX *December 2, 1729*[2]

. . . I differ from you extremely in your opinion of Swift's pamphlet . . . for so far from neither liking nor disliking it, I do both in a great degree. We are to have an Opera tonight, the royal interposition having found means to mediate between the incensed heroines, and compose the differences which arose on Stradina's name having the pas of Merighi's in the libretto. The latter, in the first flush of her resentment on the sight of this indignity, swore nothing but the Parliament should make her submit to it. You think this perhaps a joke of mine; but 'tis literal truth, and I think too absurd to be imputed to anything but Nature, whose productions infinitely surpass all human invention, and whose characters have so indisputably the first place in comedy. She has a fund of ridicule and a variety in her pieces, that every day, every hour, and every personage, convinces one is inexhaustible. I take my dear Ld Lovel,[3] who is at present the darling idol of the professed wits of this good city, [4]tout ridicule qu'il est,[4] to be but a faint sketch of her excellence in this style.

[1] *See ante*, p. 17.

[2] Ickworth.

[3] Thomas Coke of Holkham (1697–1759) was raised to the peerage in 1728, as Baron Lovel; and was created Earl of Leicester in 1744. The title lapsed with him, and was later re-created.

[4–4] In Hervey's writing.

Old beaux of fifty talking more plausible nonsense than his Lordship over solitaires: grey-haired coquets in gauze—heads and moutonnées . . . : people who proclaim against the corruption of the times, and will cheat you of half a guinea at quadrille: and all the little scrub-actors with bad hearts and worse heads, that one sees squeezing, bowing and smiling at Court, or that one hears canting in the Parliament or in the pulpit. All these, with a thousand more I could enumerate, are characters as much more entertaining than my Ld Lovel in my opinion, as the little, transparent cunning of a natural monkey is more amusing than the affected, taught, noisy gambols of an irritated bear, which generally proves the folly of its audience more than its own, and gives one as much contempt for their taste as it's own performances. . . .[1]

Let me tell you before I bid you Adieu, that you are always dear to me. Always appear amiable, to deserve my best wishes and services, and you shall always have them as fully as you can deserve them. On Saturday, thank God, I shall see you,

In dull equality, the sandy store
Of Time, still parcels out the measured hour.
Could I in absence cut the tedious day,
With interest when we meet the debt to pay?

[1] A good story of a conversation between Lord Lovel and Lord Chesterfield a few weeks after this, is related by Lord Perceval (*Egmont MSS.*). Shortly, Lord Lovel said that if he voted in the future with the Court, he expected to be paid for it with a rise in the Peerage. "That," said Chesterfield, "is impossible: that is asking what the King cannot do." Lovel reminded him that he had already been created a Baron in this reign, and asked him to explain his meaning. "Why if you will have it," replied Chesterfield, "it is a maxim of our law that the King can do no wrong."

CHAPTER IV

1730

With a new year, 1730, Hervey's letters swing back to a number addressed to Henry Fox.[1] In May 1728 Henry had made a third attempt to get into the House of Commons, this time at Old Sarum, a seat under the control of Thomas Pitt, Earl of Londonderry, who had been appointed to an office of profit. Winnington wrote in the autumn, "It was your fortune to lose the election by one voice only; for Pitt, not suspecting any opposition, had but two votes there, except the person who voted for you." [2] Since that time he had been managing the Redlynch property while his brother was abroad, and by living there was keeping it warm for him. Stephen wrote to Henry on January 17, 1729/30, that he had spent a day, the first of the session, in the House of Commons. "We had so long and entertaining a debate that the House did not rise till a quarter after twelve. Winnington took notes, and intends to send you a particular account of it. . . ."

A series of debates followed. The Treaty of Seville was debated in the House of Lords on January 27. In the Commons, on Wednesday, 28th, Henry Pelham, then Secretary at War, moved to maintain 17,000 land troops: and on February 3, came a debate to continue for a year longer 12,000 Hessian troops in British pay.

TO HENRY FOX *January 15, 1729/30*[3]

I must begin my letter with assuring you, dear Count, that 'tis neither laziness nor negligence that has hindered me writing sooner; I enquired of your brother what he intended to send you by the coach, and found his diligence to entertain you had left mine nothing to transmit. . . .

The Address in the House of Lords was moved by Lord Falmouth, and seconded by Lord Findlater; in the House of

[1] Neither the Melbury series nor the Ickworth copies contain any letters between December 1729 and June 1730.

[2] There was no house in the constituency, and only seven voters! Fox's opponent apparently did not blame him for any underhand plot. T. Harrison was Lord Londonderry's successor.

[3] Holland House.

Commons by Lord Fitzwilliams,[1] and your Hindon antagonist, Mr. Andrews. Lord Fitzwilliams' performance was darker, thicker and heavier than the fog of this day, in which I am now writing and yawning and vainly wishing for light. I am sorry when God thought fit to send such a piece of original obscurity and chaos into the world as that head, that he did not think fit to dispel the mists of it by the same methods which Moses tells us he made use of to enlighten the rest of the universe. Human aids, I am sure, can never bring it about; and without the immediate word of God, " Let there be light ", I am convinced that impenetrable, palpable cloud can never receive it. To say truth, I am afraid his dullness is contagious; for though the House sat till eleven at night, I neither heard one argument above the style of a Coffee House, or one joke above the mirth of an Ale House. Alterations at Court there are as yet none; and none, 'tis said, will be, till the end of the Session. I have seen Ld Sunderland, who enquir'd much after you. I wish for you very often and very sincerely when I am alone in my Library. The agreeable commerce of so clear a head and so pure a heart, in the midst of the *poverties*, hypocrisy and trash one meets with amongst the rest of the world, is what I am capable of putting so just a value upon, that, let your acquaintance be never so general, I may venture to assure you none can ever be more sensible of your merit, than, my dear Count, your ever faithful, humble servant, H.

TO HENRY FOX *London, January the 24th* [*1729/30*] [2]

You see, dear Count, by this second letter, how little I insist on the form of a reply, and that I am not partial enough to such small favours as to expect more thanks for them than they deserve. I have nothing to send you; but for fear you should imagine your receiving nothing from me might proceed from a negligence, and not an impotence to entertain you, I write to prove what most people would be reluctant to own. There

[1] Richard, Viscount Fitzwilliam of Merrion, who died in 1742. M.P. for Fowey in Cornwall, 1727–34. The debate in the Commons is related at some length by Lord Perceval. (*Egmont*, i, 3.)

[2] Holland House.

is a ballad about town, which they say is a satire upon the Court ; but people are so very cautious and discreet about it, that I can neither get a copy nor a sight of it. You will think me grown very grave, when I tell you there was a masquerade on Thursday, and that I was not there ; but I have got so violent a cold that I do nothing but cough all night and blow my nose all day. Your brother, Lord Sunderland,[1] and Lord Portmore [2] had last night the honour and pleasure to be admitted into the fraternity of Free Masons. I have not seen any of their simple countenances since the operation.

Winnington is in a sort of inactive state as yet. There has not been business enough in the House to make him once open. When the Hessians break cover, I suppose both packs will be in full cry.[3]

My own affairs are at a full stand, as well as every other body's that has any expectations or tenures from the Court ; no alterations of any kind, they say, will be made there till the end of the Session. I pass my time in a hum drum way, neither to be envied nor much to be pitied. I have too few pursuits to have many disappointments, and too few possessions to have many pleasures. My prudence makes me avoid wine, and my ill-fortune wont let me fall in love ; so that I live in a privation of the joys of this world, without any enthusiastic satisfaction of foregoing them for those of another, and have neither passions enough to give me a pleasure in indulging them nor a merit in withstanding them. I am of Dorinda's mind, who says " è perduto tutto il tempo che in amar non si spende " ; and can't help thinking 'tis a cruel disposition of Providence, that when one loves where one would that one cant love as long as one would.

We now turn to the foreign side of politics. Since the last session the Treaty of Seville had been concluded, as we have seen ; and this

[1] Charles Spencer, 5th Earl (1706–58) who succeeded his brother, Robert, two months before this. Their father had died in 1722, and their mother in 1716. He became 3rd Duke of Marlborough on the death of his aunt, Henrietta, Countess of Godolphin and 2nd Duchess of Marlborough in her own right.

[2] Charles Colyear, 2nd Earl (1700–85). Envoy to Don Carlos, respecting Pavia and Placentia, 1731–2.

[3] *See* p. 47.

had greatly strengthened Sir Robert Walpole's position. It had been negotiated by Colonel William Stanhope, a Vice-Chamberlain, until 1727 Envoy in Spain, and later Plenipotentiary to the Treaty at Aix and Soissons. He was shortly after created Lord Harrington, and succeeded Lord Townshend as Secretary of State for the Northern Department. The latter was becoming on worse and worse terms with his brother-in-law, Sir Robert, and had finally resigned office.

TO HENRY FOX *Thursday night [January 29, 1729/30]*[1]

I have so much business, dear Count, upon my hands to-night, that I have only time to thank you for your letter. Continue to write to me, though it be only to transmit *poverties*, as you call them. The character and tone of voice of one that one sincerely loves gives one always a pleasure, exclusive of the particular subjects on which this or that may be employed. The world is more politic-mad than ever. Sh—n[2] talked very open (and they say guarded) treason yesterday in the House: and with ironical panegyrics on the K., said, upon the account of what forces would be necessary to be kept up this year being presented by Mr. Pelham to the House, that tyrants and usurpers only had recourse to violence and a military Government to support them. The debate on the Hessians, which has set everybody's expectations agog, comes on on Wednesday. Your brother and I go out of town to Lord Bateman's[3] to-morrow morning for three days. Lord Sunderland is ill. Lord Bingley[4] did not vote with the minority, and spoke against them in the great debate in the House of Lords on the Peace. Je n'ai plus de temps ni des nouvelles.

Hervey wrote to Henry Fox apparently on February 4:[5]

I give you a thousand thanks for your letter. Your natural sentiments must always be agreeable, whether conveyed in sounds

[1] Holland House.

[2] Shippen, the well-known Jacobite. The debate was on the War Office vote.

[3] William Bateman, created a Viscount in 1725. Died in 1744. He married, in 1720, Anne, 2nd daughter of Charles, 3rd Earl of Sunderland, a granddaughter of Sarah, Duchess of Marlborough.

[4] Robert Benson, Lord Bingley (1676–1731), Treasurer of the Household.

[5] Holland House.

or upon paper. But if yesterday had left me spirits and words enough to transmit my arguments, I think I could produce many good ones against some round assertions in yours, which I take [to] be absolutely begging a question which you and I have often disputed, and I believe shall dispute to the day of our deaths.

I refer you to your politician—quid-nunc—correspondent Winnington for an account of yesterday's debate on the Hessians.[1] It lasted so long, that I did not sit down to dinner till near eleven. Your antagonist, Mr. Heathcourt,[2] [*sic*] made a flaming speech against the Court, which he had collected from a common-place book on tyranny and arbitrary power and extracts of treatises on a free Government; and which would have served just as well for any debate that ever was or ever will be in Parliament as that to which it was applied. I took this opportunity to wish Sir Robert (with whom I dined) joy of his new friend, and asked him if he did not think his pains well bestowed. Adieu. I am so stupid, my eyes, ears, thoughts, and every sense so clouded, that I can not utter one syllable more.

TO HENRY FOX *Feb. 17, 29/30*[3]

I find nothing in your letter, dear Count, but what is agreeable, but do not find every thing that is so; since it does not mention

[1] The following is part of Winnington's Report. The debate is also reported in Perceval's *Diary* (*Egmont*), i, 24, *et seq.*

"We had a long debate upon the Hessians, which was only managed by the small artillery, the great guns not firing. Those who were against them said they were now unnecessary, unless they were intended for the support of the Hanover Dominions, which we ought not to defend under the Act of Settlement. Those who were on the other side, said we were obliged to keep them in pursuance of our alliance, and so make the Treaty of Seville effectual. Your friend Mr. Heathcote made a speech against them out of the depths of Whiggism. To say the truth, Majesty and the German Dominions were treated with great familiarity. Ld Hervey spoke for them very well. The question was whether the Estimate should be referred to a Committee. Ayes 248. Noes 169. . . ."

[2] George Heathcote sat for Hindon with Townshend Andrews. "The whole power of the Ministry was exerted to give him admittance in the House, to the exclusion of Mr Fox, who was generally supposed to have the fairer right." Lord Perceval's *Diary* (*Egmont*), i, 27. Lord Hervey's speech was largely extempore. He acted as Teller.

[3] Holland House.

your having any design of letting me see you soon in London. The ease and freedom of your tête à têtes are relaxations which I assure you very sincerely my mind often wishes for, to unweary itself after the fatigue of being in masquerade for weeks together. I have particularly of late longed for it, on some occasions too long to be repeated and too nice to be reported in a letter. Things almost incredible have happened, and that would have surprised anybody but one who has had so general an acquaintance with human kind, that he can wonder at nothing but people's acting either reasonably, honestly or consistently. For which reason, I recur to my old maxim of wishing to be in love; for, as there is no pleasure without liking and wishing well to the people one lives with, so there is no way to have those sensations for them but being under some circumstances that make you deaf and blind to those things which, without being so, you must discover every hour to their disadvantage. But for my sins, that happy privation of one's senses I am cured of, and labour in vain to be re-infected by so charming a disease that I should be glad to keep my bed of it the rest of my life. You see by what I have said I am incorrigible, and that neither precept nor example can influence my opinion. There may be some amusement in the pursuit of other points, but there is no pleasure in the possession of anything but that.

I can't send you what you desire me; upon my word it is not in my power. As to pamphlets, you have had all that have been written. I send you by this post the Lords' Protest [1] and a Satire of Swift's. You never send me your opinion of anything, though you know I do not only think you *la balance à la main*, but as good a thing, *which is* le bon goût à la tête. . . .

People's expectations are mightily raised by the affair of Dunkirk [2] which comes on on Friday se'enight. Tout le monde s'embourbe plus que jamais dans la politique. I am upon this

[1] Against the Pensions Bill.

[2] On February 12, Sir W. Wyndham brought a motion on the subject of the destruction of the Dunkirk fortifications, "that these had been a manifest violation of the Treaties". Walpole obtained an adjournment of eight days, and on February 27 produced an order from Louis XIV for demolition, and carried the House against the motion. Thus "Dunkirk Day" became proverbial, even in that century!

occasion just in the same situation with people who go *randying* [1], and hate tobacco. They detest smoking, can't do it, make themselves sick with trying at it, and live in a cloud of it every day of their lives. Mais le moyen de l'éviter ?

TO HENRY FOX *[February 19, 1729/30]* [2]

The enclosed is supposed to be written by Dr. Croxal,[3] upon the House of Commons not desiring him to print a sermon preached before them the 30th of January, on this text :—" Take the wicked from before the throne, and the people shall flourish." I believe I don't repeat the words right ; but they were to this effect. I think the letter indifferent enough, but 'tis new ; and that you say is always a recommendation. I am in a great hurry, going to a masquerade at Lady Tyrconnel's, where the K., P., and every creature in London of the known world are invited. Adieu.

Thursday night.

TO HENRY FOX *March the 3rd, [1729/30]* [4]

Dear Count,

I am but just come from *Sophonisba*,[5] the new play, and 'tis so late that I am afraid my letter will not be time enough ; yet can not help thanking you for your's and telling you (not complimentally) how glad I am to hear you will be soon in town. There is nothing worth one's concern at a distance, either in time or place. 'Tis a maxim of your own ; cherish it, and live up to it as well as the rules which follows it, and never forbear making any pleasure as sweet as you can, for fear of shortening it. One's stomach had better recoil than one's taste never be

[1] i.e. ranting.

[2] Holland House.

[3] Dr. Samuel Croxall, D.D. (d. 1752). His sermon on the anniversary of King Charles's death was printed. He wrote a number of books and verses, including lines entitled *The Fair Circassian*, addressed to Miss Anna Maria Mordaunt, one of Queen Caroline's Maids of Honour. This obtained some notoriety, and was often reprinted. It first appeared in 1720. (*See also* pp. 75, 145.)

[4] Holland House.

[5] A Tragedy, by James Thomson (1700–48).

gratified. You enquire about Dunkirk. All I can tell you is that the House sat till four in the morning ; and instead of voting any censure upon the Administration, as the malcontents gave and conceived hopes of, an Address of Thanks to His Majesty for his early care, and congratulations upon the success of that care, was resolved upon by a majority of 270 to 149. I stayed it out : went afterwards abroad to dinner, sat up till six, rose again at ten, walked to Kensington, and was as well next day (and have continued so ever since) as ever I was in my life. Are not times well mended with me ? Adieu. Love me always, and believe me most gratefully and warmly,

Your's.

In the Ministerial changes which took place in May, Lord Hervey secured the recognition for which he asked in his letter to Sir Robert Walpole, and was made a Privy Councillor and Vice-Chamberlain. He was appointed to succeed Colonel William Stanhope, created Lord Harrington. In order that Hervey should receive re-election before the end of the session, the gold key was sent for from Harrington, who was still abroad ; and it was handed to him on May 7.

Lord Townshend, consequent on these changes, retired to the country, and refused to take further part in the business of the nation : but never allowed the breach with his brother-in-law to interfere with their private relations. On Lord Carteret's return from Ireland, where he had served for six years as Lord Lieutenant, he was offered the Lord Stewardship, but refused it. He was to replace the Duke of Dorset, who was going to Ireland ; and that Court post was then given to Lord Chesterfield, notwithstanding his recent collaboration with Lord Townshend.

As no letters are forthcoming in May, we hear nothing directly of Hervey's appointment ; but we find references to it in June, when his letters to Stephen recommence. The first is dated from Windsor, June 13 :

TO STEPHEN FOX[1]

. . . You love the facts of gazettes I know : and therefore I wish I could retain the stuff my eyes and ears every hour involuntarily receive. You don't know the compliment I make to you in that wish, when I would carry that rubbish for you which no other consideration would bribe me not to disburden my

[1] Ickworth.

mind of as fast as I could. Lord Harrington arrived here this morning. On parle encore de la Paix. Last preparations are making for *Thursday*.[1] His Grace of Dorset is to be the Sir Clement Cotterell[2] of that day's ceremonial. I have already had my lecture of instructions, as to bows, steps, attitudes, etc., being to walk and officiate as Lord Chamberlain.

The King is gracious to me and in constant good humour; and if the want of you was not always sufficient to leaven the whole lump of all my other pleasures, I should be happy. Adieu.

TO STEPHEN FOX [*Windsor*] *June 19th, 1730*[3]

. . . I was yesterday from seven a clock in the morning till two this morning constantly upon my legs, excepting half an hour that I was at dinner, and about an hour that I lay down in the afternoon; to compensate for which trouble I had the recreation of seeing one set of performers, bowing till their backs ached four hours in the morning, another set eating till they spewed and drinking till they reeled at noon, and a third dancing and sweating till they were ready to drop at night. Your brother was here with Hamilton.[4] I got them both into the Chapel and the Hall; but they went to London before the ball. Lord Sunderland dines with me today. Why are you not of the party? What are you doing at Redlynch? You are as much present in my mind as if I had seen you but this morning; and yet it seems as long as if I had not seen you these seven years.

Lord President[5] died suddenly at two a clock this morning. D. of Dorset was declared this day Ld.-Lieutenant of Ireland, in Council; and Lord Chesterfield had his staff at the same time.[6] Adieu.

[1] St. George's Feast. [Note in Horace, Earl of Orford's writing.] For the explanation of these notes, *see* Preface, p. xiv.

[2] Died in 1758. Master of the Ceremonies.

[3] Ickworth.

[4] Charles Hamilton, of Painshill (1694–1756), youngest son of James, 6th Earl of Abercorn, a devoted friend of the Foxes. Later in life he became an authority on gardening and arboriculture.

[5] Thomas, 1st Lord Trevor of Bromham. Judge. Lord Privy Seal 1726–30. He was made President of the Council in May, but died a month later.

[6] As Lord Steward.

Several letters in July follow full of friendship and affection for Stephen, but of no special interest. Late in August, however, we find three which may be printed.

TO STEPHEN FOX *Windsor, August 21st* [*1730*] [1]

What are the Royal pleasures you talk of my dear, dear Ste., which are not given equally to every subject? Do the trappings of Royalty make the amusements of the country more agreeable? Are our chaises easier or our boats safer for being gilt? Is the air sweeter for a Court; or the walks pleasanter for being bounded with sentinels? What entertainment does Windsor afford that cannot be found at Redlynch? But transpose that question, and I should quickly answer—the greatest joy I ever did or can know. Do not then ungratefully to me, and unjustly to yourself, any more imagine but that the privation of that dear something unpossessed,

Corrodes and levens all the rest.

* * * * *

What joys I have you may partake,
And all I taste, 'tis you must make.

For this reason I beg you would not encourage yourself in supposing that the walks of life we are thrown into have so few paths of communication, that one of us must go out of his way whenever we meet. Why should we only see one another by visits, but never have a common home. Think, if you please, that it is not easy to contrive it, but take care of concluding it impossible. For though one is not rebutted by difficulties in obtaining what one likes, impossibilities of obtaining it quickly cure one of liking it; and I am convinced people have much oftener failed of the possession of what they desired from the weakness of their pursuit than from the strength of the obstacle. So much for moralizing and pleading my own cause; and now for the indulgence of your quid-nunc lechery, I must acquaint you with a piece of Prussian news, which has for these ten days last past furnished the subject of every whisper and consultation in Windsor,

[1] Ickworth.

and in ten more will furnish the *Gazettes* of every State in Europe. The abridgement of the story is this. His Prussian Majesty,[1] bearish as he is, being yet more a bear to his son than to any other body belonging to him, by a constant series of brutality put that into his son's head which naturally occurs to every body upon the sight of a mad savage—which is running away. But as this poor Prince, either for want of caution in concealing his measures or honesty in those he trusted, was discovered in his design before he could execute it, his father has put him and all his supposed accomplices (except one page who has made his escape to Holland) in different dungeons. This was the news of the last express. How the monster intended to proceed no body could guess ; but as he has been often heard to applaud the conduct of the Czar [2] with regard to the Czarawits [*sic*] as the greatest part of his character, the relations of this Czarawits, I find, are in great apprehensions of the King's bringing this matter to an extremity of which there are so many Eastern examples, though there is yet but one Northern one. Send the peacocks when they will be best, but give me notice.

TO STEPHEN FOX *Windsor, August 26th, 1730* [3]

I have just this moment received and read your letter with that sort of sensation, which I am only acquainted with in occurrences where you are concerned. How one devours flattery from the hand of those one loves ; what a feast it is to one's taste, and what wholesome nourishment to one's heart ! Though I own that it is entirely according to the cook who prepares it ;

[1] Frederick William I reigned from 1713 to 1740 in Prussia. His abominable treatment of his son, who succeeded him as Frederick II, is fully told by Thomas Carlyle in his *Frederick the Great*, and is elsewhere described. Lord Perceval (*Egmont MSS.*, i, 103) gives as the reason for the Prince's flight, that his father was planning to make him marry the Archduchess, and turn Papist.

[2] Peter the Great, who reigned in Russia from 1685 till 1725. The Czarevitch Alexeis, his son by his first marriage, was born in 1690 ; and was father of Peter II. A weakling from birth, he fled to Vienna, in terror of his father. From thence he was decoyed back to Russia, and although he renounced his succession to the throne in favour of his son, he was thrown into prison, where he died at the age of twenty-eight, after torture and the knout.

[3] Ickworth.

for, as I frequently see it served up here, it turns one's stomach. What strong digestions then must they have, who can swallow all day without surfeiting that which will make a stander-by sick only with seeing it brought to the table. These Court ostriches are my perpetual astonishment, who are so used to these iron morsels that lighter food is not felt in their stomachs. They are like people who use themselves to drams. They come at last to value no liquor for the flavour, but to consider it only for its strength. You are my Eau de Barbade, that intoxicates my spirits without vitiating my taste, and are so much superior to common draught in every particular that one need not blush for being drunk with you. At least I dont, and own I languish as much for want of the daily dose of you which I have been so long used to, as Lord Scarsdale can do for his three flasks of claret, and feel as sensible a decay of spirits in a transition to any other company, as he could do upon being reduced to water. If you are not as fond of hearing of yourself, as I am of talking and thinking of you, mon Dieu, comme mes lettres vous ennuyent. I approve of your manner of spending your time, taking exercise whilst 'tis cool, loitering and reading when 'tis hot, and eating only when you are hungry ; but if every body was to follow your example and do nothing by habit or prescription, but every thing by choice and impulse, how many idle people there would be in the world. Fools are obliged to custom for the little they enjoy ; those who are not fools would enjoy much more if they were not constrained by it.

The abdication of the King of Sardinia, King Victor Amadeus II (1675–1732), in favour of his son, is described in the letter of August 31 to Stephen Fox. The King had succeeded to the throne in the year of his birth. He married Princess Anne of Orleans, grand-daughter of Charles I of England, but was constantly quarrelling with Louis XIV: and defeated the French at the siege of Turin in 1706. He was made King of Sicily at the Treaty of Utrecht in 1713 : but in 1718 was forced to exchange the Crown for that of Sardinia. Upon his resignation of the throne to his son, Victor Amadeus III (d. 1773), he retired to Chambéry, and married the Comtesse de San Sebastien (created Marchesa di Spigna). Her influence was exerted to make the old King reclaim the crown; and in consequence, as we shall see, he was arrested by his son's orders, and died in prison in 1732.

Unfortunately the letter is badly torn, and several important lines at the conclusion of it are lost. It seems worth publishing, however, even in its mutilated state, as neither the *Memoirs*, nor Coxe, in his *Life of Sir Robert Walpole*, make any mention of the incident. Indeed, both these prime authorities skip the two ensuing years, and recommence their narrative in January 1732/33.

It is impossible to judge the reason for the gap, as no notice at all is taken of it in the *Memoirs*, nor is any attempt at explanation given. The matter is discussed in the Preface (*see ante*, pp. x, xi).

Lord Hervey's letters now before us, therefore, gain importance, disjointed though they are, in supplying information on incidents which do not come within the purview of the *Memoirs* as they have come down to us.

TO STEPHEN FOX *Windsor, August 31st, 1730* [1]

You have too good an understanding to be surprised at many things ; but what I am going to relate I dare swear will astonish you. The King of Sardinia has resigned the Crown to his son. Do not imagine this is only rumour : 'tis undoubted, certain truth. About nine a clock last night, whilst we were at play in the King's private apartment, the Duke of Newcastle came in, like Prince Guicomar, " haste in his steps and wonder in his eye ", to let [2] the King [2] know that the Chevalier d'Ossorio [3] was that moment come from London, upon the arrival of a courier from Turin, to acquaint [2] his Grace with this piece of news.[2] This morning the Chevalier notified to the King in form, and delivered his [message . . . to] the King. The old King . . . (*mutilated*) . . . to let him know that his reason for [taking this serious] step, was his being wearied with the weight and labours of a Crown which he had worn for fifty years : and that the infirmities of age and a broken constitution made him incapable of undergoing the same fatigues of business which he had hitherto submitted to for the good of his people. He would give the reins into the hands of his son, whose youth he had taken care to fashion for what he was born to, and who was now capable of executing the lessons he had given him and following the example he had shown him. That it was upon the most mature deliberation that he had taken this step, as well

[1] Melbury. [2–2] Added in Lord Hervey's writing.
[3] The Sardinian Minister.

as for the good of his own soul as the advantage of his subjects, who might have suffered under an enervated Government ; and that for the future the Chevalier must look upon his son as his Master ; he having that very day signed . . . [*the rest mutilated.*]

Early in September, on the 4th,[1] Hervey seems to have driven to London from Windsor to attend a royal party. Such was Court life in those days.

The bustle of yesterday getting up by five a clock, and sitting up till past two, has half killed me ; but I must be quite so, before I neglect to thank you for any mark of your kindness. I have lain abed most part of this day, and am this moment stepping into the coach to return to Windsor. It went off much better last night than things of that form generally do. Every body was gay, easy, and seemed pleased ; but particularly the P.[2] and Duchess of M.,[3] who are so taken with one another, that I am not sure it will not end in a flirtation. Adieu. My head aches so much that I can not write one word more.

TO STEPHEN FOX *Windsor, September 7th, 1730*[4]

There is no part of my time I repine so much at not being master of, as the hours I wish to dedicate to you ; and though this is a misfortune that happens to me every post day, it is one I am as impatient under as if I was not accustomed to it. The King is this moment come from a horse-race, where popularity I believe carried him, as it does a stag-hunting ; for sure the pleasure of both these entertainments were calculated for much better eyes than His Majesty's. The last letters bring but indifferent accounts of the poor P. of Prussia ; his father's severities increase daily towards him and all his adherents ; in so much that I should not be at all surprised to hear of his having proceeded

[1] Ickworth.

[2] Frederick Lewis, Prince of Wales (1707–51), who had arrived in England for the first time in December 1728. He is first mentioned in these letters on p. 49.

[3] Henrietta, 2nd Duchess of Marlborough (1681–1733), daughter of John, 1st Duke of Marlborough, whom she succeeded in the title in 1722. She married Francis, 2nd Earl of Godolphin, who died in 1766.

[4] Ickworth.

to extremities for which I know but one example. I shall never have done wondering at the K. of Sardinia ; he is as incomprehensible as the Trinity.

I cannot resist giving you an account of the Princess of Holstein's wedding. I read it in a private letter from one of the King of Poland's family, who was present at it, to an Hanoverian officer now at Windsor. She was called Countess of Rosinski [*sic*], is natural daughter to his Polish Majesty, his declared mistress, and privately well with her brother the Count Rotoski.[1] The King, tired of her, insisted on her marrying this Prince of Holstein; and he, tired of being poor, consented to take her with a pension of 12,000 German crowns which her father offered to get rid of her. The lady, who liked being a w—— in jack-boots better than a Princess in petticoats, and preferred drinking in a camp to curtseying in a Drawing Room, told her future spouse, that though he did marry her, she would not only continue to lie with those she liked, but would upon no terms ever consent to lie with one she did not, and that inflicting his name upon her should never be a plea for his inflicting his person. The wise Prince, thinking of nothing but the 12,000 crowns, very loyally and philosophically told her that he thought himself obliged to obey his King, and would trust to her goodness and his own unwearied endeavours to please her for the reversal of so hard a sentence as what she then pronounced. Upon these terms the nuptials were solemnised in the most pompous manner. The day passed in feasting, balls, shows, etc. At night the lady was laid with the usual ceremonies in bed; the husband was afterwards brought dead drunk by the bride-grooms (whom she

[1] This lady's history is fully told by Thomas Carlyle in his *Frederick the Great*. He mentions her as one of Augustus the Strong's 354 children (King of Poland (1670–1733)), and calls her Countess Orzelska. Carlyle palliates Count Rotoski's relations with her, by remarking that he too was one of the illegitimate sons, and that he probably had no idea of their relationship. Of the lady he wrote, " Her history is not to be touched, except upon compulsion, as if with a pair of tongs ". An account of her is given by Pöllnitz at some length.

The Prince of Holstein was a Major-General in the Saxon Service, a brother of the Prince of Holstein-Beck, who Carlyle tells us sold his appanage in order to buy plate, whence he became known as " Holstein-Vaisselle ", i.e. " Holstein Plate " !

had bribed with gold or beauty to make him so), and laid in the bed by her. The company was no sooner gone out of the room, but she rose, went into another apartment, and slept very quietly all night. The husband waking in the morning would have followed her, but found the room fortified, the lady determined not to capitulate, and so was forced to raise the siege. She told him, as Evadne does Amintor,[1] this was no affected coyness for a night, but that he was never to expect more favour at her hands; and his inclination being much weaker than her aversion, and his love of 12,000 crowns so much stronger than that he had for her person, he submitted: and said since she insisted upon it, he saw no great difference between beginning the part of a husband at the fifth act or the first. And since the indifference they felt for one another was what all married people must come to, he thought a little sooner or a little later would make no great odds in their happiness, and that very possibly their having never been fond, might make them civil with less constraint. The truth of this was soon proved, by his going in two days with her to a convent, to see a natural child she had there at nurse, with as much sang-froid as if he had begot it. Adieu, this history perhaps may tire you, but it entertained me.

TO STEPHEN FOX *Windsor, September 9th, 1730*[2]

I have been hunting all this morning with the King in the worst country, the worst weather, and with the worst dogs, that ever poor sportsmen were cursed with. I fancy the King says to himself every hunting morning, take *physick pomp* [*sic*], as the King does in Hamlet, and has put himself into a course of these Royal medicines for the good of his body politic. For my part I was so tired, I went to bed the instant I came home, dined there upon chocolate, and am now writing from thence. Your account of your colleague, [3]Sir Edward Des Bouverie,[3]

[1] Characters in *The Maiden's Tragedy*, by Beaumont and Fletcher, 1619.

[2] Ickworth.

[3-3] [Added in a later hand]. Sir Edward died in 1736. He was an ancestor of the present Radnor family.

being too great a man to take shelter from the rain in a coach diverted me. The Sir Edward of our Castle, from the same way of reasoning, came home from the horse-race an hour before I received your letter, wet to the skin in an open chaise, whilst we *chickens* of his suite chose the ignoble safety of a dry coach with glasses drawn up.

If everybody's composition was not made up of inconsistencies, I should wonder with you how the same thought could ever enter the heads of the King of Spain[1] and King of Sardinia; but as the wisest sometimes differ from themselves, it is no wonder they sometimes agree with the weakest. I am sorry to hear when you have supposed yourself a King, that you could believe it possible ever to be weary of being so, for fear that abdicating principle should be predominant too in your real possessions, and that you may be one day tired of reigning in a heart that can never be tired of being under your dominion.

I see Lord and Lady Bateman very often. I dine there, they dine here; they hunt with us in the morning, play with us at night, and seem to take very kindly to the Court. The P. is most particularly civil to them. Old Marlborough[2] is come to the Lodge, and lets Lady Di. sometimes be of the party. [3]Thereby hangs a tale. She[3] invited me to dinner, and used me like a dog for trying to get this little Park for my friend Charles.[4] She took that occasion to hold in a hand upon her daughter's character, till her nose worked, her cheeks flushed, and her whole fabric trembled.

I hear nothing of the Courts removing to Kensington.

[1] Philip V is indicated, who abdicated in 1724, in favour of his son Louis. The latter died a few months later, when Philip resumed the Monarchy. The simile thereby, as we shall see, became even more apparent.

[2] Sarah Jennings (1660–1744) married John Churchill, later created Duke of Marlborough in 1678. He died in 1722, having had a son, who predeceased him, and four daughters. The eldest, Henrietta, as we have seen married the Earl of Godolphin, while the 2nd, Anne, married the 3rd Earl of Sunderland, as his 2nd wife, but died in 1716. The youngest daughter of the Sunderlands, Lady Diana Spencer, lived with her grandmother; their eldest was Lady Bateman, whom the old Duchess detested.

[3–3] In Hervey's writing.

[4] Lord Sunderland. Was Hervey trying to get the Rangership for his friend?

TO STEPHEN FOX *September 14th, 1730*[1]

. . . We jog on here le vieux train. A little walking, a little hunting and a little playing, a little flattering, a little railing and a little lying : a little hate, a little friendship, and a little love : a little hope and a little fear, a little joy and a little pain. They are the ingredients that compose the daily vicissitudes of Court meals, and though some of them are rather [2] hard of digestion ; yet if one knows the quality and manages the quantity of them, I think, with some caution, not too nice a taste, and a good digestion, it is possible to live at such a table and escape both starving and surfeiting. For though one is forced in civility to take a dab of every one of these dishes upon one's plate, one need swallow only what one likes, and give the rest away. Monsr. Deggenfield [Degenfeld], the Prussian Envoy (whose name I know not how to spell), has at last had his audience of the K. They say he has cried *Peccavi* in form in his Master's name, for the affront done to our's, in the person of Sir C. H.[3] How true it is, God knows. All I know is that his public reception was as cold as his climate. Sir Luke Shaub [4] is going Envoy to Poland. The Queen was taken ill last night with a touch of the gout. Celâ sent la Gazette ; c'est un récit qui m'ennuit. Adieu.

TO STEPHEN FOX *Windsor, September 16th, 1730* [5]

. . . I have persuaded Ld Bateman to be at Old Windsor [6] when you are here. Not that I will lend you for a moment of the day or night that I can have you ; but in order, if I can

[1] Ickworth. [2] In Hervey's writing, replacing the words " a little ", erased.

[3] Sir Charles Hotham, the British Representative in Berlin. Lord Perceval (*Egmont MSS.*, i, 100) gives an explanation of this entry. Hotham had been sent to Berlin, to try to obtain the recall of Reichenberg, the Prussian Envoy in London, who was in the habit of trying to stir up every possible discord between the two Courts. Hotham produced a letter to the King of Prussia, which proved his case ; but which the latter, instead of reading it, threw at his head. Sir Charles at once retired, and, refusing to close the incident, as being an indignity to his master, left Berlin without taking leave, although the King had perceived his gross mistake, and did his best to get the matter hushed up.

[4] Sir Luke Schaub (d. 1758), diplomat, and Ambassador in Paris 1720–4. His brother Col. Schaub held a high post in the Prince of Wales's Court.

[5] Ickworth. [6] The Batemans had a house there.

so contrive, that the hours you are not with me may not lie as heavy upon your hands, as I always find those in which I can not be with you ; for I can with a great deal truth upon this occasion say, as Lady Mary [1] does upon another :—

In crowded Courts I find myself alone.
And feel no commerce grateful, but your own.
Prudence, not taste, makes other walks my care,
For ev'ry line of pleasure centers there.
And whilst a thousand objects I pursue,
They're all as tasks or debts to custom due ;
I practice others, but I live with you.

I have often thought, if any very idle body had curiosity enough to intercept and examine my letters, they would certainly conclude they came rather from a mistress than a friend ; but it must be people that were unacquainted with you who made that conclusion. Otherwise, they might know that reason would make one as fond of your society, as passion could make one of any other body's. . . . Lord Bateman is grown quite a courtier. Adieu, mon bien aimable, mon bien aimé.

TO STEPHEN FOX *December 12th, 1730* [2]

. . . I was last night to see *Medea*, the new tragedy. The house was in one continued roar of laughter from the beginning of the 3d act to the end of the 5th. Mrs. Thurmond run mad, Mrs. Porter came from Heaven, and Mr. Wilks stabbed himself, all to the infinite mirth and satisfaction of the whole audience. The Epilogue was more tragical, or ought to be so for the author; for he certainly deserves to have every bone in his skin broken for his insolence. 'Tis a stupid, impertinent lampoon on my Lord Abergavenny, whom he might just as well have named as described in the colours he has chosen.[3]

[1] Lady Mary Wortley-Montagu (1689–1762) was daughter of Evelyn, 1st Duke of Kingston.

[2] Ickworth. There are a number of other letters in December, but of no special interest.

[3] The reference is to a recent and successful case of *crim. con.* brought by

I never hear any absurdities of any kind (and God knows I am seldom without hearing 'em of some kind or other), that I am not astonished how creatures of your species can be guilty of so many, or that you, who are of their's, can be exempt from them. There is but one [1] I know belongs to you, which is the being capable of feeling a kindness that I know no mortal on earth but yourself ever deserved. But 'tis some consolation to me [1] for not being like you, to think you could love me better if I were. To what purpose then should I wish it? And what good could it do me?

> Whilst I maintain my empire in that breast,
> Each wish is answer'd, and each good possess'd.

The time has arrived to attempt some reasoned explanation of Hervey's impassioned adoration of Stephen Fox, which was reaching its zenith about this time. To eliminate entirely the constant flow of expressions of affection with which his letters abound, might be to give an incorrect representation of their mutual relations. We have thought fit, however, while retaining the more ebullient passages, to cut drastically the avowals of devotion, which tend to become tedious and even mawkish by continual repetition. But in all this sentimentality, Hervey makes it clear that what was in his mind was true friendship. He seems to have felt an urgent call for someone to whom he could discreetly and safely confide his thoughts, to whom he could look for comfort and for real sympathy in a hard and exacting life.

And so in the early months of King George II's reign he came to the conclusion that Henry Fox was his man, although nine years his junior: and decided, wrongly as it turned out, that he had all those qualities for which he was searching. What occasioned that selection nowhere appears, but clearly they had met at Bath. Henry, however, was tried out and found wanting. He proved too restless, too ambitious, too exacting, to fill the niche into which Hervey tried to fit him. Henry, even in those early years, had his eye on the future, as became a provident younger son. They remained, however, the best of friends and regular correspondents, until in later years

Lord Abergavenny against the lover of his wife who had recently died. Hervey related the whole circumstances in detail in an earlier letter, but they are so unpleasant, that we have omitted them. *Medea* was acted only three times. The author was Charles Johnson. (Genest's *History of the Stage*, vol. iii.)

[1–1] In Hervey's writing.

Enoch Seeman (?), pinxit

JOHN, LORD HERVEY

political considerations drove them apart. But as soon as Hervey found that their paths seemed unlikely to run parallel, he turned his batteries at close range on the elder Fox brother within the first few months of their acquaintance. His success was instantaneous.

Stephen Fox was cast in a very different mould to that of his younger brother. He was as easy-going as Henry was turbulent, and had few decided aspirations to success in public life. He was content to live in the country, to cultivate rural pursuits, and to learn the duties of an owner of property. He thus had far more time on his hands to respond to urgent calls for sympathy and appreciation, even though life in London was of little interest to him.

Hervey's character was full of complexities and perplexities. But one aspect, which is brought into bold relief in his many portraits, was enlarged upon by his enemies and his detractors. Pulteney's phrase, " Little Master-Miss " : and Pope's " Amphibious thing ", that " now trips a Lady and now struts a Lord " : his " Lord Fanny " : and the " Lady of the Lords ", in the lines on his first speech in the House of Lords, by one of the *Craftsman's* scribblers,[1] are not so far from the truth as one might imagine. Nature had created him effeminate in appearance. Illness had added to the pallor of his complexion, to obviate which he was not above painting his face. These disabilities endowed him with a species of inferiority-complex which even led him on occasions to compare himself with a woman. " He seems in this relationship ", says Mr. Sedgwick, " irresistibly impelled to visualise himself as a girl." We agree. That seems to be the real explanation ; and he himself made no bones about it. He confessed quite frankly that Lady Deloraine scored a bulls-eye, when she said at Court to him and Miss Fitzwilliam, a Maid of Honour of masculine appearance, " that in her opinion a woman could never look too much like a woman, nor a man too much like a man ". All this fits in closely with the remarkable admissions made by Hervey in letters at this time, that they might be taken for those from a mistress ; though he laid great stress on the fact that no one who knew Stephen could come to that conclusion. And aga in, note his confession that he had blushed deeply on hearing his friend's name mentioned by mistake in a toast when he was not present, and felt just as " his favourite mistress " might have done. It is noticeable, however, that in all the scurrilous attacks on Hervey, we can find nothing to implicate Fox in the charges which Pulteney, Pope and the hack-writers so continuously hurled against the first-named, for there is little in Pope's verses entitled, *One thousand, Seven Hundred, and Twenty-eight* which applies to him, though brother Henry comes in for a share of the kicks.

[1] See Appendix C (*a*), p. 296.

Another remarkable feature in these effusions addressed to Stephen are the ultra-sentimental expressions with which Hervey was wont to terminate his letters, and which continue throughout the series. " Mon cher, et très cher, carissime " ; " caro et carissimo, et sempre caro " ; " mea cara et sola voluptas " ; " le plus aimable et le plus aimé qu'il y est au monde " ; are specimens of the superlatives with which Hervey interlarded his *Adieus*. In the earlier letters these endearing appendages are not so noticeable. It was after their journey to the Continent that they began to reach their maximum ; and there seems no doubt that Hervey realised that his friend had saved his life by his devoted and disinterested attentions on that trip. His health when he started, as we have seen, was at its worst. He came back a different man, cured temporarily at least of his worst symptoms, and fit to take up the life at Court, which was to be his constant occupation and delight until Queen Caroline's death eight years later. Gratitude for such services became an obsession, and coloured their everyday intercourse until Stephen's marriage to his child-bride in 1736, of which we hear nothing in the letters. But it is noticeable, after his meeting with Voltaire's friend, Count Algarotti, about the same time, that Hervey began to transfer similar endearments to this new acquaintance. The same old epithets begin to appear, though in a lesser degree, in his correspondence with him, and resemble those to which we became accustomed earlier in the letters.

CHAPTER V

1731

In January we find several letters of interest at Ickworth, as indeed there are throughout the year 1731, which is not covered by the *Memoirs*, although for the first six months the series is disjointed.

TO STEPHEN FOX *St. James's, January 5th, 1730/31* [1]

My dear Ste. I am going to tell you in manuscript what perhaps you may have seen already in print ; mais n'importe. Ld Wilmington is President,[2] and the Privy Seal in commission between Mr. Stanyan [3] the Turk and Jackson the Swede. Sir Robt. Rich [4] has Ld Deloraine's Regiment : Cathcart, Sir Robert's : and Hargrave, Cathcart's. Sir R. W., the D. of N., [Newcastle] and toutes les grosses têtes, are gone to dine and lie at Cassiobury. Political revolutions never surprise one ; but last year I should have thought it just as likely to hear of them at Cranford or Dawley.[5] Old Marlborough is come to town, cross as the devil, and flaming like Mount Vesuvius, and from as unknown a cause. I have had my flame too, but no irruptions : I burn all inward, and am really very uneasy. I am to sup on Thursday with the Prince at the younger [6] Dss of Marlborough's. The party was put off at his desire till my return. . . .

TO STEPHEN FOX *St. James, January 6th, 1731* [7]

I have left the King above, playing at hazard in a hot, sweaty, stinking crowd, to come and tell you with what content and satisfaction I every moment think of the return of you and

[1] Ickworth. [2] President of the Council, to succeed Lord Trevor.

[3] Abraham Stanyan (1669–1732), British Envoy in Constantinople 1719–20.

[4] Sir Robert Rich, 4th Bart. (1685–1758), a distinguished soldier, and a staunch supporter of Walpole. Field-Marshal later in life.

[5] The country houses of Lord Berkeley and Lord Bolingbroke.

[6] In Hervey's writing. [7] Melbury.

happiness : there is none for me without you. I dare now venture to thank you too for the charming punctuality you have shown ever since we parted, in writing to me almost every post. Had I done it before, I should have feared I owed the continuance of it to your complaisance or my importunity, when I would only be indebted to your kindness and your inclination for it.

I dined today at 19's [1] [Sir Robert Walpole], and was entertained, though not with an entertainment in the same style with the last, nor one I can venture to repeat. I can not imagine what people mean, when they sigh over the degeneracy of the age and the badness of the world. In my opinion, and to my taste, they are both delightful. I had rather live in these times than in any times or country I ever read of. When people talk of the falsehood, insincerity, treachery, dishonesty and ingratitude of mankind, they only complain, like drunkards, of a disease of their own making. Why do they put it in the power of anybody to hurt them by those qualities ? What do I care, or what need I care, for the want of generosity in people of whom I don't ask favours : for the want of secrecy in people I dont confide in : for the ill-nature of people on whom I am not dependent : for the truth of those whose information I never rely on : or for the insincerity of people whom I never believe. To be sure there is such muck, mire, and mud in the world ; but why people who have eyes need walk into such dirty ways and travel such nasty roads, I can not imagine. Or if they must frequent them, let them be but well clothed and thick covered, and none of the filth can penetrate or do them any harm. For my own part, my mind never goes naked, but in your territories. When I stir out of them I am fenced like a stage-coach-postillion, and should expect if I was not, to be as much bespattered. Adio Carissimo.

I have writ in such a hurry, that I dare say I have writ a great deal of nonsense, but won't read it over.

The sequel seems unfortunate, and shows clearly that the life of a Vice-Chamberlain at the Court was anything but a sinecure !

[1] Most of the explanations of these code numerals which follow in various letters are in Hervey's writing.

TO STEPHEN FOX *January 7, 1730/1*

[1] "My dear Ste. I am so dispirited, and my head aches so violently with sitting up till three this morning, *ex officio*, that I have not eat a morsel, and have been on the bed almost all the day. It is now seven a clock, and in an hour I must attend His Royal Highness to the Dss of M.'s where we are to sup, and I fear will sit up again. All these misfortunes will hinder me from saying much to you this post. . . .

A letter written four days later, gives us a circumstantial illustration of the uncertain state of Lord Hervey's health. Clearly he had what in these days would be colloquially termed a "black-out". Part of it has already been published by Mr. Sedgwick; but we feel that it should be again included.

TO STEPHEN FOX *St. James's, January 11th, 1731* [2]

For fear some officious paragraph in a news-paper should alarm your kindness for me and make you uneasy, I write this to give you a short account of a very disagreeable accident that happened to me yesterday morning in the Queen's Drawing Room. As I was talking to the Prince in as good spirits and health as ever I was in my life, I dropped down at once without the least warning, as if I had been shot. Sir Rob. Walpole, Charles Churchill [3] and Ld. Scarborough [4] carried me into the Queen's Bedchamber, where they pulled off all my clothes, half drowned me with water, and crammed drops and gold-powder into my mouth. The King assisted with more goodness than his general good-breeding alone [5] would have exacted, and has sent here perpetually. I was brought down, God knows by whom, sometimes fainting, sometimes recovered, to my own lodgings, and immediately then blooded in both arms. I took in an hour after

[1] Ickworth.

[2] Ickworth. Printed in *Memoirs*, ed. Sedgwick, p. xxiv.

[3] Natural son of General Charles Churchill, and himself a soldier of distinction, as well as M.P. for Castle Rising for many years. He had a son, also Charles, by Mrs. Oldfield: and died in 1745. Hervey later spoke of him as one of his best friends.

[4] Richard Lumley, 2nd Earl (1688–1743), a favourite at Court, and generally loyal, although at one time he came much under the Chesterfield influence.

[5] In Hervey's writing.

a remède ; at night finding my head still charged and heavy I was ordered to be cupped, and this morning have taken physic. I felt neither pain nor sickness the whole time, and feel myself to-day astonishingly well. The Prince sat with me all yesterday, and has promised to so again to-day ; but all these honours do not compensate for the disagreeable circumstance of this accident having been so public. You know how I detest being talked over. Adieu. Sick or well, absent or present, dear Ste.—wholly your's.

No reference appears in these letters to Lord Hervey's duel with William Pulteney which took place late in January, although Henry Fox acted as his second. There is little correspondence to be found attributable to that spring and summer, and doubtless both brothers were in town. The accepted explanation of the quarrel was an anonymous pamphlet, so common in the political world at that time, entitled *Sedition and Defamation Displayed*, with a preface, *The Dedication to the Patrons of the Craftsman* (i.e. Pulteney and Bolingbroke), replying to a violent attack in the *Craftsman*, the organ of the Opposition, first established in 1726, upon Walpole and his Administration. Pulteney took into his head that Hervey had written them, and replied with *A proper Reply to a late Scurrilous Libel*, by Caleb D'Anvers, a personal attack on his erstwhile friend couched in coarse, and abusive and indecent language. Hervey flatly denied the authorship of the pamphlet (according to Coxe, in his *Life of Sir Robert Walpole*, it had been written by Sir William Yonge) : but Pulteney even after he knew that he was in the wrong, refused to withdraw his allegations. Croker in his edition of the *Memoirs* (i, xxxvi) suggested that Hervey did write the *Dedication* (but not the pamphlet) pointing to a marginal note in what he believed to be Hervey's writing on the copy of the pamphlet at Ickworth, as a proof of the fact. Mr. Sedgwick is also in agreement with this statement : and we too have now had the privilege of examining the book at Ickworth which is entitled "Pamphlets relating to the *Craftsman*". This contains a fly leaf, the whole of which is in our opinion most probably, or even certainly, written by Lord Hervey ; and was evidently removed from the original packet containing six manuscript pamphlets before they were bound together. It is in fact a list of the contents. One of them is entitled, exactly as written, "Sedition and Defamation displayed. The dedication by Ld. H." For the sake of accuracy, therefore, we should point out that there is no marginal note on the pamphlet itself, but that the entry in question is in this index. We do not, however, attach any special significance to this correction.

An undated letter in the Ickworth series referring to some " Dedication " (*see* p. 160), on the diction of which Hervey expresses an opinion and rather a scathing one, does not seem to be connected with this incident.

TO STEPHEN FOX *Tuesday night, April 4* [*1731*] [1]

I cannot keep up the vieillerie of writing after the Opera, for there has been none. Strada is sick. Lord and Lady Bateman dined here, with Dicky and Mrs. Upton. They all came together from the Bath last Saturday. We adjourned after dinner to the play to see the new farce called *The Lottery*, ill-written, ill-acted and ill-sung, but well attended and well applauded. *Henry the 8th* was the play that preceded it, in which the ceremony of the Coronation was represented ; and when the Champion threw down his tin-glove, some waggish footman threw a dirty wash-leather one out of the gallery. This made a great laugh, clapping and noise ; which frightened the Champion's horse, set him a-plunging, made him kick the players, overturn the Coronation dinner, set everybody near him running, everybody at a distance laughing, and put the whole house in an uproar. For my part, I own myself so enfantin que ces tours de page me divertissent extrèmement, et [2] j'ai ris comme un fou.[2] . . .

Lady Hervey wrote to Stephen Fox at his house in Burlington Street, on July 3,[3] from Ickworth.

'Tis impossible to tell you how much I was disappointed last night to hear from my Lord that the Norfolk journey is put off. I never thought any letter from him could have been so disagreeable to me. 'Tis too much in one week, to see what one does not like, and to hear one shan't see what one does. I beg however you'll be so good to let me know how he looks, and what spirits he is in. Is there no hopes of his making us a visit this summer ? And won't you keep your word with me ? I can assure you the park is in the full perfection of beauty ; but, as Lord Chesterfield

[1] Melbury.
[2]–[2] In Hervey's writing. The rest of the letter is missing.
[3] Melbury.

(when he was Ld Stanhope) used to say of Bretby, "There's something in the house extremely disagreeable." [1]

Anyhow Lady Hervey had not so long to wait to see her husband as she had feared: for the Ickworth copies in July contain four letters to the Prince of Wales, three of them from Houghton, Sir Robert Walpole's house in Norfolk, and one from Ickworth. Of these, the first may be omitted: but the account of Houghton in the second is important. First, Campbell, and then Ripley, were the architects, the latter of whom, then Master Carpenter, succeeded Vanbrugh as Comptroller of the Department of Works in 1726. Clearly Kent was also involved.

TO FREDERICK, PRINCE OF WALES

Houghton, July 14th, 1731 [2]

Sir,

Your Royal Highness commanded me to give you a very particular account of this place, and as I have no pretence to the character of a connoisseur, I hope you will neither expect I should give it in proper terms, nor with any remarks of my own. As to the style of a virtuoso, I own I am not ambitious to learn it, for, by the technical jargon of a true follower of Palladio and Vertuvius [Vitruvius], one would imagine that a modern architect must have as great a contempt for his mother tongue as his grandfather's taste; but as I am not learned enough to be proper in my dialect, I may have some chance to be ignorant enough to be intelligible.

In order to give your Royal Highness a notion of what is done here, I should first let you know what materials Sir Robert had to work upon. I believe he will forgive me, when I say the country and situation are not what he would have chosen, if chance had not chosen for him. The soil is not fruitful, there is little wood, and no water: absolutely none for ornament, and

[1] In a letter from Sir Thomas Robinson to Lord Carlisle of Dec. 12 in this very year, he mentioned that the family lived in "a tenant's old house in the park, so very bad a habitation that I am astonished how so large a family have so long made a shift in it. The old mansion house was pulled down about 20 years ago." (*Carlisle Hist. MSS. Comm.* Report XV, 6, p. 87.) The present great house was erected by Lord Hervey's son.

[2] Ickworth.

all that is necessary for use forced up by art. These are disadvantages he had to struggle with, when that natural leaning to the paternal field and the scene of his youth, a bias which everybody feels and nobody can account for, determined him to adorn and settle at Houghton.[1]

He has already, by the force of manuring and planting, so changed the face of the country, that his park is a pleasant, fertile island of his own creation in the middle of a naked sea of land. The manuring has given it verdure, and the plantations thrive so well, that it will very soon be far from wanting wood.

There is a garden of 23 acres to one side of the house ; and to the other three, the park comes close up without any interruption. The house itself is 164 foot in front. There are two ranges of offices of 100 foot square, joined to the house by two colonnades of 68 foot each, which makes the front of the whole from out to out just 500 foot.

The building is all of stone, and its chief ornaments four cupellos at the four corners, which were obstinately raised by the master, and covered with stones in defiance of all the virtuosi who ever gave their opinions about it. The base, or rustic story, is what is chiefly inhabited at the Congress.[2] There is a room for breakfast, another for supper, another for dinner, another for afternooning, and the great arcade with four chimneys for walking and quid-nuncing. The rest of this floor is merely for use, by which your Royal Highness must perceive that the whole is dedicated to fox-hunters, hospitality, noise, dirt and business.

The next is the floor of taste, expense, state and parade. The first room is a hall, a cube of 40 foot finished entirely with stone, a gallery of stone round it and the ceiling of stucco, the best executed of anything I ever saw in stucco in any country. The ornaments over the chimney and doors are bas-reliefs of stone ;

[1] Another account of Houghton is given in the *Carlisle* papers, p. 85,—a letter from Robinson to Carlisle, Dec. 9, 1731. The "cupellos" mentioned as insisted on by Walpole, are, on Professor Richardson's authority, taken from a book of architecture by Decker.

[2] "The Norfolk Congress", i.e. Sir Robert and his political friends. The *Memoirs* tell us that this took place twice yearly, ten days in the summer, and twenty in November, about the time of the King's birthday.

round the sides marble bustos, and over against the chimney the famous group of Laocoon and his two Sons. Behind the hall is the salon, finished in a different taste, hung, carved and gilt large glasses between the windows, and some of his finest pictures round the three other sides of the room (this room looks to the garden). On the left hand of the hall and salon, this floor is divided into a common eating room, a library, a dressing room, a bed-chamber, and withdrawing-room for ordinary use ; and on the right hand (which is the only part yet unfinished) is to be the great dining room, and the State apartment. The furniture is to be green velvet and tapestry, Kent designs of chimneys, the marble gilded and modern ornaments. Titian and Guido supply those that are borrowed from antiquity.

The great staircase is the gayest, cheerfulest and prettiest thing I ever saw ; some very beautiful heresies in the particulars, and the result of the whole more charming than any bigotry I ever saw.

The upper or attic story is divided all into lodging-rooms. There are twelve of them, of which ten have servants' rooms belonging to them : and by deviating from orthodoxy in the proportion of the windows on this floor, he has not only dared to let in light enough for the poor inhabitant to be able to read at noon day (which the Palladian Votaries would fain have prevented), but he has made the building much handsomer on the outside than without this successful transgression it could possibly have been. In short, I think his house has all the beauties of regularity without the inconveniences ; and wherever he has deviated from the established religion of the architects, I believe Your Royal Highness would say he had found his account in being a libertine.

I beg Your Royal Highness to remember that whatever I wrote of, and from this place, you gave me your word should go no farther than of chaise-party in the morning : and must take the liberty to insist on not being put into the Burlington-inquisition for want of implicit faith.

We have already sent and received messages to Lord Townshend, who is to dine here to-morrow. . . .

TO FREDERICK, PRINCE OF WALES

Houghton, July 16th, 1731[1]

. . . When you imagine, Sir, that politics can put my old friends (as Your Royal Highness is pleased to call them) out of my head, you very much mistake both me and our employments here. Politics have very little share in our conversation, and the friend you mean so great a share in my heart that he is in no danger of being dislodged by that or any other force. Lord Townshend dined here the day I received Your Royal Highness's letter. It is difficult to answer for hearts; but as far as words and countenances go, we were all in mighty good humour. Houghton was extremely commended; and to-day we are to go and commend Raynham. Yesterday we all dined at Lord Lovel's;[2] he is situated within a mile of the sea. It is at present a most unpleasant place; but he comforts himself with a park in embryo, and a Burlington house with four pavilions on paper. We have a whole house full of people, but everybody does so much what he pleases, that one's next room neighbour is no more trouble to one here than one's next door neighbour in London. I do not, upon recollection, think that I have illustrated the ease we live in here at all well by what I have said last; for considering the house from which I now write, I might have remembered that one's next door neighbour in London is now and then a little troublesome . . .

TO FREDERICK, PRINCE OF WALES

Ickworth, July 21st, 1731[3]

. . . Our company at Houghton swelled at last into so numerous a body that we used to sit down to dinner a little snug party of about thirty odd, up to the chin in beef, venison, geese, turkeys, etc.; and generally over the chin in claret, strong beer and punch. We had Lords spiritual and temporal, besides commoners, parsons and freeholders innumerable. In public we drank loyal healths, talked of the times and cultivated popularity:

[1] Ickworth.

[2] Holkham. For Lord Lovel, *see ante*, p. 41.

[3] Ickworth.

in private we drew plans and cultivated the country. On architecture Mr. Arundel [1] was consulted, in planting Ste ; whenever I threw in my opinion, it was commonly en ignorant, and always rejected. We went to see Sir Andrew Fountaine's,[2] which is absolutely the prettiest trinket I ever saw. My Lord Burlington could not make a better ragoust [*sic*] of paintings, statues, gilding and virtû ! Lord Townshend's place [3] is really a beauty, of a superior rank, and strikes one with a pleasure very different from that of a toy-shop. It is great, noble and complete. It has all the advantages Nature can bestow in the situation, and all the additions Art can make in the finishing. Wood, lawn and water can produce nothing more beautiful than the park ; Kent, gilding and expense can add nothing to the house. It is not the worse for his having seen Houghton, though I believe he is. For if he had liked that house less I fancy he had liked the Master better : ce cy est seulement entre nous. But Hephaestion never dares to offer the signet to Alexander : he depends and trusts, but does not dictate and enjoin. . . .

TO STEPHEN FOX *August 12th, 1731* [4]

. . . The Prince drove me yesterday to dinner at the Dss. of Marlborough's. We talked of you by the way. Lady Stafford [5] was quatrième. We were good company ; elle brillait dans la

[1] Richard Arundel, 2nd son of 2nd Lord Arundel, of Terice, who died in 1759. He married, in 1732, Lady Frances Manners, daughter of 2nd Duke of Rutland.

[2] Narford.

[3] Raynham. Hervey's remarks in the *Memoirs* (pp. 84–5) may be recorded. " Before Sir Robert Walpole built this house . . . Lord Townshend looked upon his own seat at Raynham as the metropolis of Norfolk, proud of the superiority, and considered every stone that augmented the splendour of Houghton as a diminution of the grandeur of Raynham. Had Sir Robert raised this fabric of fraternal discord in any other county in England, it might have escaped the envy of this wise rival. . . ." In other words, he suggested that this was a basic reason for the disagreement between the two brothers-in-law.

[4] Ickworth.

[5] Claude Charlotte, daughter of Philibert, Comte de Gramont, married, in 1694, Henry Stafford-Howard, 1st Earl of Stafford. She died in 1737.

naïve. Sixpence [Lady Deloraine][1] has met with a terrible rebuke from 13 [the Queen], and was all day yesterday in tears. 7 [Miss Vane][2] was not sorry for it. Things go worse between 92 [the King] and Penny [Miss Mordaunt].[3] Adieu. I am just sent for to the Prince, and must dress before I go, for it is public day. . . .

TO STEPHEN FOX *August 14th, 1731*[4]

I have just left the King at dinner to come and thank you for your travelling letter, with a hundred different dates, which I received this morning. I conclude you are gone mad, and that you saunter up and down the country with court-cards sown upon your coat and straws in your hair. Does Mr. Hamilton accompany you as infected, or to take care of you? I should be

[1] Mary, daughter of Charles Howard, married, in 1726, Henry Scott, 1st Earl of Deloraine, who died in 1729. A very pretty woman, but was Hervey's pet aversion; so we shall hear more of her in his letters. She had been appointed Governess to Princesses Mary and Louisa after her husband's death; and became the King's mistress, after Lady Suffolk left the Court, but for a short time only, as she re-married in 1734. Her portrait, with her two little daughters, but with her back to the spectator, is in the foreground of Hogarth's great conversation-piece, the *Conquest of Mexico*, painted in 1731–2. A reproduction faces p. 90.

[2] Hon. Anne Vane (1710–36), daughter of Gilbert, 2nd Lord Barnard, one of the Queen's Maids of Honour, known as "The beautiful Vanella", and a lady apparently lacking in moral sense. She was at this time mistress of Lord Hervey; but left him for the Prince of Wales in 1731. The latter's growing attachment to Lady Archibald Hamilton, and the suggestion of his approaching marriage, caused him to break off relations with her in September 1735. In point of fact, however, she had already returned to Lord Hervey (see *Memoirs*, p. 477). She died early in 1736, and her son also about the same time. Lord Perceval (*Egmont*, i, p. 235) spoke of her as "that fat and ill-shapen dwarf," and wrote that she had nothing good to recommend her that he knew of, "neither sense nor wit".

The story that Hervey gave "Bussy" Mansel a letter to her, nominally about a midwife, but in reality abusing her for using her influence against him, is given in *Egmont*, i, 264. But is it surprising? for she was clearly backing Dodington against him.

[3] Anna Maria Mordaunt, another Maid of Honour. She was known as "the Fair Circassian", from verses written to her by the Rev. Samuel Croxall (*see ante*, p. 49). She married Stephen Poyntz in 1733 (*see* p. 145).

[4] Ickworth.

glad to know; but whether it is by contagion or office, I should still envy him. He is with you, and I am not; and no contingencies can make me not wish to exchange those circumstances.

The Duke of Dorset [1] has just taken his leave to go and King it in Ireland. I am sure he will be happier in that Drury-Lane employment than any other man upon earth; and is at this moment ranging his maces, his two battalions of Guards, and his twelve Chaplains, for the first Church-day. He will not dislike haranguing his Parliament, especially if Carey [2] makes a good speech, and Dean Swift does not put it into doggerel verse; but those are two very doubtful suppositions. The Court hunted again yesterday. I had the good fortune to be too late, and to be shut out of the park; for the ways of Richmond on those days are like the ways of Heaven—"strait is the gate and few there be that enter thereat." The King had no sport, and consequently a great deal of pleasure; for he was back again by twelve a clock, to the great satisfaction of his heart and ease of his derrière. I ride as usual every morning with the Queen; but Lord Halifax [3] has taken it into his head of late two or three times to se fourrer dans la partie, et m'ennuye à me faire pleurer. Poor Lady Betty Nightingale is dead in lying in. I did not know her; but people that did, say they are sorry. Whether they are or no is another point; I have known ladies shed tears for a dead friend that they hardly curtsied to alive. Adieu. . . .

TO STEPHEN FOX *Hampton Court, August 17th, 1731* [4]

. . . I long to tell you a droll history of the reconciliation I made between 92 [the King] and Penny [Miss Mordaunt]. You will wonder how it could come in my way to be concerned in it; but it was all absolutely my doing. We began hunting last Saturday in Richmond Park. I never saw the hounds, but rode as usual the whole time by the Queen's chaise. Sir Robert

[1] Lionel Cranfield Sackville (1688–1765), created Duke in 1720. He was recalled from Ireland in 1735, but as Lord Scarborough refused an offer to succeed him, he returned again until 1737.

[2] Secretary to the Lord-Lieutenant.

[3] George Montague, Earl of Halifax (1685?–1739).

[4] Ickworth. Part published in the *Memoirs*, ed. Sedgwick, xxiii.

received the King at the Park gate, dressed in green and gold and a cap as Ranger, with the leash cross his shoulders, which gave occasion to a joke which I shall transcribe, and that we all sung the whole day. You know the stanza in Lady B.'s [1] song :—

> " Caroline, ma douce maitresse,
> Partage mes bons tours de main,
> Nous menons son mari en lesse,
> Et nous nous mocquons du genre-humain."

It was thus turned upon this occasion :—

> " Pult'ney soyez en allegresse,
> Du beau triomphe de ce jour.
> Nous menons Sir Robert en lesse,
> Il faut que chacun ait son tour."

I dined after the chase with Her Grace,[2] where I had the pleasure of talking of you and finding my taste so well confirmed, that everybody's good opinion of you is proportioned to the degree in which they are acquainted with you. It is unimaginable how many thousand nameless accidents and indescribable sensations prove to me every day how much I am engrossed by one thing. What I am going to tell you is so foolish an incident [3] to relate, yet I am almost ashamed to do it ; though it may serve in some degree to illustrate what I wish so much I was able to make you thoroughly sensible of. T'other day at dinner at Lord Harrington's, Sir William Irby [4] sat next me, and Lord Chancellor designing to drink his health and taking him for you, called to him by your name ; when, without the least affectation I assure you I coloured, and felt just as I imagine your favourite mistress would have done upon the same occasion. Don't despise me for these little particulars ; but flatter your vanity with reflecting that to teach such a way of thinking to so good a courtier is not a less proof of your power, than it would be to establish Christianity in Turkey or chastity in Swallow Street.

The next letter again reintroduces the complications on the Continent, which arose owing to the ambitions of Elizabeth Farnese, wife

[1] Lady Bolingbroke?
[2] Duchess of Richmond.
[3] In Hervey's writing.
[4] Later Lord Boston.

of Philip V, King of Spain, and her determination to find suitable States in the North of Italy for her younger sons. The Second Treaty of Vienna, concluded in March, had arranged for the installation of Don Carlos, the second son, in Parma, the Duke having died childless in January : [1] and that the Imperial troops who had occupied it on his death, should be evacuated. The landing of Spanish troops at Leghorn was to be made an international affair, and this took place in October, notwithstanding the French refusal to participate in a dispute as to the precedence of the British and French Admirals.

Sir Charles Wager, who had blockaded Cadiz in 1726–7, was sent out in July to take command in the Mediterranean. Henry Fox, as we shall see, who was going on a pleasure trip to Spain and Italy, was given a passage on his flagship, and accompanied him to Seville.

TO STEPHEN FOX *Hampton Court, August 23rd, 1731* [2]

I find your Itinerant Madness is at last settled in Redlynch (with a *y*)—observe my obedience ; and am extremely glad to hear your amusements are so numerous and your spirits so good. Poor Mr. Hamilton [3] makes a *sad hand* of it ; I pity him, and dare say you insult him. Does Hill [4] follow his function in visiting the infirm, or does he follow his pleasure in accompanying you ? We were all alarmed yesterday here by the Prince, who was taken ill on Saturday after hunting, and grew so much worse the morning after, that he was convulsed and light-headed. Upon being blooded he grew better, and upon clearing the room, quieter. He desired I might be left with him alone, and after talking to me half-an-hour, without receiving any other answer than, " Sir, we'll talk of that to-morrow. Pray, compose yourself now ", he dropped asleep and slept two hours, which he had not done in the whole preceeding night. He has grown gradu-

[1] Antonio Farnese, the last Duke, born in 1679, and succeeded to the Dukedom in 1727. Don Carlos (1716–88) succeeded to the throne of Spain after his half-brother's death in 1759 as Charles III.

[2] Ickworth.

[3] Charles Hamilton (*see ante*, p. 51), who seems to have had an accident to his hand.

[4] Rev. Samuel Hill, the clergyman at Redlynch, and later Canon of Wells, the great sporting parson constantly mentioned in a MS. " Memoires de la Chasse " of the Fox family, now at Melbury : and their willing butt. He died in January 1753, " much regretted by all who knew him."

ally better ever since ; slept very well last night, has very little fever to-day, and is now talking very cheerfully to the Queen, whom I left this moment by his bedside.

There came letters from Sir Charles Wager on Thursday from Cales [Cadiz], and yesterday from Seville. He was received with great distinction by the King and Queen of Spain : and has been visited already by above twenty Grandees, who every one made him a speech in form as long as that he made to the King. The Commander of the Spanish Squadron made him the first visit upon his arrival at Cales [Cadiz] and invited him to dinner and saluted him with guns or flags, I know not which ; but in short with the highest maritime honours that can be paid. The Spanish fleet is not ready. They will pique themselves upon fitting out more ships than they can man ; and though they press tailors and cobblers and every creature they can lay their hands on, there is not one vessel that has a quarter of its complement. But as the Great-Duke [1] has signed a Treaty to regulate the most minute article relating to the reception and establishment of Don Carlos in Florence as eventual successor, it is concluded here that the Court of Spain will not suffer this unreadiness of their fleet to make any demur in the embarkation of the Infant, but that they will send him on board Sir Charles Wager immediately to Italy. Nobody any longer imagines the Duchess of Parma with child ; and an express is every day expected to communicate the news of her having declared herself not so. It was thought this declaration would have been made in form the tenth of this month, our style. Voilà bien des nouvelles politiques. . . .

Three days later Stephen was given the news of the untimely death of Henrietta, Duchess of Marlborough's only son, by her marriage, in 1698, with the Earl of Godolphin, a tragedy which had a permanent effect on the fortunes of the Spencer-Churchill family. The young man had married two years before, Maria Catherina de Jong, the daughter of a Dutch burgomaster. Lord Perceval (*Egmont*, i, 201) wrote of him that he had several good qualities, and was very charitable. His only fault was drinking and loving low company. He was vertuous as to women, was pious, and had no sort of pride or ambition.

[1] Of Tuscany.

TO STEPHEN FOX *Hampton Court, August 26th, 1731* [1]

Lord Blandford's death is so much the conversation of to-day, that I cannot help beginning my letter by telling you of it. He died suddenly of a drunken fit or fever at Oxford. It is a fine accident for our lucky friend, Lord Sunderland. He will be no longer obliged to manage that unloving, capricious, extravagant Fury of a Grandmother. I could not help reflecting how particular it was, that the only remaining branch of such a family as the Lord Treasurer Godolphin, and the head of such a family as the late Duke of Marlborough, should go off so universally unregretted, especially when nobody ever pretended to say he had not sense, good-nature and honesty. With those three qualities to want one friend is very extraordinary.

The people who are about the Prince (I have not seen him these three days) say he is better, though weak beyond imagination for so short an illness. He has this morning begun the bark, and cut off his hair. I should say many things to you if you were here, which I shall not trust even to a cipher. Solomon you know says, " Speak not in Palaces for the walls have ears ; nor of Princes for the birds of the air will reveal it." The King has a defluxion fallen on one of his eyes in so violent a manner that he can hardly see. I forgot whether I sent you word that Lady Di. Spencer was going to be married to Lord John Russel,[2] and am not sure it is so ; though Common Fame (the greatest of all liars) says it is all concluded. I have been blooded to-day, so cannot use my arm to write any more. Adieu. I love you, and love you more than I thought I could love anything. I have received a letter from you to-day which nobody who loved you less could deserve. Adio, Carissimo.

TO STEPHEN FOX *Hampton Court, August 27th, 1731* [3]

I write to you to-night, because to-morrow until the hour the post goes out will be taken up between hunting and Her Grace,

[1] Ickworth.

[2] Lady Diana Spencer was, as we have seen, grand-daughter of Sarah, Duchess of Marlborough, and sister of Lord Sunderland. Lord John Russell, her cousin, was 2nd son of Wriothesley, 2nd Duke of Bedford. He succeeded his brother Wriothesley in the titles in 1732, as 4th Duke, and lived till 1771.

[3] Ickworth.

who mourns in nothing but her manteau,[1] [2]I assure you,[2] for Lord Blandford. You say you wonder how I could be instrumental to a certain reconciliation. The particulars are too long for a letter, and will keep cold longer than the reconciliation kept warm. The Prince is much better; he has been up to-night, and had a natural salivation these last four and twenty hours which has wet seven and twenty handkerchiefs, and given him vast relief. I am this moment come from him. I pity and envy Mr. Hamilton excessively. How willingly would I sit for months with my hand in salt and water in the same company, and how little should I regret the loss of any other amusement: but as this is not his case, I compassionate the mortification he feels and wonder at his insensibility to the recompense.

It is true that Sir Robert Walpole had a fall, but not that he was blooded or that he received any hurt. Lord Malpas and the Polish Envoy did not come off so well, for they were both hurt and blooded; and Mr. Fitzwilliams who fell last hunting day broke one of the bones of his wrist. I wonder who is to be the sacrifice for to-morrow's sport; not one chase has yet been had gratis, bad as they have been. I have a notion the King's eye will pay part of the tax; for it was this night so violently inflamed that we played only by one candle: and by what one may reasonably imagine (though Kings are above having their motions stopped by diseases or influenced by accidents) His Majesty's eye would be much better accommodated to-morrow morning with a poultice of bread and milk and a dark room, than with the dust of the chase and a noonday sun.

There came an express yesterday from Parma, but (as the King related the contents of the letters) with very inconsistent accounts. He says they write him word that the incredulity as to the Duchess's[3] being pregnant increases every day, though her belly does so too. The whole puts me continually in mind of the

[1] *Sub rosa.*

[2]–[2] In Hervey's writing.

[3] Lord Perceval wrote that she was well watched (*Egmont*, i, 201). He added, "This will revive the opinion that the Pretender's birth is spurious, King James's Queen being of the same family and house."

Rabbit woman,[1] but old Dorothea watches her too close for any juggle (if they intend one) to succeed. The six thousand Spaniards are to go immediately, but not Don Carlos. Sir Charles Wager is already sailed for Gibraltar to take up some of our troops; and from thence he goes to Barcelona, whither theirs are marching cross the country, and where they are to embark. Adieu. 'Tis almost twelve a clock; I am so near being asleep, that I am not quite sure whether I am writing to you or dreaming of you. Most of my nights and days pass in that vicissitude: all my agreeable ones at least do so now, and will till we meet.

TO STEPHEN FOX *Hampton Court, September 2, 1731* [2]

. . . It is impossible at this distance to satisfy your curiosity about what I did not dare trust to a cipher. The Prince is quite recovered; and the King's eye worse, so bad that he did not

[1] The whole story of Mary Toft or Tofts appears in the *Dict. Nat. Biog.* under her name. It is the tale of an elaborate hoax, which completely took in many of the leading surgeons of the day in the year 1726. Her story was that she had been frightened by a rabbit in the fields; but in the end her imposture was discovered, and she made a complete confession. St. André and Molyneux were both well-known surgeons of the time. The medical name for her condition is now called a "hydatidiform mole". The quotation is from Lord Hervey to H. Fox, December 2, 1726, "There is one thing that employs everybody's tongue at present, which is a woman brought out of Surrey who had brought forth seventeen rabbits, and has been these three days in labour of the eighteenth. I know you laugh now, and think I joke; but the fact as reported and attested by St. André, the surgeon (who swears he delivered her of five), is something that really staggers one. I was last night to see her with Dr. Arbuthnot, who is convinced of the truth of what St. André relates. Every creature in town, both men and women, have been to see and feel her; the perpetual emotions, noises and rumblings in her belly are something prodigious. All the eminent physicians, surgeons and men-midwives in London are there day and night to watch her next production. St. André's printed account of the whole progress of this affair is to come out to-day, and if I can get it time enough to send with the other things, you shall have it. Mr. Molineux (who married Lord Essex's sister) swore to me that he himself, when she was in labour, took one part of one of the rabbits out of her body. In short the whole philosophical world is divided into two parties; between the downright affirmations of the one hand for the reality of the fact, and the philosophical proofs of the impossibility of it on the other; nobody knows which they are to believe, their eyes or their ears."

[2] Ickworth.

hunt yesterday, and did not dine in public today. Winnington is here. He talks of going to Maddington from Basingstoke. I do not fancy it can be above a day's journey ; I should think that nothing from hence, should you think the other a great way to meet me there : and could not meeting your sister be a pretence ? In short I long and pine and fret to see you. What does one live for, but to be happy ; and what happiness can one have, when one loves one single thing better than all others in the world bundled together, and does not possess it. Adieu. I am called to dinner.

Two days later Hervey wrote :—

TO STEPHEN FOX *Hampton Court, September 4th, 1731* [1]

I had not time in my last to answer your question concerning the Duchess of Marlborough's concern for her son, but can assure you she is neither so unaccountable, as [not] to feel any affliction, nor so ridiculous as to affect it. She very truly says that his behaviour towards her must justify her being at least indifferent to his death ; and that anybody who had any regard to *Papa's* memory must be glad that the Duke of Marlborough was now not in danger of being represented in the next generation by one who must have brought any name he bore into contempt. The death of her son makes a very great change in her present circumstances, and a much greater still in what must devolve upon her at her mother's death : but to do her justice, I believe that consideration of interest affects her (though daughter to the Duke and Duchess of Marlborough) as little as it would anybody I know. I dined there yesterday with Lady Stafford, whose chit-chat is really lively, natural and amusing. It is a sort of wit I like ; her imagination is constantly at work without labouring, and her observations not sought though uncommon. I own I have an aversion to those wits by profession, who think it incumbent upon them always to reflect and express themselves differently from the rest of the world ; they are a sort of mental postermasters in company who think they must distort themselves to entertain you, and often give me pain, but never give me pleasure.

[1] Ickworth.

Pope is the head of this sect. If he had never talked, one should have thought he had more wit than any man that ever lived, and if he had never written he would have talked much better ; but the endeavouring to raise his character as a companion up to the point it stands at as an author, has sunk it as much below its natural pitch as he has endeavoured to put it above it. But this is a rock many have split upon as well as him. Many fail of pleasing from being too solicitous to please, and many make very ill figures in company by endeavouring to think like others, who would have made very good ones if they would have been satisfied with thinking their own way. I am so much of a virtuoso that I love all originals and hate copies. I like the company of my dear, handsome, silly, natural Lady Tankerville,[1] better than that of all those fine ladies put together, whom seeing the world has made half-wise, reading novels half-mad, and hearing Lord Chesterfield half-wits. She absolutely and fairly thinks a loud ; her mouth is the outlet to everything her eyes and ears take in. And do not you think like me, that such a creature, who, like a looking-glass, returns every image it receives just as it comes to it, worth a hundred of those daubers who will paint and varnish and polish everything that comes from them, till there is nothing more of nature in their words than there is in Lady Mary's complexion ? We are to lose Lady Tankerville this week ; which will be a great mortification to the whole Court as well as to her, and a pleasure only to poor Lady Deloraine, who is grown lean with hearing her commended, and I believe has never slept since Lady Tankerville has taken her place at the King's commerce-table. The Prince is quite recovered excepting his looks, his flesh and his strength. He was yesterday abroad for the first time in a coach, and afterward came to the Queen's Drawing Room. He has made the two Lords and Grooms who were in waiting during his illness presents, to thank them for their care and reward them for their diligence : to Lord Tankerville a couteau de chasse, to Lord Baltimore a pocket book, to

[1] Camilla, daughter of Edward Colville, of Whitehouse, Durham, married Charles, 2nd Earl of Tankerville, K.T., who held several Court offices. She was a Lady of the Bedchamber to Queen Caroline, but was apparently retiring at this period.

Mr. Townshend a watch, and to Schutz a gold étui, to his physician a purse of hard money, and to all his pages rewards in the same solid specie. He never loses any occasion to ingratiate himself, and *does those things from goodness of heart and a natural disposition and desire to give pleasure* which every Prince, though he did not feel,[1] would do in policy and interest, if not from inclination. No debts are ever paid with such beneficial, as well as agreeable interest, as those that are laid upon peoples' hearts; and if I were a King I am sure I should be better pleased with the voluntary contribution of their good wishes for my prosperity so raised, than with all the taxes power could make them pay for the support of my grandeur. Don't think this common bant, for I protest I feel it as sincerely as I feel friendship for you, which is as strongly as I ever can feel anything. Adieu.

On the 9th, Hervey wrote a letter to Stephen, from which we extract a few fragments: [2]

. . . You have already heard, I suppose, of Daniel Pulteney's [3] death. It was very sudden; if an infirm man's can properly be called so. Horace Walpole [4] has been very near tipping off in the same way. He is now out of danger. . . . I do not know whether I sent you word of Lady Di.'s match with Lord John Russell being quite agreed. He is at this moment lisping love in her flippant Ladyship's ear at Blenheim. It has been kept secret from Lord Sunderland and the Batemans, till three days ago.

TO STEPHEN FOX *Hampton Court, September 11* [5]

By my having no letter from you today, I conclude you were

[1] " the same impulse," erased. The above interlineation is added later.

[2] Ickworth.

[3] Daniel Pulteney, became M.P. in 1721. A friend and follower of the 3rd Earl of Sunderland.

[4] Horatio Walpole (1678–1757), Sir Robert's younger brother. He held many posts, both at home and in diplomacy abroad. He was Ambassador at The Hague in 1722 and 1733–40; and in Paris 1723–30. He was at this time Cofferer to the Household.

[5] Ickworth.

either on the road to Maddington [1] last post day, or that, when you are retired to that Little Trianon (sacred to sweat and spaniels), you are determined not to be troubled with [2] any business foreign to any of the place. So if perhaps you have resolved to receive no [2] more despatches than you send, then my trouble in the enclosed will be thrown away. Voiture [3] or Balsac [4] would tell you that, as Apollo and Diana were brother and sister, there would be nothing inconsistent if you suffered poetry to amuse your mind in all the leisure hours your body must allow for rest, and that this God himself had his harp in his hand as often as his bow and arrow. You see how earnestly I plead, and what pompous names I bring in evidence to prove this intrusion upon hunting not impertinent. To tell you I don't like these verses myself would be wrong, because to you I profess being sincere ; and to tell you I do is unnecessary, since I send them where I always wish to appear agreeable. . . .

The next letter, two days later, is addressed to Henry Fox in Spain.

TO HENRY FOX *Hampton Court, Sept. 13, 1731* [5]

I received a letter from you yesterday, my dear Count, dated from the Bay of Cadiz, Aug. 15/26, for which I return you my best as well as earliest thanks. It is so delightfully particular, that

[1] Maddington was Stephen Fox's shooting-box on Salisbury Plain, set up in 1727, a few miles west of Stonehenge. "There were but two beds in all, and those very bad ones," reports the *Memoires de la Chasse*. The shooters were usually four ! From there they seem to have ranged at will over the south-western and southern areas of the Plain, often shooting from horseback. No details of the bags were kept till 1736. Blank days were by no means unknown. But the outlook was not always as black as that. Stephen Fox, a very good shot, was reported to have killed 19 partridges on the first day of shooting in 1733 ; and the total bag of partridges for 1734 was 315. In 1736, Stephen was reported in these volumes to weigh 9 stone, and Henry 12 stone. (*See Henry Fox, 1st Lord Holland*, i, 49 etc.)

[2–2] In Hervey's writing.

[3] Vincent Voiture (1597–1648). French writer. An associate of Corneille, and celebrated as a society wit.

[4] In an unknown handwriting. Jean Louis Guez de Balzac (1594–1654). French author. His letters to his many literary friends, when published, established his high reputation.

[5] Holland House and Ickworth.

I am personally as well acquainted with the Spanish Court as if I had been spewing three weeks on board S^r. Cha. Wager, and sweating three more at Seville. There is but one part of your description that I can give no credit to, which is that relating to the person of the Queen.[1] I have so long figured her a long, lean, raw-boned Tarmigan [*sic*] with a shrill voice and fierce eyes, that it is quite impossible for me to fix any other idea to her name. The Prince and Princess of Asturias[2] walking upon the shore whilst the barges of music row up and down the river, I think so purely ridiculous, that I can very easily believe His Highness like my Lord Car[narvon][3] throughout. I suppose if Madame la Princesse happened to have the same fears of a coach that she has of a barge, she would walk the streets holding by the door, whilst her footmen lolled on the seats. You brag of never being better in your life (as I am informed) fort mal à propos ; for though you bear the heats of Spain so easily, I hear those of England did not agree quite so well with your constitution. . . .

To be sure you have heard long ago of your friend, Lord Sunderland's good fortune by the death of Lord Blandford. He gets nothing immediately but an independency on Mount Ætna,[4] who never gave him any thing in present, and who, if she was as partial to him as she is prejudiced against him, would now certainly never think of leaving him a shilling at her death. Lady Di. is to be married in a few days to Lord John Russell. Negotiation has been carried on with so much affected secrecy by old Ætna, that it has never been communicated to Lord Sunderland and Lady Bateman till last week, tho' it has been in every mouth and Gazette within a hundred miles of London this month.

The Prince has been very ill, but, his flesh, looks and strength excepted, is quite recovered. The King has had a very sore eye

[1] The celebrated Elizabeth Farnese, 2nd wife of Philip V.

[2] Prince Ferdinand (1713–59), Philip V's 2nd son by his 1st wife, and therefore half-brother to Don Carlos and Don Philip. He succeeded to the throne of Spain as Ferdinand VI, and had married Maria Magdalena Barbaro, daughter of John V, King of Portugal.

[3] Henry Brydges, Marquis of Carnarvon, eldest son of James, 1st Duke of Chandos, whom he succeeded as 2nd Duke.

[4] Hervey's nickname for Sarah, Duchess of Marlborough.

these last three weeks, which he seems to propose curing by reading all day, walking in the dew all the evening, and sleeping with his windows open all night.

I expect you to keep your promise of writing to me again very soon, and with a thousand particularities. I am as fond of little facts as Ste.; therefore let me have frequent and very minute details of everything you hear, see and do. If you should meet with Cochi [1] at Florence, make my court to him; you know how to do it, where you have a mind. You will like him, because he has no affectation; and he you, because you have no belief. Adieu, I hope you are, and will be, well diverted; but begin to despair of seeing you this winter at Redlynch.

TO STEPHEN FOX *Hampton Court, September 16th, 1731* [2]

. . . I have lately had two very long letters from the Count, the first from Cadiz after his return from Seville, the other from Parma. There was three weeks difference in their dates, though but three days in their arrival here. In that from Cadiz he gives me a full account of his journey to Seville, where he went along with my brother,[3] Lord August Fitzroy, Lord Loveless [4] and five more, to accompany Sir Charles Wager. They were all admitted at the close of Sir Charles's audience, and presented to the King and Queen of Spain. Her Majesty he describes plump, with a lively look, and extremely marked with the smallpox; but I have been so used to figure her up, a long, lean scold, with a shrill voice and fierce black eyes, that I can never fix any other idea to her name. The King, he says, is like my Lord Tyrconnel, only shorter and fatter: as stupid and as nasty [as] I always imagined him. Don Carlos is like Fitzwilliams, the King's page, with fair hair, a sensible, good humoured contenance, and a wanton childishness in his behaviour which, he says, becomes him. Don Philip he describes handsome and serious; and the Prince of Asturias like Lord Carnarvon. The Princess of Asturias's person he says is as handsome as her face is ugly, which

[1] Dr. Antonio Cocchi, the friend of Sir Horace Mann. A Florentine physician and student of letters, who died in 1758.

[2] Ickworth.

[3] Hon. William Hervey, R.N.

[4] 6th and last Lord Lovelace, of that creation. He died in 1736.

is in excess. The Palace they all live in was built by the Moors, irregular, ugly and ill-furnished, or rather unfurnished. They have no diversions but music upon the water, and to that nobody goes but the Prince and Princess of Asturias (who both love music) and their retinue. The Count went thither every night. He talks much of the delightful evenings, how well the heats agree with him, and quite en gourmand of the water melons and iced liquors. The King's hours, for a man who has a great deal of religion and no pleasure, are very extraordinary ; for he never dines till six at night, and often does not go to bed till six in the morning. Patino [1] is everything at the Court. The sea, the West Indies and the finances are immediately in his province : and the Marquis de Castelar, Ambassador in France, is his brother. He dined on board Sir Charles Wager the day before your brother wrote to me ; and the next morning the fleet was to set sail for Gibraltar. From thence it was to go to Barcelona, where the six thousand Spaniards were to meet them.

The Count's last letter was dated from Parma. It does not say where he left the fleet, but that Sir Charles Wager sending my brother, Will. before to Leghorn, with some instructions for Coleman,[2] he went with him ; and Coleman being at Parma, they both went on thither. The first news they met at their arrival was that the Duchess had declared herself not with child in form the day before. She retired to her country-house, the Regency is dissolved, and the Emperor has taken possession, or rather guardianship, of everything, in the name of Don Carlos ; who, I conclude, by what I hear from our Ministers, will now, if the fleet is not already sailed from Barcelona, go along with it. My brother is to return to the fleet with dispatches from Coleman relating to its reception at Leghorn : and your brother intends not to return with him, but to take this opportunity to make the tour of Italy, and join the fleet when it is to come back to England. He sets out for Rome, he says, in a fortnight, and stays a week at Florence to make Cocchi talk religion.

So much for foreign articles. As to domestic affairs, I hear

[1] Don José Patiño (1666–1736). He held the post of Chief Minister 1726–36.

[2] Francis Colman (died 1733), father of George Colman, the elder, dramatist. He lived in Florence as British Minister. His wife was a sister of Mrs. Pulteney.

there is likely to be a dispute in the Marlborough family about the inheritance of what Lord Blandford died possessed of. Mount Ætna says it is to come immediately to Lord Sunderland, which I own to me seems absurd; for whilst the Duchess of Marlborough lives, the law always supposes she may have a son, and if she should have one, it would be mighty odd to have the estate vested in Lord Sunderland now, and taken from him again upon that birth. Adieu. I have written till I am half blind and quite tired; it is but eight a clock yet, so I am still in hopes I may have a letter this morning. The tea is ready, and I drink your health. C'est à dire, à tout ce qui me fait plaisir. Adio, Carissimo. . . .

TO STEPHEN FOX *Hampton Court, September 18th, 1731* [1]

You guess very ill about the conquest you imagine Lady Tankerville's *agréable folie, naïvèté charmante et beauté naturelle* made in a certain heart. You must know as little of its sensations to imagine it an easy prize, as you must of its value, if you were to think it a considerable one; for though [2] there have been many sojourners there, I promise you there have been but few governors.[2] And as to *la petite personne* you mention, I assure you she has had orders to decamp long ago, though not to make room for a successor. Don't pity Lady Delo[raine], I beg you, in so pathetic a style; for she is such an idiot that every look tells it, every word makes one sick, and every action makes one peevish. But the story I am going to tell you of her will make you think me prejudiced perhaps. Miss Fitzwilliams [3] and I (on purpose to make her fret), maintaining the other day the beauty of one of her daughters, who is a cherry-cheeked, buxom girl, against the other, who is in her own pale, languishing, sickly style and her favourite, we both agreed that the cherry-cheeks would turn out the prettiest woman, to which her Ladyship answered that she could never think the delicacy of her favourite an objection to a girl, any more than it would be an advantage to a boy; for that in her opinion a woman could never look too much like

[1] Ickworth. [2–2] In Hervey's writing.

[3] Miss Fitzwilliam, one of the Maids of Honour, a masculine-looking girl.

W. Hogarth, pinxit

CHILDREN'S THEATRICALS. DRYDEN'S *CONQUEST OF MEXICO*

At the house of Mr. Conduitt, of the Mint. 1731–2

Wm. D. of Cumberland Prss. Mary and Prss. Louisa

D. of Richmond Dss. of Richmond

Css. of Deloraine, and two children

Lady Caroline Lennox (Cydaria) Lord Lempster (Cortez) Lady Sophia Fermor (Almeria) Miss Conduitt (Alebeck)

a woman, nor a man too much like a man. Considering the two people she said this to, it was certainly well said; and I can forgive her having bragged of it to every creature she has seen since; as it was the first time she ever chopp'd [*sic*] upon common-sense, and I dare say will be the last. But I cannot forgive my own ill-fortune, that, since Balaam's miracle was renewed and that God did open the mouth of the ass, it should happen to me, who had suffered so often by its braying, to suffer too by its articulating. I remember Aureng-Zebe [1] says:—

> "Nature herself is chang'd to punish me,
> Virtue turn'd vice, and Faith Inconstancy."

And I find like him,

> Nature herself is chang'd to punish me,
> Folly turn'd Wit, to Satire, Idiocy.

À propos to idiots, I must tell you a dialogue that passed yesterday in the Drawing Room between that ecclesiastical blockhead, the Bishop of Rochester [Wilcocks] [2] and Her Majesty. He is that to the Knights of the Bath, that the Bishop of Salisbury is to the Knights of the Garter, and being yesterday at Court for the first time with the badge and red ribbon about his neck, the Queen came up to him and complimented him on wearing the Order, of which she very modestly said her son had the *honour* to be the head. To which his Episcopal Politeness replied: "Madame, the Duke of Montagu is our Master". "Yes, my Lord, and you are Prelate, but my son is at the head of the Order." "May be so, Madam, I know I am Prelate or Dean or something: and the Duke of Montagu, I know, is called Master. The Duke, Madam, is a very fine prince." So ended the conversation, his Lordship acknowledging the Duke for a fine prince, the Duke of Montagu for his Master, and himself he did not know very well what. Nobody else, I believe, would be puzzled to determine. I was close behind him all the time

[1] In Dryden's Tragedy of that name (1676).

[2] [In a later hand.] Joseph Wilcocks (1673–1756), Bishop of Gloucester, and later of Rochester in 1731. Also Dean of Westminster. He was a learned Antiquarian, as is related in 1735 by Hervey. (*Memoirs*, p. 500; and later in this volume, p. 234.)

he was thus adroitly making his Court, had like to have made the Queen laugh in his face; and was swingingly chid by her at night for behaving myself as much like a child as he did like a fool.

All the stories you have heard about the Duchess of Marlborough's receiving joy, and not mourning, I assure are quite groundless lies. I am to dine there to-day with the Prince. The Princesses are gone under Sir Robert's convoy to hunt in Windsor Forest for the first time this year. The King's eye is too well to serve for an excuse to stay at home. So fine an autumn was never known in England; the days have the clearness, and the evenings the softness of June. I hope they are just the same at Maddington. The description you give of the place, since you write it from thence, does not hinder me wishing myself perpetually there; for wherever you are,

"Ille mihi praeter omnes
Angulus ridet . . ."[1]

TO STEPHEN FOX *Hampton Court, September 25th, 1731*[2]

It is so uneasy to me to neglect doing anything that gives you pleasure, that I am sat down to write to you this morning at eight a clock though the post never goes till five at night; for fear of being prevented by some unforeseen accident, as I was last Thursday, when, as I returned from walking with the Queen, I found Lord Bateman in my lodgings, and his staying with me all day hindered your having a letter. I find by him things go very bad between him, my Lady and Mount Ætna. As soon as Lord Blandford died, she wrote a letter to excuse her not acquainting Lord Sunderland with his sister Di.'s match sooner,[3] and said the reason was, for fear he should have told Lady Bateman. . . . The old Beldam of Bedlam, after offering £50,000 with Lady Di. to Lord John, gives but £30,000; which is in reality giving but £14,000, for 16,000 Lady Di. has of her own. We are all here in great expectation of the D. of Lorraine's[4]

[1] *Horace*, Carm. II Ode vi. [2] Ickworth. [3] In Hervey's writing.

[4] Francis, Duke of Lorraine (1708–65), later Emperor Francis I (1745). He was 2nd son of Leopold, Duke of Lorraine who died in 1729: and married Maria Theresa, daughter of the Emperor Charles VI, in 1736.

arrival. The King told me that Lord Chesterfield had written such an account of him, that it looked like a love-letter : but I cannot think it any good sign for his understanding in his situation, and with his vast expectations if his presence is not necessary in his own Dominions, that he should be anywhere but at Vienna. How childish it is for him to be rambling about Europe to see sights, when he should be cultivating the favour from which he expects an Empire. You know how necessary I think it always is, to keep in people's sight in order to keep in their affection ; and how soon any impressions not so renewed wear out. Human minds were no more for lasting characters than sand, and those of princes are the most sand of all. The deepest you can make there want to be so perpetually retraced, that, if they are not, they might as well never have been made. . . .

TO STEPHEN FOX *September 27th*[1] [*1731*]

I had time last post to thank you but very slightly, and can never thank you enough for your agreeable letter I that morning received from Maddington. As to your dislike of writing, I think one can no more in general say one loves or hates it, than one can say in general one loves or hates eating or kissing,[2] both which depend entirely on the food and the object. One hates talking to people one dislikes ; but to those one does not dislike, it is pleasant even to talk upon paper ; and the only reason why it is less pleasant to speak to their eyes than to their ears, is that one is forced to speak slower and a little more constrained, from being more afraid of being overlooked than one is of being overheard. But because one has not all the liberty one wishes, is that a reason why one should not enjoy all one possesses ? I could no more deny myself the satisfaction of writing to one I loved when I had no other way of conversing with them, than, if I was a prisoner, I would always stay stifling in my dungeon, because I had only a little garden of two or three acres within my limits allowed me to walk in.

Quand on ne peux pas ce qu'on veut,
Il faut vouloir ce qu'on peut.

[1] Ickworth. [2] Corrected in Hervey's writing.

. . . I have run this dissertation on poor Fanny's exit [1] into a great length, especially considering I prefaced it by allowing you had already said in six lines everything that could be said upon it. But I am really jealous of her character on this occasion, and quite hurt by those impertinent and simple people who endeavour by such paltry comments to detract from it. I liked her living, and honour her dying. I dare say if it could be known, Adrian, Anacreon, or Petronius did not die with more unconcern. Cato made much more bustle about it; though he makes so much a better figure in Lucan and Addison, than she does in *Fog* and the *Craftsman*.

Nor are these all the absurdities I fret at and grow leaner under upon this occasion. There are full as many bad moralists who descant on this subject as ignorant anatomists; and I am forced to sit and hear things advanced by my brother-Courtiers, which if they did not make me peevish would infallibly make me laugh. I dare make no answer to them, because I am sure, if I should dash their redundant stream of folly with one drop of common-sense, those inexhaustible sluices, their mouths, would be never shut: and I should either be hooted through the Palace for an atheist for want of being understood, or at least run the gauntlet through staring eyes and pointing fingers wherever I went. Mr. Schutz [2] t'other day foamed at the mouth, and his eyes struck all the fire his phlegmatic composition could supply, at my barely saying in cool blood and a meek voice, that I thought she had done mighty right. He talked of flying in God Almighty's face, of not being our own masters, of self-murderers being deserters, and all the common-place galimatias which orthodoxy often preaches without believing, and good Christians generally receive without understanding. You will easily imagine I did not enter

[1] The reference is to Miss Fanny Braddock, sister to General Braddock, later Commander of the troops in North America. She had gambled away the little money she had at Bath, and finally was found hanging in her apartment, much to the sorrow of her friends. "Poor Fanny," said her brother, "I always thought she would play till she would be forced to tuck herself up." (*Horace Walpole*, *Letters*, ed. Toynbee, iii, 334.)

[2] Augustus Schutz, Master of the Robes and Privy Purse to George II. A special favourite with the Queen and the Princess Royal, and not to be confused with his brother, Colonel Schutz, who was a member of the Prince of Wales's entourage.

into an argument. I should as soon think of reasoning with a kicking horse or a biting dog. All one has to do upon such occasion is to get out of the way. . . .

TO STEPHEN FOX *Hampton Court, September 30th, 1731* [1]

I believe you were quite tired with my long moralising lecture by the last post. I very often think on these subjects till I think nonsense, and as I always write and speak to you just as I think, it is very probable I might write till I write nonsense. If I desired to entertain you with nonsense of a more common style (though a very uncommon degree of it), it should be with the recital of your beauty, Lady Deloraine's ordinary conversation. She really works miracles in idiocy; for nobody yesterday thought she could be a greater fool today, and nobody today believes she can be a greater still tomorrow. Yet one she has proved, and t'other, I, who have more faith in the progress of folly [2] than other people,[2] dare answer for her, she will prove. One day at dinner, Lord Scarborough was commending the beauty of her two daughters, to which with a sigh and tears in her eyes, she replied: "Oh! my Lord if you had seen my son, you would never have thought these girls deserved to be named with him." Lord Scarborough with a great deal of surprise said:—"I swear, Madam, as much as I lived with your Lord I never knew you had a son." "No, my Lord, you never saw him, poor dear thing. I miscarried of him at five months end; but so beautiful a creature"—here her tears stopped her voice, and putting her handkerchief to her eyes gave the whole company an opportunity of looking at one another with that applause to her Ladyship's speech that it deserved. This is true, upon my honour, au pied de la lettre.

There is a girl, one Miss Mekensy [*sic*],[3] the prettiest creature that ever was looked on, just taken into the Family in the quality

[1] Ickworth. [2–2] In Hervey's writing.

[3] *Court and Society*, by 7th Duke of Manchester (ii, 330), gives details of Miss Mary McKenzie, a niece of the attainted Kenneth, 3rd Earl of Seaforth. He relates that an attempt to poison her was later made by Lady Deloraine, who was jealous of the attentions paid to the young lady by a certain Mr. Price. After her recovery Miss McKenzie and Mr. Price were very happily married.

of dresser to the Princess Louisa, which puts the poor girl immediately in my Lady Governess's power. She is so hurt at the other's beauty that she exerts that power in making her cry regularly once or twice a day, by putting her out of countenance and telling her of her Scotch Highland awkwardness. The other day at dinner, to show that the girl had a high forehead and thin hair, her Ladyship pulled her pinners back to the crown of her head, tore off a handful of hair (no doubt) in the operation, and scratched what remained over her temples, crying, " Look here, do you see how bald she is ? " The poor girl coloured like scarlet ; and everybody at table commended her the rest of the dinner, though she sat all the while coiffée by my Lady Governess directly like Mrs. Cibber in the play of the *Amorous Widow*, when the old aunt has pulled her niece's head over one ear to hinder her lover from thinking her pretty. Voilà les scênes dont je m'amuse ; and whilst her Ladyship is so good to treat the Court with such farces, it is impossible to be sorry that the King does not think fit to transport Drury Lane hither. When God Almighty made her, he made a much better comedy than Congreve or Vanbrugh ever wrote ; and to give her Ladyship her due, poor Mrs. Oldfield never acted her part more to the satisfaction of the audience than her Ladyship performs her's ; though 'tis as the Italian players act at Paris—all she says is an impromptu, nothing is given her but the character, and it is kept up with such spirit and with so much approbation, that one may say of her performance, as I have somewhere or other read of *the Cid*, that,

> " A hundred nights a crowded audience drew,
> A hundred nights performed, it still was new."

So much for her Ladyship. I must now tell you a short story of the Duke of Newcastle, whom you know I hate as much as one can do anybody one so heartily despises. He was t'other night most excessively drunk, and the next morning fearing he might have said or done something improper to the Princess Royal with whom he had had a great deal of conversation, he came to her, making a thousand excuses for his conduct, to which she very graciously answered : " Mon Dieu, vous étiez charmant ;

vous ne m'avez jamais si bien diverti de votre vie. Je voudrais vous voir toujours ivre." He was so well satisfied with this compliment that he bowed ten times de suite down to the ground, and was both pleased and proud to hear that he was never so agreeable as when he was least himself. Adieu. J'attends le 8 d'une impatience que—divinez le reste. Je n'ai plus de papier.

Since I wrote the enclosed, I have been walking with the Queen, who has been talking over a piece of news to me that came by an express last night from Turin. The young King [1] has been obliged to seize and put his father under arrest. The reason and manner of his doing it, were as follows. The old King, who it seems has left Chambéry for some time and resided in the neighbourhood of Turin, having a mind to resume the crown, has been long tampering under-hand with the first people of the Country, to see if they would give in to his scheme and assist him in the pursuit of it. This conduct soon came to the young King's ears; and upon the intelligence he received of it he went to visit his father, begging him to desist from such measures, and not drive him to the extremity of using force to maintain what he was determined, as a duty to himself and to the State, never to give up. The King's letters from Allen [2] go so far as to say the young King threw himself at his father's feet, and conjured him by all the tenderest expressions not to urge him any farther: for that his affection had already made him reject the counsel of all his Ministers, who, in their advice, had considered only his treason, whilst he still remembered that it was committed by a father, and therefore came himself to expostulate, instead of sending to punish.

This had so little effect on the old King that he still went on. Among many other steps he took, he sent a copy of his Act of Renunciation to the President of the Parliament of Turin, desiring him to study it, to see if there was no flaw in the form of drawing it, and if it was indisputably binding. Of this the President informed the young King, who immediately sent at midnight to seize his father's person. He was taken out of bed from his wife (now called the Countess of Spigho [Spigna] and formerly Madame St. Sebastien), was carried to Rivoli, and is now confined

[1] Of Sardinia. *See ante*, p. 55. [2] No doubt British Minister in Turin.

there and under a guard. Madame Spigho (whom he married since his abdication) is sent to a castle in Savoy : and all the other people as yet taken up for being in the old King's interest are the Grand-Veneur, the Governor of Turin, the old King's physician and the physician's son. Everybody condemns the old King and speaks of him as a madman, at the same time that they applaud the just and mild conduct of his son. Mr. Allen says the young King is in the greatest affliction imaginable. It is certainly a very disagreeable situation : and what an exit is this for the greatest Prince of his time ?—last year to have committed such a folly as his abdication, and this year to endeavour to retrieve that folly by such an injustice as this resumption would have been. For whatever [1] he was, he is now his son's subject; and to endeavour to take the crown again is being as much a rebel as any private sentinel who stands at the gate of his Palace would be, if he should endeavour to usurp it. Adieu. If I hear nothing from you, I will certainly be at Hartford Bridge the 8th, by dinner.[2]

TO HENRY FOX *Hampton Court, October 1/12, 1731* [3]

. . . I sent you word in my last of Lord Sunderland's good fortune, but nobody (not he himself) then knew it was so good as it proves ; for notwithstanding he is only heir presumptive to the young Duchess of Marlborough, the words of the will (the oddest that ever was made in this particular) put him exactly in the place of a Lord Blandford, the title only excepted : that is £8,000 a year rent-charge comes to him immediately, and £12,000 a year more at the death of his grandmother. What I find so very extraordinary in this disposition is that such vast wealth should be lodged anywhere, a temporary, precarious possession ; for if the young Duchess should have a son, all this would revert from Lord Sunderland to him. And if Lord Bland-

[1] In Hervey's writing.

[2] Between Bagshot and Basingstoke :—a useful and convenient rendezvous for the two friends, to meet for a few hours' conversation, when Lord Hervey's Court duties did not enable him to go as far as Somerset.

[3] Holland House and Ickworth.

ford had died immediately after the Duke of Marlborough, and this little Lady Mary[1] had proved a boy, the case I put had actually happened. Lady Di. is to be married next week. Old Ætna, after all her golden promises, gives her but £15,000. Her own 15,000 makes her fortune in all 30,000.

Send me word if you have talked with Cocchi, and if he answers. The people who have his turn of reflecting seldom fall off. Mr. Jackson is sensible, thinks quick and clear, and expresses himself so too. He believes nothing.

The Duke of Lorraine is expected here next week, he embarks at Rotterdam on Tuesday ; part of his equipage is already arrived. He comes incognito, as Count de Blamont, to avoid the embarras of all ceremonials and forms. God knows how we shall entertain him ; je crois qu'il s'ennuyera, et nous nous ennuyerons, great and small. He is to be lodged at Count Kinski's, the Emperor's Minister. Lord Chesterfield has sent such encomiums upon him from Holland, that the King told me one of his Lordship's letters looked as if it had been written by the Duke of Lorraine's mistress. But you know I never mind his Lordship's accounts of people ; his decisions are always extravagant and capricious. I have heard him say as much on dispraise of the Dss. of Queensberry's[2] person, as he can say in panygyric on the D. of Lorraine's parts. He loves to paint in strong colours, and never considers likeness. Adieu, dear Count ! Write to me often and very particularly. Little things at a great distance either of place or time always amuse. Contez-moi quelque chose des extravagances de cette folle la Duchesse de Buckingham.[3] Je suis sûr qu'elle en a fait cent milles pendant qu'elle était en Italie.

[1] Lady Mary, the 2nd Duchess's youngest daughter, married Thomas, 4th Duke of Leeds in 1740.

[2] Catherine Boyle, daughter of Henry, Earl of Clarendon and Rochester, married 3rd Duke of Queensberry in 1720. She was forbidden to attend at Court on account of her partisanship of the poet Gay, who was not a *persona grata* with their Majesties. *See ante*, p. 17.

[3] Lady Catherine Darnley, natural daughter of James II and Catherine Sedley. She married John Sheffield, Duke of Buckingham, as his 3rd wife, and died in 1743, a few months before Lord Hervey's death, to whom she had left Buckingham House for life. She had strong Jacobite leanings and was constantly intriguing on the Continent.

[TO STEPHEN FOX] *October 2nd, 1731* [1]

. . . The Duke of Lorraine is expected on Sunday at Hampton Court for the first time, so I should be obliged to leave you early [2] . . . I think you are in the right about the *Free Briton.*[3] I told 19 [Sir R. Walpole] there were whole paragraphs I would swear to. That part of the D. of Marlborough's will relating to Lord Sunderland is very odd, but very clear. Mount Ætna and Lady Di. are come to town. The latter is to be married as soon as the writings can be finished. Ld Portmore is come back from Paris without any new fashion but a pair of very extraordinary shoe-straps, which look like Mercury's wings, to his feet, blacked. I hear he is to have the Green Ribbon. I was surprised at coming to town today, with a report among all sorts of people from St. James's to White Chapel, that the Queen died suddenly in the night. The report they say, was a contrivance of the Spital-Fields weavers to sell their crapes and black clothes. It succeeded ; for in three hours, Mr. Hoare told me, they were all bought up. It sounds incredible, but it is certainly true ; the Queen so well all the while that I was two hours with her this morning, and never saw her in better looks, spirits and humour in my life. I must send you a bon-mot of a Roman Cardinal to the Duchess of Buckingham ; and must tell it in the language I heard it. " Votre Éminence " (dit-elle) " ne peut pas imaginer quel plaisir je sens en revoyant mon frère, et combien de tendresse mutuelle il m'a temoigné." " C'est apparemment par principe, Madame," (lui répondit-il) " puisqu'on vous dispute à tous deux la naissance ". I do not believe the story ; but si non è vero, è ben trovato.

I write to you from the Duchess of Richmond's, where I am to dine. She has a belly up to her chin and looks mighty well. His Grace is in great anxiety for her welfare, and a boy. I am so, for fear of any unforeseen accident preventing our meeting on Friday.

[1] Ickworth. [2] At Hartford Bridge.

[3] " My wife brought me from London the *Free Briton*, a weekly paper writ by Fra. Walsingham Esq. (a supposed name), which author owns himself to be the writer of *The Remarks on the Craftsman* . . ." (Lord Perceval, June 28, 1731, *Egmont*, i, 196.)

'Tis you alone my fears and wishes make,
From you my thoughts their various tincture take.
With every good, whilst you are present, blest,
Of all, when you are absent, disposses't,
Each hour at best a blank, not one enjoy'd,
A tedious waking, or a sleeping void.
And whilst the present I should strive to taste,
I wish the future, or I weep the past.

It is ridiculous to say one writes in a hurry when one write in rhyme, but 'tis true. And you know I do not lie, when I say I sometimes can write as fast in verse as I can in prose. Adieu. Dinner is on the table. . . .

TO STEPHEN FOX *Hampton Court, October 12th, 1731*[1]

. . . The Duke of Lorraine is not yet come. The wind is contrary, and keeps him at Rotterdam, where he has been ever since last Monday. . . .

Lady Di. was married yesterday ; nobody was present but her two brothers, Lady Bateman, D. and Dss. of Bedford, and Lady Essex. Lord Bateman and Lord Essex were here, where there was a great Court and a ball at night ; and the two eldest Princesses (for the first time in public) danced country dances, the Prince with one, and the D. of Grafton with the other. The Prince supped after the ball in his own apartment with ladies, of which Lady Hervey was one (I went to bed). He has given her the prettiest watch I ever saw ; it is lapis-laselli [*sic*] set with diamonds. La Mouche[2] had no supper, nor no present, and consequently has no comfort ; elle est au désespoir. Voilà une fade Gazetté de Cour. But if I was never to write to you of anything but what is uppermost in my thoughts, you would no more hear of anything but yourself, than you would see anything else if you were to live always before a looking-glass. Adieu. Novembre me paroit furieusement éloigné.

[1] Ickworth.

[2] Clearly Lady Deloraine, for Lord Hervey mentions her nickname at Court as "Fly." (*Memoirs*, p. 747.)

TO STEPHEN FOX *Hampton Court, October 14th, 1731* [1]

To say I wrote to you in a hurry, when it is yet but seven o'clock in the morning, and the post to set out at five in the afternoon, may sound odd, but so it is; for I have two long letters about business more to write, and at nine am to go as usual to the Queen. As soon as I come from her, I must dress to be ready to receive the D. of Lorraine in the King's suite, who will like to have all us Show-Officers at his door upon that occasion. His R.H. is to see the King first in private in the closet. He came on Tuesday night to Greenwich, lay on board the yacht, and came next morning through the City to Count Kinski's. It must have given him a great idea of the largeness of London; for the Bridge and Hanover Square, you know, are almost the two extremities of the town. We talk of nothing here but the Count de Blamont (the name he goes by), so in all probability for some time you will hear of nothing else. Unless he can divert himself with eating and drinking at great dinners and suppers, he will s'ennuyer furieusement. For I hear of no other amusement cut out for him but that, and an English play which he does not understand, and a bad pack of hounds which he does understand.

I was yesterday with the Prince at Kew. He has made two charming, pretty rooms there, and is going to do a great deal more. We played at nine pins all day, and did not dine till five a clock: à la Redlynch, as to the hours, not a bit in any other particular. You know then how well I was entertained. I was forced to leave him there, and come back to Hampton Court in the dark and the cold, on horseback, with my dinner in my throat, in order to be time enough dressed to play with the King. . . .

TO STEPHEN FOX *Hampton Court, October 15th, 1731* [1]

My dearest Ste. We are to set out so early to-morrow morning to hunt in Windsor Forest for the entertainment of the Duke of Lorraine, that I am forced to write to you to-night. I have had no letter from you since I saw you: and consequently

[1] Ickworth.

no pleasure, for you know what relates not to you is pretty indifferent to me.

We had a great bustle here yesterday with the reception of the D. of L. He was first in private with the King, then with the Queen, and then with the Prince, after which he came to the circle in the Queen's Drawing-room, and stood by part of the time they were at their public dinner. Monsieur Kinski intimated to everybody that he would have no title given him in conversation but Monsr le Count [*sic*]. Since he was not to receive all honours, he would have none. We went all this morning from Hampton Court, every courtier from Sir Robert down to Lifford,[1] to London to wait upon him. I dined at the D. of Devonshire's, in a fine house with charming pictures ; an honest clown for the master, bad jokers [2] for our conversation,[2] and loud laughers for the guests. The D. of L. is a pretty figure of a man, though low and rather thick : ill-made and worse dressed. He wears his own hair, has a very handsome face, like the King of France, but a more sensible, more lively and a more good-natured countenance. He seems very easy and very well-bred. He run the gauntlet yesterday through a crowd of starers and whisperers without being disconcerted ; and received all to-day with as little constraint as if he had been amongst us this seven years. . . .

TO STEPHEN FOX *Hampton Court, October 19th, 1731*[3]

. . . What I said would be, has been. The D. of Lorraine was entertained on Saturday with a bad pack of hounds, and yesterday with a bad play. I thought his not understanding it would be a misfortune, but I have changed my mind ; for if he had, I should, as a damn'd proud Englishman, [have] blushed for two hours together. The play was *The Recruiting Officer*,[4] and one of the jokes, a fellow's saying that, " the King of England was greater than any Emperor in Christendom ". How disagreeably foolish this would have been, had the men, for whose entertainment the play was given, known what they were saying. On Saturday after hunting, he dined in private with the King

[1] Lord Lifford. *See* p. 112.
[2–2] In Hervey's writing.
[3] Ickworth.
[4] By George Farquhar.

and Prince and twelve men more at table, and a mob of about a hundred people looking on. He goes to Newmarket on Monday, comes back on Thursday; the day after the Birthday, goes to Euston for five days, from Euston to Houghton for five more, and then returns to London, where they say he will continue till the meeting of the Parliament.

Lord John Russell and his bride came here from Windsor Lodge last Sunday. She was as fine as lace and brocade and jewels could make her. I asked her if she liked being married as well she fancied she should; and she said she thought it was the charmingest thing in the world. Lord John had a very conjugal languor about him; he does not seem so much as one of those coursers who the first *week* with vigour run. Old Marlborough has heard, talks and thought so much bawdy upon this occasion, that she is as coquet as if she was eighteen, and as rampant as if she were drunk. . . .

TO STEPHEN FOX *Hampton Court, October 23rd, 1731* [1]

. . . The Birthday, after many changes in our resolutions, is at last finally determined to be kept in London, where we all repair on Thursday next. The Monday following the Court goes to Richmond for a fortnight, and as the Duke of Grafton is not come to London till December, I have resolved to take this fortnight in hand rather than wait for that month in the bush; and that I may lose no time, I start from London [2] the same hour the King leaves it for Richmond. . . . With the King you know there, I have nothing to do as Vice-Chamberlain, and hope I shall not be wanted of evenings as Lord Hervey. . . . The more I see of the D. of Lorraine the better I like him. He is well-bred with more nicety, more ease and more constant presence of mind than anybody I ever met with, and has the most beautiful, most sweet, and most sensible countenance I ever beheld. The Countess, his namesake,[3] has mustered all her charms, and every night lets off her whole artillery of smiles, oglings and

[1] Ickworth. [2] For Redlynch.
[3] Clearly a play on the word, "Deloraine".

languishing from every corner of the table at which he plays; but he returns these advances no more than a blanket would return her voice, and they were quite lost to everything but the observances and ridicule of the spectators.

Charles Churchill is come back in perfect health, to my great satisfaction. He is one of the very few people I love, or desire to be loved by, or that I think deserve to be loved. He has brought me a seal from Italy qui est charmant, and clothes from France for the Birthday, which I believe will not be here time enough; for they are at present only on their journey, and nobody knows where.

Your news about Lady Drogheda [1] and Meadows has no more truth in it, I believe, than if it came from Court, or than any she ever spreads. But it is so absurd a thing for both of them to do, that I am astonished there should be no better foundation for the report.

The Duke of Lorraine dined yesterday at Standish's [the D. of Newcastle]. There was a most magnificent entertainment, and everything that depended on his servants was in perfection. Whether it was trim-tram,[2] I know not, but can give a shrewd guess.

7 [[3] The Prince [3]] told me he and I were not in favour enough to be two of the forty that were invited: he said it with some warmth. All the answer I made him was, that whoever showed their dislike to me, by coupling me with him, I should always say, like the song, "Ces affronts sont des faveurs". He replied immediately, "You take every occasion to be agreeable, and they to be disagreeable." I saw he was hurt, and was glad to observe at night that Standish saw it too. It put him in a real fidget, equal to any he ever put on when he had a mind to appear a man of business. I know it would have been much righter for 7 [[3] the Prince [3]] to have seemed quite indifferent upon this occasion, and for that reason I ought to have been sorry that he did not; but I own I was pleased. Adieu. . . .

[1] Charlotte, daughter of 1st Viscount Falmouth, and widow of Henry, Lord Drogheda, who died in 1727. She died in 1735.

[2] An absurdity.

[3–3] In Hervey's writing.

TO STEPHEN FOX *Hampton Court, October 26th, 1731* [1]

. . . I was on Sunday in town at a vast feast made by Kinski in honour of the day, which, it seems, belongs to the Saint whose name the Emperor bears. We were 26 at table, 14 foreigners and 12 English. We dined at a long table with 38 dishes at a course, 12 removes, 2 courses, and a dessert of arches, pyramids, giants, beasts, trophies, eagles, etc., of barley sugar and sugar plums, painted of different colours, and raised to such a monstrous and ticklish height that I believe it had been three weeks building and was full half an hour in setting on. The dinner lasted three hours and a half. The last two hours the doors were thrown open to the street, and everybody that had curiosity to see, and strength enough to push, came into the room. I never was so hot, so sick, and so tired in my life. The stink of all that dead flesh before, and all that live flesh behind, made the stench insupportable; the women scolding, and the children squalling for being squeezed, entertained one's ears no better than the other did one's noses; and in short altogether it was one of the most expensive tawdry, ill-understood, disagreeable German pieces of magnificence that ever was seen. . . .

TO STEPHEN FOX *London, October 28th, 1731* [1]

After walking round Hampton Court Park this morning with the Queen, we all came to town time enough for the Council, after which there was a Drawing Room; from thence I went with Sir Robert Walpole and Mr. Churchill to the King's Arms to dinner. At six I went to the play with the King; and 'tis now past ten, and we but just come back again. By this account you see I have had to-day but little time to write; however, it stands fixed for me to leave this place on Monday. As it is moonlight, I will come on to Basingstoke if I can. So if you come, send or call at the posthouse to know if I am there; though upon recollection I think 'tis Maidenhead we used to go to, and I love all vieilleries where you are concerned. Regnier is just come to consult about my Birth Day clothes, of which there is not yet one stitch set. The stuff for the waistcoat arrived

[1] Ickworth.

but to-night, and the coat is not yet bought. Adieu, mea vera & sola voluptas. The D. of N. gives the D. of Lorraine another feast on Saturday in town. [1] I am honoured with an invitation.[1] Lord Sussex is dead. Voilà des nouvelles dont vous ne vous souciez guère.

We now come to three letters, written to the Prince of Wales, from Redlynch, early in November. The first speaks of the call of Lord Hervey and Stephen Fox at Lord Pembroke's, Wilton.

TO FREDERICK, PRINCE OF WALES

Redlynch, November 6th, 1731 [2]

. . . The day after my last in my way hither I called and breakfasted at Wilton. Old Pem.[3] received us with great civility and courteousness. My Lady was sent for down; and we were carried with great form and method through every room of a very fine old house. It is directly like an Italian Palace. There are a great many very fine statues, and a great many more with only very fine names, to which I believe his Lordship stood sole godfather. He was dressed in a pale blue damask night-gown and a black velvet night cap, which I suppose in the Antiquaries' style was emblematically to signify the youth of his body and maturity of his head. Whether my Lady Countess will allow of this interpretation I cannot tell; but I know of no other body that can confirm or contradict it. She knew the history of every busto as well as his Lordship. I do not wonder at his having endeavoured to bring her into a taste for antiques; but I question much whether her taste is so established, that if the antique in her bedchamber was to be exchanged for a modern, she would be much afflicted. I daresay she would have skill enough to find out the difference, but I shrewdly suspect that she would hardly be virtuosa enough in that case to give antiquity

[1–1] Added in Hervey's writing. [2] Ickworth.

[3] Thomas, 8th Earl of Pembroke, and 5th Earl of Montgomery (1656–1733). His third wife was Mary, daughter of 1st Viscount Howe. After his death she married in 1735, Hon. John Mordaunt. Lord Pembroke was President of the Royal Society 1689–90. Vertue's sketch of him (Walpole Society, *Vertue*, Vol. V, 101) presents him in much the same costume which Lord Hervey describes. Lord Pembroke claimed to have saved the Raphael Cartoons at Hampton Court from complete ruin and destruction. (*See Egmont*, i, 218.)

the preference. The Duke and Duchess of Queensbury, Lord Cornbury, and Sir William Wyndham, who is now at Amesbury, had dined at Wilton the day before we were there. His Lordship would fain have had Mr. Fox and myself stay dinner, and he was so cheerful, so jocose, so odd and so entertaining, that we had a great mind to it ourselves. But 24 Somersetshire miles after dinner in November is not an undertaking for a poulet. He said he had once come post from London to Wilton between four in the morning and dinner-time: and very jocosely at the end of his story assured us he did not design ever to do it again. One of his legs that is swelled as big as my middle looks, poor man, as if it was carrying him post another way.

It has rained incessantly ever since I left London, so that the life the Redlynch colony is forced to lead *sent plus les moines que les chasseurs.* The walls of the house are the limits of our walks, and all our employments eating and drinking, chatting and reading. We might pray if we would, for my dear friend Parson Hill is always at hand. But I like him much better in his lay calling than his ecclesiastical vocation; and, give him his due, I believe he had rather act in one than t'other, though he is really not only a good companion but a good man. As for Mrs. Digby, the only woman we have here, I know no fault she has but loving her husband better than any other man, and liking her children better than any other company. According to La Bruyère's doctrine she should be one of the most agreeable creatures in the world, for he says the prettiest human composition is une jolie femme qui a toutes les bonnes qualités d'un honnête homme. And as far as my skill goes, I think she seems to be made by that receipt.

Quant al Padrone, Signor Ste,
Le petit drôle, mon cher ami,
Il peste un peu contre la pluie,
Mais d'une humeur badin, joli,
Amusant, polisson, poli,
Fait les délices de notre vie,
Rit, cause et chante, et chasse l'ennui.

Voilà un crambo qui ne vaut rien; mais n'importe.

I have sent Your Royal Highness a picture of our life in black and white. I should be glad [1]to see[1] one of Kew. Is there anything new added by way of appendix ? Or do vieilleries reign in such undisordered, unchangeable vicissitude, that by looking at my watch I may know whether your Royal Highness is walking, playing, dressing, *raccommoding*, eating or sleeping ? If it would not be too bold for Hephæstion to pry into the sanctum sanctorum of your employments, I would ask whether Roxana or Statira is at present in favour ? Is La Moscula [2] still flattered by the Hackney *piper of Dudley's and Trevor's* ? Or do you say like Ovid, " Non oculis grata est Atthys ut ante meis ? " . . .

> No more my eyes thy beauty charms,
> No more my heart thy beauty warms,
> No more I languish for thy arms.

Upon reading over this galimatias I feel some doubts arising whether I ought to send it or no, especially without covenanting that it shall be exposed to no eyes but your own. . . .[3]

TO FREDERICK, PRINCE OF WALES

Redlynch, Nov. 8th, 1731 [4]

It is impossible for me to tell your Royal Highness with how much real pleasure I received the honour of your last letter. All the expressions of kindness it contained seemed so natural, notwithstanding the partiality of them, that I could not help flattering myself they were something more than the common effects of a temper universally obliging, and really thought they carried the marks of a heart particularly kind. The favours of princes are generally bestowed with little benevolence, and acknowledged with little sincerity ; but I am sure the manner in which I feel your's is a strong exception to one part of this rule, and, if the manner in which you confer them is not an exception to the other, you conceal an indifference to those you oblige with

[1–1] In Hervey's writing.
[2] Lady Deloraine.
[3] We have not reprinted the long set of verses which follow, and to which Hervey has above alluded as " this galimatias," for they appear in Mr. Sedgwick's edition of the *Memoirs* (i, xxxvii).
[4] Ickworth.

more art than in many occasions you can want to make you agreeable. J'enrage que je n'étais pas du souper que vous me dépeignez. Those little snug parties are my delight. Je ne m'étonne point que vous vous ennuyez dans un autre endroit dont vous me parlez ; but if I was Prince of Wales, healthy and but four and twenty years old, I fancy I could find ways to cut out my time in such a manner que je ne m'ennuyerais pas.

I was yesterday for a party of pleasure with Ste. and Mrs. Digby, to see Parson Hill and his wife, an old, fat, stupid, good woman, who has no signs of life but sitting upright, and according to his account has no joy in it. . . . There were two female things more there, one of which was a young girl, at whom he licked his lips ; and the other, her old aunt, who licked her lips at him : a scene which, if Molière had had the cooking of it, I assure Your Royal Highness, would make no ill figure upon the stage. To entertain these guests, he borrowed my box with Your Royal Highness's picture ; and though neither of these she-asses had ever seen you in their lives, the comment one of them made upon it was that a periwig would become you much better she believed than your hair ; and the other, that she thought the picture was an extraordinary good likeness. Ceci, tout sot qu'il vous doit paroître, est tout vrai au pied de la lettre. Et voilà, quand on ôte le nez d'un livre, comme on s'amuse à la campagne.

I shall be in town on Friday. The motions of Court once resolved are so like the Persian laws, that I make no doubt of Your Royal Highness's leaving Kew that day too. And as the days shorten, the leaves fall, the winds whistle, the rains beat : and in short that it is now cold, wet, dirty, confirmed, absolute winter, I make as little doubt of your being glad to change your solitary, paper dwelling at Kew, for the comfortable séjour de Londres.

TO FREDERICK, PRINCE OF WALES

Redlynch, November 10th, 1731 [1]

. . . I do not repine I own at the thoughts of being about to get *en train* for the winter. Short days and bad weather are the

[1] Ickworth.

most sociable things I know. In summer and sunshine, people are always straggling as long as 'tis light, and sleepy as soon as 'tis dark. *Cela ne vaut rien.* Books and cards, wine and tea, are the only implements we have made use of here to *désennuyer.* Yesterday we had an incident extraordinary to entertain us. It was a trial of pochers [*sic*], which from the justice of the prosecution and the oddness of the circumstances I fancy would have entertained Your Royal Highness. The Judge was deaf, the Somersetshire witness as unintelligible as if he had been dumb. Ste. plaintiff; Parson Hill his counsel; and a poor frightened farmer's son, two broken tradesmen, a ragged spaniel and a brace of greyhounds were the defendants. After they had all talked at a time for about half-an-hour, the Court broke up. The Judge set his mark to a warrant; the criminals were ordered to the House of Correction, because they could not pay the penalty; and after whining, canting, and weeping my friend Stephen into compassion, they were all dismissed and forgiven; and I believe at this moment are poaching afresh. Voilà une Gazette de campagnard assez ennuyeuse; mais si je parle de ce que je vois et ce que j'entends, il faut qu'il soit dans ce style.

What game you poach, Sir, what you hunt, what you catch, or what runs into your mouth, I don't pretend to guess. If you think fit to tell me, I shall soon be in the way of being informed. In the meantime I beg leave to assure Your Royal Highness, I am with the greatest respect, warmth and truth.[1] . . .

TO STEPHEN FOX *St. James's, November 18th, 1731*[2]

. . . Why did you not come to my lodgings for a minute after the Opera? I did not a stay a quarter of an hour with the Prince. He went immediately to bed; and I came home. As it was uncertain how long he would keep me, I could not ask you to come; but that uncertainty would not have hindered you trying to see me, if you had felt what I did, with thinking it would

[1] This last paragraph seems to suggest a possibility that Hervey already knew that there was trouble in the offing. It is interesting to compare it with the letter to Stephen Fox of December 14 (p. 123), and that of December 25 (p. 127).

[2] Ickworth.

be two months before we should see one another again. Mais j'ai tort de toutes les façons de vous reprocher, car les reproches ne corrigent jamais. Elles ne font tout au plus que rendre meilleurs hypocrites ceux qu'on voudroit changer. I passed the evening at the Dss of Richmond's, and wished myself a hundred times in the great chair we squabbled for at Basingstoke. The winter is begun in form, and all the unalterable vieilleries en train. L'Ennui est retabli dans son trône à St. James's, et tout-le-monde reconnoit son Empire. [1] Le Roi [1] s'ennuit avec [2] my Lady Suffolk : la Reine [2] s'ennuit avec my Lady Charlotte : [3] le Prince s'ennuit avec ses sœurs, et ses sœurs s'ennuient avec lui. Les Filles d'Honneur s'ennuient de coucher seules : et les Courtisans s'ennuient de les voir au Drawing Room ; et pour moi, si le déplaisir de vous perdre n'étoit pas quelque chose au delà de l'ennui, je m'ennuyerais aussi. . . .

TO STEPHEN FOX *St. James's, November 20th, 1731* [4]

You are by this time en train (as you call it) at Redlynch, and as you generally are more desirous to be in *a track* than solicitous about *what* track, I may very fairly for you, and disagreeably for myself, conclude you are now as well pleased and as well satisfied there as you was a fortnight ago. It is charmingly convenient to be of such a temper, and most unfriendly in me to wish it altered. It is like some digestions that turn even distasteful things into nourishment ; or if you do not meet with anything that it is impossible to convert into nourishment, at least it is never painful. It passes off as iron does through the ostrich's stomach ; and if you receive no benefit, at least you receive no hurt. I can't help seeming to grudge you this inestimable gift of

[1–1, 2–2] In Hervey's writing.

[3] Lady Charlotte de Roucy (d. 1743), sister of Frederick William, Earl of Lifford, so created about 1699. He died in 1748/9. They were sprung from a Huguenot branch of the family of Rochefoucauld. Lord Hervey thus mentions them in the *Memoirs* (p. 383) : " Two poor miserable Court drudges, in more constant waiting than any of the pages of the back-stairs : were very simple and very inoffensive, did nobody any hurt, nor gave anybody but His Majesty any pleasure . . ."

[4] Ickworth.

Providence wherever I am concerned; and do not think I am unreasonable for so doing since I cannot share it.

The Duke and Duchess of Richmond dined here yesterday; we drank your health. The Duke of Lorraine is chosen a member of the Royal Society. He hunts to-day on Wimpleton [*sic*] Common, and is to dine afterwards with the Prince at Kew. I was invited, but the King going to the Opera, and the Duke of Grafton not being in town, I could not go. The Prince is to give him a clock that plays tunes and cost £600: a very fine, dear, ugly thing, but if princes do but give, it is sufficient; it never signifies what, farther than the price.[1] The Duke of Lorraine, they say, is to go away Tuesday sennight. I hear he is to be made Governor of the Austrian Netherlands; and the present fat, ugly, pious, stupid Governess is to go into a convent. . . . Adieu. I am just going to Kensington with the Queen.

TO STEPHEN FOX *St. James's, November 25th, 1731* [2]

I received a letter yesterday from you, and another from Rome from your brother. I was glad of both, but it was a very different degree and sort of gladness which they gave me. By the negligence of Mr. Jackson[3] (to whom he trusted for intelligence), the fleet was come to Leghorn, the troops were landed, and Sir Charles Wager sailed again, before ever your brother knew of their arrival; upon which he intends, he says, to go to Venice, and from thence by the Tyrol to Paris, where he desires me to direct my next letter. . . .

I am half dead to-day with a headache, the consequence of dancing, supping and sitting up last night at the Duke of Newcastle's; and suppose I shall from the Prince's ball to-night be carried off in a hearse. The entertainment last night was the most magnificent, the easiest, the best understood, and the best ordered thing, I ever saw in my life. The Duke of Lorraine is as great a romp as you or me. I write this from the Council Board: and hear so much of the Indies, Plantations, ships, troops,

[1] Corrected by Hervey.

[2] Ickworth.

[3] Apparently a protégé of Lord Hervey's (*H. Walpole's letters*, ed. Toynbee, i, 120, etc.), by whom he obtained a post at Leghorn, and had been Consul at Genoa.

etc., that I am quite confounded in what I write. However, I must try to recollect a French epigram I heard last night repeated on the Cardinal Fleury. The bitterest, the cleanest and the strongest satire I ever saw in my life :—

> Confondant du passé le leger souvenir,
> Ébloui du present, sans perçer l'avenir ;
> Dans l'art de gouverner, décrépit et novice,
> Punissant la Vertu, récompensant le Vice.
> Malgré sa tête altière, accablé de son rang,
> Fourbe dans le petit, et dupe dans le grand,
> On connait dans ces traits, sans même qu'on le nomme,
> Le Maître de la France, et le Valet de Rome.

Adieu, my dear, dear Ste.

TO STEPHEN FOX *St. James's, November 27th, 1731* [1]

The Duke of Newcastle's and the Prince's balls have almost demolished me. I have been in a fever with the sitting up, and giddy, like drunkenness, with the senseless motion ever since. I lay on the bed all yesterday till the Drawing Room hour, and then went in with the King, but was so sick and so afraid of accidents, that I left His Majesty to be lighted out again by whom he could get, which, for so good a courtier as you know I am, is a strong proof how ill I thought myself. I have had recourse to Indian root, and am better ; so much that I ventured to the Opera to avoid owning I was sick. I have tasted nothing but tea, bread, and hartshorn drops this four-and-twenty hours ; and am now freezing by the fire-side, my blood and thoughts quite stagnated, and nothing warm about me but that corner of my heart which you inhabit.

The King and Queen took care to exempt themselves at the Opera from the inconveniences we freezing plebeians shook under, by wrapping themselves up in velvet lined with ermine from head to foot. Lord Herbert [2] and Lord Albemarle [3] were there

[1] Ickworth.

[2] George, Lord Herbert (d. 1751), later 9th Earl of Pembroke, the "Architect" Earl.

[3] William Anne, 2nd Earl (1702–54), married, in 1723, Louisa, daughter of 1st Duke of Richmond.

shivering without waistcoats. The latter will pay for that air o. strength within this week about twelve ounces of blood, three blisters, and as many ounces of the bark. His doing these things, because that Goliath, Samson and Hercules—Lord Herbert—can stand them, is so absurd, that if he should take it into his head to show himself invulnerable in the extremes of heat as well as of cold, I do not think it would be at all more extravagant for him to strut through his kitchen fire, because Shadrac, Meshec and Abednigo walked unsinged in Nebuchadnezzar's furnace.

The Duke of Lorraine is gone to-day to Chatham. He comes back to-morrow, and goes for good and all next Saturday.

The Princess Royal of Prussia's [1] marriage is at last consummated with the trumpery Margrave of Bayreuth's eldest son; a fine exchange, poor thing, from the K. of England's. The P. of Prussia was sent for back to Berlin, and reconciled to his father upon this occasion. It is reported in town that the condition of this reconciliation was that [2] he should never marry a daughter of England.

If I am not better soon, when His Grace of Grafton returns I shall go to Ickworth for a little country air and quiet. If you were here to go with me, I should take that journey as a cordial; as it is I shall take it as physic.

On November 30 follows a letter full of advice to Stephen as to remedies for a twisted knee. "I thought the Opera tonight would never be finished, they encored so many songs; and I have wanted this hour and half to come home and thaw myself by a good fire, and write to you."

TO STEPHEN FOX *St. James's, December 2nd, 1731* [3]

You're not mentioning your knee in yesterday's letter makes me hope it is better; if it is not, be sure you do not neglect it. Winnington has been with me all this morning. He talks of going to Redlynch, but I fancy he will only talk of it. He goes to the masquerade to-night with His Royal Highness, who is to be dressed himself like a shepherd, an Adonis, or an Apollo

[1] Princess Wilhelmina, Frederick the Great's adored sister. She had been selected for Frederick, Prince of Wales.

[2] Added in Hervey's writing.

[3] Ickworth.

(I have forgot which), and to have eighteen huntsmen in his suite. The huntsmen are to be dressed after a drawing of Kent's, in green waistcoats, leopard-skins and quivers at their backs, bows and arrows in their hands, tragedy buskins upon their legs, breeches trussed up like rope dancers, antique gloves with pikes up to their elbows, and caps and feathers upon their heads like a Harry the 8th by Holbein. I was upon the list for a performer in this harlequinade, but pleaded chicken, headache, fear of sitting up, etc., and got off. I blushed with the thought only of being set forth in all this prettiness ; and am sure I should have died with shame in the executive part, as soon as ever I found myself in the room, with a mob of about four or five hundred squeaking idiots in our train, which will infallibly be the case of those who have obedience and courage enough to stand the trial. I know it will be monstrous to go at all after refusing to go with him, but I cannot resist the curiosity I have to see this fraternity I have deserted, run the gauntlet, and shall take a malicious pleasure in swelling the number of their persecutors. I have not said one word in ridicule of this project to Winnington. Think of him and his Grace of Devonshire in the antico-moderno accoutrements I have described. I would fain have them go in at the head of a pack of hounds ; nothing else could improve it.

The Duke of Lorraine was yesterday at the Duke of Norfolk's [1] from three a clock till ten. The dinner was splendid, and Sir Robert Walpole of the party. Such revolutions have long ago done surprising me ; and when I wonder next, it will be at things keeping in the same track, which is just as likely to happen, as it is to have it day or night for 24 hours together. There was a ball at night ; a great deal of good, and a great deal of bad, company. Adieu, mon cher and très cher. I choose dealing when one drops a card ; but all good players say it is a disadvantage.

TO STEPHEN FOX *St. James's, December 4th, 1731* [2]

You did not guess so well as you are apt to do on most occasions, when you imagined I was the author of the French

[1] Thomas, 8th Duke (1683–1732). The Duke and Duchess may have been under the suspicion of leanings towards the Pretender, owing to their religion. Hence Hervey's remarks. [2] Ickworth.

epigram on Cardinal Fleury ; it came from a much abler hand. I approve of your criticisms. " Punissant la vertu, recompensant le vice " is not in his character. But as he has lately, upon so scandalous an occasion as *Père Gerard's* acquittal, and so foolish a one as *Abbé Paris's* miracles,[1] interested himself in the Ecclesiastical disputes, and been so unjustifiably partial *to* the Jesuits, and *against* the Jansensists ; so I think if the author of the epigram had turned that line, and by saying, " Opprimant la vertu, et protégeant le vice ", had [2] made it relative to these two disputes, in which it was impolitic, out of his way, and beneath him to meddle. Though the words thus had been less strong, they would have been more severe, because more applicable.

I went to the masquerade as I told you I would, and found everything as I thought I should. When I saw that fraternity I had deserted, lugged and twirled about as I imagined they would be when I resolved to desert them, I laughed, like Madame *Sévigné, dessous ma coïffe* : and felt the same sort of pleasure, that I fancy a little *miscarriage* or a child that died in the month, would feel in Abraham's bosom, when he looks down and sees the troublesome follies and all the noisy, senseless bustle of a world he was originally designed to be a member of, and which he had the good luck to slip out of. The D. of Lorraine was there, happy as the night was long, flying about, talking to everybody he met, pleasing and pleased. He was to have gone away to-day, but at the King's request has put off his journey to Wednesday. I dined with him t'other day at the Danish Envoy's, where the only two Englishmen invited were the Duke of Newcastle and I. Je trouvois celà drôle. Lady Bell. Tufton was married two days ago to Lord Nassau Pawlet : [3] her sister's friend looks dissatisfied and disappointed. The Duchess of Cleveland [4] they

[1] François de Paris (1670–1727), theologian and supporter of the Jansensists. His grave in the cemetery of St. Medart became an object of pilgrimage, until it was closed by the order of the French King.

[2] In Hervey's writing.

[3] Youngest son of 2nd Duke of Bolton. Lady Isabella was daughter of 6th Earl of Thanet.

[4] Anne Pulteney, aunt of William Pulteney, second wife of Charles, 1st Duke of Cleveland, who was son of Charles II (1662–1730). She married Philip Southcote in August 1733 ; and died in 1746.

say is certainly going to be married to your friend, Southcott, the Duke of Norfolk's disagreeable, cherry-cheeked captain. Such an exploit will make her Grace's name sure as proverbial for idiocy as her defunct spouse's of foolish memory. The selling herself once to a fool with a great title and a great estate was a common and consequently excusable prostitution: but to buy a fool without either title or estate, and deprive her age of the comforts for which she sacrificed her youth, is a madness, a weakness and an infamy which nobody can forgive her, and which in a month she will not forgive herself. If, as Shakespeare says, the heyday of her blood was not yet over, she should, like my more experienced dames, Lady K—y and Lady Fitz—r, have made a regiment pass in review before her, singled out the strongest and ablest fellow, and listed him in her service. 'Tis with such ladies' lovers, as with their chairmen. When they want them for a present job, and pay them so much a pitch, there are twenty crowding at the call; but those they take by the year are never in the way, always grow idle and good for nothing.

. . . I left the King at the Opera to come home and write to you; because the Prince, as soon as the Opera is done, has engaged me to go and sit with him. *It is well he is so secret when one is serious, and so entertaining when one is so gay; otherwise the frequency of these parties would be rather too much.*

Part of the next letter has already been printed by Mr. Sedgwick. It refers to one of those attacks which we have already noticed, affecting Hervey from time to time, and as it was symptomatic of his curious state of health, we reproduce it here.

TO STEPHEN FOX *St. James's, December 7th, 1731* [1]

I have been so very much out of order since I writ last, that going into the Drawing Room before the King, I was taken with one of those disorders, with the odious name, that you know happened to me once at Lincoln Inn Fields' Playhouse. I had just warning enough to catch hold of somebody (God knows who) in one side of the lane made for the King to pass through,

[1] Ickworth. The first paragraph is printed in the *Memoirs*, ed. Sedgwick, i, xxv.

and stopped till he was gone by. I recovered my senses enough immediately to say, when people came up to me asking what was the matter, that it was a cramp took me suddenly in my leg, and (that cramp excepted) that I was as well as ever I was in my life. I was far from it: for I saw everything in a mist, was so giddy I could hardly walk, which I said was owing to my cramp not quite gone off, and was so sick I thought I should have vomited in the room. However, to avoid giving suspicion, I stayed and talked with people about ten minutes, and then (the D. of Grafton being there to light the King) came down to my lodgings; where without taking anything to promote vomiting, I began to strain, and brought up a good deal of blood. I am now far from well, but better and prodigiously pleased, since I was to feel this nasty disorder, that I contrived to it à l'insû de tout le monde. Mr. Churchill was close by me when it happened, and takes it all for a cramp. The King, Queen, etc. enquired about my cramp this morning, and laughed at it. I joined in the laugh, said how foolish an accident it was, and so it has passed off. Nobody but Lady Hervey, from whom it was impossible to conceal what followed, knows any thing of it.

I have had another letter from the Count, dated from on board a boat on the River Po, between Ferrara and Venice. Write to him soon, and direct it to Mr. Alexander, his banker at Paris. By his letter I should guess him fretful, ennuyé and impatient.

The Duke of Lorraine goes to-morrow for certain, repining and regretted. He walked this morning in Kensington Garden with the Queen. We were all wet to the skin, and coming back full gallop in open chaises, all bespattered and covered with dirt, like so many stage-coach postillions.

Henry Fox was still in Italy: but was moving homewards, via Nice, where he was staying with Mrs. Strangways-Horner, the châtelaine of Melbury in Dorset, at her villa. He spent the autumn of 1732 in England, and was at Goodwood, the home of his future bride, Lady Caroline Lennox, then a child of nine, for Christmas. Shortly afterwards he left for the Continent, again for Nice, and did not make his reappearance in this country until the early months of 1735.

TO HENRY FOX *St. James's, December 8/19, 1731*[1]

I have two letters, my dear Count, to thank you for, one from Rome, the other from the River Po. By all I can collect from them, you are dissatisfied, ennuyé, and fretful. . . . You relate Mr. Jackson's neglect so naturally, that I half believe your coming back by land owing to that accident; though before you left England you know I said you would do so, and from another cause. You see how well you can deceive, or how easily I am deceived. But since it will flatter the vanity of both of us to believe your success on this occasion, owing to the first of these reasons rather than the last, let us indulge ourselves in that belief and nourish that charming quality, that gives being to almost every pleasure one tastes.

I saw Lord Sunderland, Sunday, Monday and Tuesday, which is every day he has been in town since his sister was married. He is grown so confirmed a fox-hunter, that he has two packs of hounds, in order not to lose one day in the week besides the Sabbath. Lord John and Lady Russell, Lord and Lady Bateman, and Dicky,[2] *one* Mr. Mordaunt, and *one* Mr. something else, and three or four more anonymous misters, have been with him at Althrop [*sic*], where I hear their recreations all day were galloping and hollowing, and their pleasures all night stale beer and tobacco. . . . How essential riches must needs be to happiness, when people with twenty thousand pounds a year take the same pleasures with those who carry chairs and burdens for two or three shillings a day, and which each of them may purchase for a groat. I am sorry you was not of the party. What pity it is you should be losing your time poking into the mouldy, rusty, shattered remains of Rome and Athens, and informing yourself in the unprofitable knowledge of how the ancients employed themselves; when you might actually partake of all the more eligible amusements of the politer moderns, who have found out so much a better way of passing their time than any of our ancestors, that I would fain have them take for their mottos, "*Meruere decus; vestigia prisca ausi deserere.*"

Lady Russell, whom you inquire after, is at present very happy. She lives in Grosvenor Street, and with the same people she used

[1] Holland House. [2] Upton.

to do. My Lady Rich's restoration was the first act of her new reign; it immediately succeeded her coronation. The Dss of Man[cheste]r frets,[1] shrugs and barks there as usual; but whether Her Grace has swallow'd or spit out again the tips of all the noses she has bit off since you left England, I am unable to inform you. The only reason why she has never deprived her dear Duke of his, I suppose, is that she hopes one time or other to lead him by it.

As to my own manner of life, *As it was in the beginning, is now and ever shall be, Court without end, Amen.*

The Duke of Lorraine will employ no more of my time; for he, this day, took his leave of the King and the whole Court, regretting and regretted; and is at this moment on board the yacht at Greenwich. King, Queen, Prince, and everybody belonging to the Court, have been as civil to him as possible. He has been five days in Suffolk with the D. of Grafton: five more in Norfolk with Sir Robert Walpole: feasted somewhere or other every day in town: and present at all the balls, suppers, Operas, masquerades, plays and shows that London affords. He is very handsome, cheerful, sensible, well-bred and obliging: and though he seems to do everything with ease and without thought, one never finds he does or says anything that is not proper, or omits anything that is. Never anybody had the good fortune of pleasing so universally. I believe his sorrow to leave us was not put on; for the etiquette of the Court of Vienna will not suit his temper, I fancy, quite so well as the freedom of this. Adieu, my dear Count. The Parliament meets the 13th of next month. When you and I shall meet I shall be glad, but can't guess. I fancy Mr. Alexander will forget something or other that is essential to your leaving the South of France.

TO STEPHEN FOX *St. James's, December 9th, 1731*[2]

. . . The Duke of Lorraine is at last departed; he embarked yesterday at Greenwich. The King gave him some very fine

[1] William, 2nd Duke of Manchester married, in 1723, Lady Isabella Montagu, daughter of John, 2nd Duke of Montagu, a niece of the 1st Duke of Marlborough. She married Edward Hussey, later Lord Beaulieu, in 1743. Sir Charles Hanbury-Williams wrote a very caustic set of verses on her.

[2] Ickworth.

English hunters ; and he has given Lord Scarborough a very fine brilliant ring. He is universally liked and regretted here. . . . Adieu, it is so cold, and I must go to the fire.

I have been to warm myself, and am come back to give you an account of an étourderie of my judicious, amiable Lord Selkirk.[1] He was the Lord in waiting yesterday when the D. of Lorraine was to take leave of the King, and whilst that ceremony was passing in the closet, my Lord, thinking it his duty to entertain Monsieur Neibourg in the antechamber, took him up to Mary, Queen of Scots' picture, and made him this speech. " Voilà le portrait de Marie, Reine d'Écosse, qui avait l'honneur d'appartenir à la maison de Lorraine. Son oncle, le Duc de Guise, était un grand homme. Vous savez tout ça ; par Dieu, la maison de Lorraine faisait alors une figure en France bien differente de celle qu'elle ne fait à cet heure "—and all this while the fool meant to be civil. Is it not astonishing that a wretch, who has been lying, flattering and stinking for these last five reigns and these last fifty years in a Court, should not have yet got the common knowledge of a page of honour or a gentleman usher ? I asked him afterwards if he thought he had made his court to Monsieur Neibourg by the compliment he had made the House of Lorraine ? And his answer was in broad Scotch. " Yas, Yas, for by God he knew it, as well as I, that it was true." My answer was, that I knew many things of England to be true which I should be shocked to be told by a foreigner. Un altra volta, caro and carissimo. Adio.

The next two letters to Stephen Fox are both dated December 14, and are individually of special interest. The first dates the moment at which Hervey's estrangement from the Prince of Wales first comes definitely under notice, though the remarks on November 10 may well give the impression of veiled hints. Up to a few weeks before, he was revelling in the latter's favour, although beginning to show signs of boredom in such company as the younger Court provided. But here we find a complete change of attitude. Hervey had clearly received unexpected evidence that Miss Anne Vane, with whom, as we have seen, he had been secretly intimate for a long time past, was deserting him for the arms of his princely rival. The second letter

[1] Charles, 2nd Earl (1683–1739). Lord Hervey elsewhere described him as, " An old paralytic Scotch Earl, the servile follower of every King *de facto*, and every Minister in power."

seems to announce the failure of an effort to get some small Government post for his friend Stephen, and his belief that it was in some way due to the machinations of the Duke of Newcastle.

TO STEPHEN FOX *St. James's, December 14th, 1731* [1]

It is grown into a vieillerie to write to you after the Opera. I am just come from thence, and am now unwearying myself, after the bustle of a disagreeable day, by my fireside in my night-gown, and indulging my thoughts in the only object they fix upon with pleasure. . . . As to my own health, it is better much within these few days, which I am astonished at; for I have been in a course of fretting for this last week. That fool 7, [[2] the Prince [2]] plagues my heart out. He is as false, too, as he is silly, and appears every thing he is not by turns but wise. Yet the mask of common-sense, if he knew how to get it, would disguise him more than any other. He could put on nothing so unnatural, nothing so unlike. I can explain no farther to you at this distance; for paper is as great a blab as a human creature. It tells everything one communicates to it: and like most go-betweens never serves you to one, without betraying you to a hundred.

TO STEPHEN FOX *St. James's, December 14, 1731* [3]

I have fretted these last four and twenty hours for a thing, which, though it only concerns you, I am sure will not vex you the hundredth part so much or so long as it has done me. The short of the story is that there [is] going to be —— [4] in the ——,[4] and my solicitation for —— [4] has not succeeded. I know you will not care much; and yet, since you care at all, I hate to have miscarried in it. The whole is a riddle, for there is one to be left open; and I am sure 19 [Sir R. Walpole] was sincere and hearty upon this occasion. And indeed what reason could he have to be otherwise, when, there being a vacancy unfilled up, there could be no competition? He said a thousand obliging things to me, and of you; and, not with the same air that he says those he does not mean, he assured me he would

[1] Ickworth. [2–2] In Hervey's writing. [3] Ickworth.
[4] The omissions are in an unintelligible cipher.

do anything in his power to please you, and begged me to take care you should not impute what was not his fault to his coolness towards you or his negligence. There is some mystery I can not fathom. Standish [D. of Newcastle], I know, has been monstrous impertinent (if one can properly call what is natural to anybody, monstrous), both to you and to me; but I dare not so much as let him see I know he has been so, for the sake of the canal of my intelligence. However, I may have it in my power to return it sometime or other, as strongly and as secretly as I feel it. . . .

TO STEPHEN FOX *St. James's, December 21st, 1731*[1]

I went to-day to make a visit to Mr. Arundel, and being so near your house called in to see it.[2] It is quite finished, and looks the smuggest, sprucest, cheerfulest thing I ever saw. Nothing can improve it but a piece of moveable goods of my acquaintance, which I expect home with more impatience than I can tell you or than you deserve I should feel, since the 10th is the soonest you design to bring it. Va-t'en, petit indigne. . . .

Your beauty, friend and passion, Lady Deloraine, came to me the other day, and complained that she was not in fashion this year, and asked me if I could conceive the reason of it. She said everybody seemed to neglect and avoid her. I told her I thought it was easy to be accounted for; that envy kept the women at a distance, and despair the men; to which she only answered, "Pshaw", turned to the glass, reflected on her conduct, and believed me.

Everybody concurs in their opinion of Pope's last performance,[3]

[1] Ickworth. This letter in the copy is dated 1732, apparently in error, for it fits properly in here in 1731.

[2] Now 31 Old Burlington Street. (*See ante*, p. 28.) Formerly Lord Hervey's.

[3] This is the *Epistle to Richard Boyle, Earl of Burlington*, known also as the *Moral Essay IV*, "On Use of Riches." In it, Pope referred to Burlington's "brother peer" as Timon, and ridiculed the lavishness of his expenditure. It was at once suggested that the Duke of Chandos was indicated; and though Pope denied the designation, he was not believed. The verses were registered at the Stationers' Hall on December 7, 1731, and the publication in folio was advertised in *The Grub Street Journal*, at that time still to some extent influenced by Pope.

and condemns it as dull and impertinent.[1] I cannot but imagine, by the 18 lines in the last page but one, that he designed ridiculing Lord Burlington as much as he does the Duke of Chandois. It is astonishing to me that he is not afraid this prophecy will be verified, which was told to him a year or two ago,

> " In black and white whilst satire you pursue,
> Take heed the answer is not black and blue."

I have sent you enclosed a paraphrastical translation of the epigram on Cardinal Fleury : a bad imitation, and a very unjust application of a very good original.[2] Lord and Lady Albemarle are to dine here; and it is near three a clock and I in my night-gown ; therefore I must bid you Adieu. When you say so to Redlynch, I shall be happy. The town is as empty as at mid-summer, which can be no great inducement to anybody to visit it, I own. . . .

TO STEPHEN FOX

From the Duchess of Marlborough's Dressing-Room,
December 23rd [*1731*] [3]

You see by the date where I am. She would not let me go home ; and I can never let myself miss one post, when you tell me so obligingly if ever I do that you are uneasy till the next. I received a letter from you yesterday to which I am ashamed to make any answer. All you say in it is so sensible and so unanswerable. I showed part of your letter to Sir Robert ; he repeated what I told you before, with such an air of sincerity, that if he is so old a courtier as to be a hypocrite upon this occasion, I own myself so young a one as to have been his dupe.

I passed yesterday in a mixed way, partly agreeably, partly much otherwise. I was with 19 [Sir Robert Walpole] in the morning, and displeased ; dined with him, not less so, received your letter and was more so. Then went to welcome old Pem.[4] to town, sat tête à tête with him an hour, heard you commended from his observation and from report ; and consequently thought

[1] In Hervey's writing.

[2] The translation has been omitted.

[3] Ickworth. There is a doubt about the year, but from the contexts it must be 1731.

[4] Lord Pembroke.

this the part of the day that was spent most to my satisfaction. By this preface he brought me into good humour enough to be able to laugh at several odd, lively, comical things he said upon Pope's letter to Lord Burlington, and Dr. Bentley's [1] behaviour when they came to consult him (as a book-doctor, so he called him) how to save the books of the Cotton Library from being ruined by the water that had saved them from the fire. From thence I went to Count Hughes, who is as incomprehensible as any of the mysteries in the Trinity, which they say he was originally educated to preach upon. The music there was fine, and the company better suited to the scrub-house than the entertainment he gave us there; though my Lord Essex was one, who is gone this morning to be kissed and stuffed at Freeholders' Christmas feastings by his Grace the Duke of Newcastle, in Sussex. You know that friendship diverts me, and the reason why it diverts me. I am not so much surprised at Dawley [2] walking to Claremont, as Macbeth was at Birnam Wood coming to Dunsinane. I have been long enough at Court to wonder at nothing in friendships but their lasting. That I have for you is the only one I know, excepting that I flatter myself you have for me, in which I have no more notion of seeing a change than I have of wishing for one. Adieu.

The next letter written on Christmas Day, in conjunction with that of December 14, seems to us to clear up once and for all the date of the commencement of Hervey's deadly hatred for the Prince. Several theories have been put forward to account for his breach with Frederick; and it has even been suggested that a portion of the *Memoirs* was destroyed to conceal the real reason. This letter, and Hervey's lines which terminate it, shows vividly how badly Hervey was taking the realisation that Anne Vane had deserted him. He may well have had some inkling of the truth early in November, or even before. Lord Perceval (*Egmont*, i, 218, 280) stated at the end

[1] Richard Bentley (1662–1742), Master of Trinity College, Cambridge, for 42 years. Keeper of the Royal Libraries, and F.R.S. The Cotton Library had been collected by Sir Robert Cotton (1571–1631), was added to by his son, and was presented to the nation by Sir John Cotton, 4th Bart., in 1700. It was housed at Ashburnham House, Westminster, until the fire in 1731, when it received serious damage. It was removed to the British Museum in 1753.

[2] Lord Bolingbroke's house, near Uxbridge.

of January 1732, that Queen Caroline had dismissed Miss Vane from her post at Court for "her familiarities with the Prince", and later chronicled the birth of her baby in June, who we learn from other sources was believed by the public to be the son of either Lord Harrington, Lord Hervey or the Prince of Wales. Evidently the Prince had few doubts, for he is said to have settled £3,000 p.a. on her, and to have given her a house in Soho Square. The story of Lord Hervey having sent her a letter is discussed in the Preface, p. xi, and on p. 75. Lord Perceval's suggestion that the King and Queen were extremely annoyed with Lord Hervey about it seems improbable, as the Queen had just removed Miss Vane from her employment.

TO STEPHEN FOX *St. James's, December 25th, 1731* [1]

Lady Mary was talking so fast, so incessantly, and so loud, at my elbow the whole time that I was writing my last letter, that I shall not be at all surprised if you are not able to understand, when you read, what I did not understand as I wrote. I have quite forgot what it was about, but I daresay it was unintelligible. . . .

I know of no news, but that the King of Sardinia has sent his father his wife again; and the King of Prussia has sent his son to Kustrein.[2] [3] It was said the monster [3] designed to give him a regiment; but it seems the regiment is to have the care of him, and not him of the regiment. I have almost every day fresh instances of the falsehood as well as the folly of —— [[3] The Prince [3]]: and since it is impossible to correct the first, wherever it is so natural, I am not very solicitous, as you may imagine, to rectify the errors of the last. Let their folly fall on their own head, and their wickedness on their own pate. They neither know nor suspect that I have detected them, nor ever shall; for the easiest, the most natural, and the justest revenge one can take upon people who imagine they impose upon one, is to let them fancy they do; and instead of being their dupe, let them make themselves their own. I have fretted at their conduct a good

[1] Ickworth.

[2] *See ante*, p. 53. The reference is obscure, as according to Carlyle, Prince Frederick was first sent to Küstrin in February 1730, and remained there till February 1732.

[3–3] In Hervey's writing.

deal : but for the future I am resolved to think of it as little as I can, and not speak of it at all. Many reasons will make me silent on this occasion : but I think people with common judgment or common prudence would keep their grievances to themselves as much as their distempers, and never trust the recital to anybody but those who were to cure them. . . .

For few or can or wish to bring relief,
And every touch we feel augment our grief,
To probe is but to irritate the heart,
And to divulge is to increase our smart.
The wise in silence therefore bear their pain,
Or only where redress is sure, complain.
Content they feel with necessary ill,
And what they must submit to seem to will.
While babbling fools, repining at their fate,
Their wrongs, their wants and discontents relate :
And ignorant of the make of humankind,
Solicit pity where contempt they find.

TO STEPHEN FOX *St. James's, December 28th, 1731* [1]

I am delighted to hear you *ennuyez* in the country. I hope you have not been one moment better pleased since you told me so than you were then. It is but just that you should feel, by absenting yourself, part of what you inflict. . . .

. . . When you talk of my staying in town to *conter fleurette et politiquer* as joys that I cannot forego or indeed as any joys at all, you make me both sick and peevish. The first part of this is just what a little, pert petit-maître with his elbows as high as his shoulders, would lisp to the Duke de la Trémouille ; and the latter part of it what would suit your friend Winnington much better than your friend Hervey. I am much too old for a coquet, and too lazy for a politician. I look with more horror on the meeting of the Parliament, than my little son does on Monday sennight, when the holidays determine and he is to go to school again. And whatever you may think of the attendance

[1] Ickworth.

Enoch Seeman (?), pinxit

STEPHEN FOX, LATER 1st LORD ILCHESTER

at Drawing Rooms, I think much the most disagreeable attendance belonging to Court employments is that which is expected from us at the House of Commons : though according to all accounts, conjectures and appearances, there never was any session more quiet than this is expected to be. Everything goes well abroad, and I hear of no complaints but the Charitable Corporation[1] at home. Adio, Carissimo ! . . .

TO STEPHEN FOX *St. James's, December 30th, 1731*[2]

Since my last I dined at Sir Robert Walpole's, with Horace [Walpole], Dodington, Winnington, Lord Wilmington, Mr. Clayton and Sir William Young.[3] Such variety of entertainment from internal speculation on what passed, I never enjoyed in any other two hours of my life. Lord Wilmington did little besides eating and drinking and taking snuff. Dodington did not only talk in character, [4] but was dressed in character :[4] for he was in a bob-wig, and an old laced coat made into a frock, which very typically expressed, though he had finery at heart, that his head was turned to appear a country gentleman, and if he still carried the ensigns of a courtier about him, it was only some reliques of la vieille Cour, and no new acquisition. His conversation was full of wit, impropriety and absurdity : whenever he gave his opinion, it was in contradiction to the Master of the house, and generally supported it with bad reasons. He had[4] a great mind[4] to fasten himself on Lord Wilmington as an

[1] A body set up in 1725, as a Corporation to assist charitable objects by private subscription. The management, however, became so corrupt, that the whole undertaking broke up, causing very serious losses to the families whom it was intended to help. See *Carlisle*, p. 36. The scandal led to the House of Commons appointing a commission to report on the whole matter, which was presented to Parliament in 1733. Lord Perceval reported the debates. Certain M.P.s were implicated, and one at least was expelled from the House of Commons.

[2] Ickworth.

[3] Sir William Yonge (1693–1755), a creature of Walpole's, whom he later appointed Secretary-at-War. Hervey thought nothing of him, but acknowledged that he was "goodnatured and goodhumoured, nobody's friend, nobody's enemy": and had "a great command of what is called parliamentary language" (*Memoirs*, p. 38).

[4]–[4] In Hervey's writing.

intimate, who seemed to decline that appearance, and did not lend him one precedent to back any of his assertions upon an appeal to him. Sir William Young and our friend Winnington told a few insignificant lies. The first said that woodcocks were so rare now to what they used to be before people shot flying, that he remembered the time when he once flushed (I think he called it) two brace out of one little holly bush. Upon which *Horace* burst out into a loud laugh, and said he remembered a lying Lord Quarrington [1] that said he once shot eleven woodcocks at one discharge of his gun ; to which a stander-by replied, it was pity the gun did not recoil and knock down the twelfth, to make them a round dozen. This did not disconcert Sir William, who laughed as loud as any of us ; nor did it deter our friend W[innington] from telling us he had made a Worcester man his implacable enemy, by sending him once, for a present and a great rarity, a chicken with a woodcock's head fastened to it for a woodcock. The man, he said, eat it, was prodigious thankful and believed it a woodcock, till another gentleman laughed at him a week after, and told him the trick ; and from that time to this the man has never forgiven him. The Master of the house and I said nothing to either of these stories, and poor Mr. Clayton [2] said nothing to anything or any body. His senses were in a fit of an apoplexy all dinner. The machine worked, but it was quite an automaton ; for he neither saw, heard or comprehended any one thing that passed, and carved, chewed, and swallowed his dinner with no more seeming sensibility than the jack that roasted it. These are the men to whose care nations are committed, who are to report truth, to see, hear and judge for others, to serve their Prince and their country, to shine in Senates, enact Laws, mend or preserve our Constitution, and teach our Senators wisdom !

I very seriously wish one could cure our friend of dealing so much in the fabulous, when he proposes to shine in company ; but it is a sort of thing, if one loved anybody never so well, one could not tell how to go about to correct them. I really wish

[1] Perhaps Lord Quarendon is indicated.

[2] William Clayton, who became Lord Sundon, husband of Charlotte Dyves, Woman of the Bedchamber to Queen Caroline (*see* p. 165).

him well ; and he has qualities that might make him make a good figure, but such a weakness, and the ridicule of it, will cover as many beauties as charity can faults. As to Sir W. Y., he has such a complication of unpleasant qualities, that curing him of one only, would go no farther towards making him agreeable, than washing one tooth would towards making him sweet. I own I admire the Man of the house prodigiously ; for notwithstanding his propensity to laughing, one seldom sees him indulge it in an improper place, or at an improper time.[1] He can suppress a smile when his heart laughs, as well as force one when it aches. His behaviour in many things that day was, under a seeming openness and negligence, devilish artful.

The P., Miss Vane and Dod. were all last night at that pretty idiot, Lady Deloraine's lodgings, whose head is no more the better for age than her face is the worse. She has taken it of late into her sweet fancy to study philosophy, and talks all day, and I believe dreams all night, of a plenum and a vacuum. She declares of all philosophers Dr. Clarke [2] is her favourite, and said t'other day if there was any justice in Heaven to be sure he took place there of the twelve Apostles. [3] One sees by this all the notion she has of Heaven.[3] Adieu. I beg you would not leave this letter as usual in your coat-pocket to be perused by your valet de chambre, who, under the pretence of brushing your clothes makes his morning lecture every day out of the writings of your correspondents ; and some things I have here written, you know I would not say to any creature in the universe but yourself. . . .

[1] This hardly seems to tally with Hervey's remarks (*Memoirs*, p. 492).

[2] Dr. Samuel Clarke, the friend of Newton.

[3–3] In Hervey's writing.

CHAPTER VI

1732

TO STEPHEN FOX *St. James's, Jan. 4, 1731/32*[1]

The news is at last arrived of Don Carlos (whose name I am sick of) being quietly settled in Parma. The Imperial troops (according to Ministerial phrase) have *evacuated* both Parma and Placentia ; and with great reluctance, I believe, left their Spanish successors the sole possession. The Queen of Spain now sees the project completed, which she has so many years pursued, and which to effectuate she has embroil'd all Europe, made treaty upon treaty, half-ruined Spain, bought Vienna, squabbled with France, courted England, and bullied Tuscany. This period to our seven years negociations happens very seasonably, as it will enable the King to meet his Parliament with a good grace and not make an ill figure in his Speech.

Sir Robert Walpole does not stir out. The news of Lady Malpas's death,[2] which came but last Sunday, is the occasion of his confinement. I have been with him these two hours, and am but just come from thence. She was his only daughter and a favorite ; and he certainly a good father and a humane man. Yet I do not think this loss sits very heavy upon him, or will affect him long. Nor is it natural it should. People may be kind, beneficent and friendly, from principle, charity and compassion. But they feel sensibly for nothing but what is conducive some way or other to their pleasure, or their interest, or their pride, three things that could none of them have any great share in his correspondence with his daughter. Besides that, people in business have their thoughts so taken up that they have not leisure to reflect on things that are not relative to their calling ; and if anything does vex them a little, unless they are put in

[1] Melbury.

[2] Mary Walpole. Sir Robert's daughter, married in 1723, George, Viscount Malpas, who succeeded his father as 3rd Earl of Cholmondeley in 1733. She died on Jan. 2, 1731/32.

mind of it frequently, they forget their own distresses as easily as they do other people's. . . .

The spring of 1732 is singularly devoid of letters. But in May one of the Ickworth copies, addressed to his mother, Lady Bristol, mentions Lord Sunderland's recent engagement to Lord Trevor's daughter, and the drastic line taken by his grandmother, Sarah, Duchess of Marlborough, on receipt of the news. With this letter we have connected three letters in the Holland House series, from the Duchess herself, two to Mrs. Strangways-Horner, the owner of Melbury and an intimate friend, of dates July 14, 1732, and March 1, 1733 and one to Henry Fox, with whom the old lady was always on good terms. They are placed in Appendix B. Fox was quite prepared to stand up to her in defence of his friend, Lord Sunderland. This she did not take it amiss, and put her side of the case to him at some length. The letters appear to us to be of some interest, besides being from the Duchess, as marking the point of severance of the Blenheim and Althorp branches of the Spencer-Churchill family.

Lady Louisa Stuart's *Introductory Anecdotes*, to the *Life and Letters of Lady Mary Wortley-Montagu*, her grandmother, do not entirely tally with the statements of the original participants in the controversy, but may be quoted as a comparison: "With the second [son of Lord Sunderland], Charles, Sarah, Duchess of Marlborough agreed pretty well till he succeeded to the Marlborough titles and fortune; when *money*, the mainspring, hidden or manifest, remote or immediate, of all family quarrels, quickly produced a rupture between them. She laid claim to a portion of her late husband's personal estate, and the affair could only be settled by what is called an amicable suit, but as a suit with her to go on *amicably* was a thing about as likely as for an oil-shop, set on fire, to be slow in burning, so the flame no sooner kindled than she insisted upon giving it full vent; and amused the world by pleading her own cause in Chancery. . . . The new Duke's habits of squandering and running into debt gave force to the sarcasm; yet people smiled when they recollected that his younger brother, Jack Spencer, who, besides equalling him in this respect, made the town ring with some wild frolic every day, kept a fast hold on the old lady's favour all the while, and in her eyes could do nothing wrong."

TO THE COUNTESS OF BRISTOL

St. James's, May 9th, 1732 [1]

The passengers in the Caravan I lately sent to Ickworth having informed your Ladyship of the hours I have been forced to keep

[1] Ickworth.

every day for this last fortnight in Parliament, and that I have never sat down to dinner till 8, 9, or 10 a clock, your Ladyship will not wonder that I have not had time or spirits to think of writing letters.

As to your account of the alarm given at Bury by the armament of the Spaniards,[1] and the parallel you draw between these apprehensions and those of the Irish in '88, I am equally surprised (considering how little you dabble in ancient history, and how much you live in the modern world) that you should know so much of what passed forty years ago, and so little of what is doing at present. I hear of nothing coming from Spain to us but an Ambassador, and nothing going from us to Spain but a pacquet-boat; so that if the conjectures of Suffolk-newsmongers and the *Bury Mercury* have given your Ladyship any other intelligence, I hope you will quiet your fears and remove such gazetteers for the future from your person and counsels.

But now I have informed your Ladyship what foreign news we have not, I should let you know what domestic news we have; and really the last full moon, together with the warm, mantling season of the year, has infected so many people with a contagious marrying madness, that the disease is almost grown epidemical. And as some of these infected persons are the heads of those matrimonial atheists, who used to be strongest in their blasphemies against that *wise* and *blessed* institution, I really begin to think it possible that the practice of marrying may possibly last another half-century, and my great-grandchildren not be as much at a loss to know what father must own them as what father begot them. The principal actors in the dramatis personæ in these present comedies and future tragedies of weddings, are Lord Cowper and Lady Harriet Nassau, Lord Grantham's second daughter; Mr. Williams[2] and Lady Frances Coningsby; Lord Carbery's eldest son and Miss Fanny Fitzwilliams; and, what will surprise your Ladyship more than all the rest, Lord Sunderland and the only daughter of Lord Trevor.[3]

[1] No doubt Spanish ships off the east coast of England.

[2] Charles Hanbury-Williams.

[3] Elizabeth, daughter of Thomas, 2nd Lord Trevor of Bromham (d. 1753) and his wife, Elizabeth Burrell, daughter of Timothy Burrell, of Cuckfield,

The first reflection your Ladyship will naturally make on this last piece of news (when I tell you the young lady is pretty and sensible, and has £30,000), to be sure will be, that bellowing Ætna, after the frequent desire she has expressed to see Lord Sunderland married, must be overjoyed; and that those streams of sulphur, fire and smoke, that used to flow in such outrageous torrents from the foul mouth at the summit of this tremendous mountain, are all converted into the soft murmurs of the Land of Canaan that flows with milk and honey. But if this is your conclusion, your Ladyship is extremely out in your conjectures; for upon Lady Russell's acquainting her Grace, at her brother's desire, with his intentions and his asking her consent, this pacific, indulgent parent, with one blister on her back, and another upon each arm, starts up in her bed, sends for a lawyer, her standish, and her will: orders the lawyer to scratch out Lord Sunderland's name wherever he found it in her will, and began to write him a letter to the following effect.

First, to tell him the ridiculous [1] choice he had made was one worthy of his understanding, and as prudent a determination as ever she expected from his judgment.

She proceeded to calling the young lady's father a madman, her mother a fool, her grandfather a rogue, and her grandmother a w——: said that Lord Blandford's choice of a burgomaster's daughter was a properer match than this for the Duke of Marlborough's heir: and that she could account for his pitching upon this woman by nothing but the artifice of his overbearing sister Bateman, who she supposed had brought it about for her own selfish ends.

She further imparted to him what she had done as to her will; and concludes, after four pages in folio of the like gentle hints and remonstrances, with saying she knows no merit this woman has but being allied to the high and mighty blood of the Batemans.

His Lordship's answer was short, but not sweet. He began with acknowledging the honour of her Grace's obliging letter,

Sussex. The fact that he was a renegade Tory, and, as Hervey wrote, "by principle (if he had any principle) a Jacobite", may have raised the old lady's objections to an even higher temperature.

[1] Added in Hervey's writing.

and telling her that he found nothing therein to induce him to change his resolutions, unless she called invectives, persuasions.

That for his overbearing sister (as her Grace was pleased to call her), he could not possibly find out any interest she could have in his being married but his being pleased ; and [1] that nobody whatever had recommended this [1] woman to him.

He said it was long since he had either expected or desired to be in her Grace's will : and concluded with telling her that this letter was the last trouble of any kind he should ever give her. "I am your Grace's grandson, Sunderland", was his ending.

I believe your Ladyship wishes your son was at the end of the trouble he is giving you too ; and therefore I shall add nothing but my being so, with great duty and obedience. . . .

Again a gap. Henry Fox spent the autumn of 1732 and the early winter in England.

TO STEPHEN FOX *Bury, August 26th, 1732* [2]

When I tell you I am now at Dean Butt's,[3] with a dozen Corporation men in the next room, you will not wonder if I say but little : and when I tell you I received last night the letter you wrote me from Salisbury, you will not wonder that I can not help saying something . . .

I came to Ickworth on Wednesday last, and am to leave it on Tuesday. I live quite easy there, hear of no Court intrigues, no politics, etc. Every thing I say takes, and every thing I do is approved. In short, I want nothing but you to be quite happy. That *But* though, I grant, is so material an ingredient to my happiness, that it is the same as if I said any body wanted nothing but legs to walk or wings to fly.

I intended giving you an account of Sir Robert's feast, at which there passed something very *particular* and very *comical*, but I have never had time to relate them. Adieu. I am all this while excessive rude to my Constituents, but extremely indulgent to myself.

[1–1] Altered by Hervey. [2] Melbury.

[3] Dr. Robert Butts (1684–1748), later Bishop of Norwich and Ely. Rector of Ickworth 1717–33.

TO STEPHEN FOX *Kensington, August 31, 1732*[1]

I came yesterday, my dearest Ste, to this place, and Sir Robt. Smyth[2] came with me. We lay at Hockrill, and though he is sensible, civil, entertaining and *chatty*, I have been there tête à tête in better company, and have been better pleased. I thought of you often at Ickworth, talk'd of you often, and wish'd for you oftener. The place seemed disagreeably altered, as it would do with all its oaks cut down. "By the waters of Ickworth I sat down and wept, when I remember'd thee O! Redlynch." . . .

I was this morning at the Duke of Richmond's,[3] who is to my thinking just as backward in his cure as he was a month ago, and backwarder much than he should have been two months ago. His surgeons are like the physicians in a Farce of Molière's; they are all of different opinions, and none of them I believe in the right. When I was there this morning, his company was the Duke of Grafton, two tradesmen, a new animal he is very fond of which he calls a man-goose [*sic*], and two West-Indian foxes. I could not help reflecting on the affinity between two-legged and four-legged animals, and, as I communed with myself, thought the company very well suited. I found things here just as I left them; every wheel of the clock goes just as it did, and the same dull figures grace the quotidian circle. This is so like a pun, that I have a mind to scratch it out again; but because I do not always know a pun any more than I do humour, I will hope I'm mistaken, and let it go. . . . I hear you have written to his Grace of Richmond, and that he intends writing to you to-night. . . .

I had like to have forgot to tell you Arundel[4] is at last married to Lady Fanny Manners. The news came this morning, and the ceremony was performed at Belvoir Castle.

[1] Melbury.

[2] Sir Robert Smyth. His brother-in-law, who had married Lady Louisa Hervey.

[3] Charles, 2nd Duke of Richmond (1701–50).

[4] For Richard Arundel, *see ante*, p. 74.

TO HENRY FOX *Kensington, September 7, 1732*[1]

Dear Count,

If you dislike my writing to you when I have nothing to say, do not blame me: but remember you drew it upon yourself when you desired me unconditionally to write, and did not bid me wait, as Quakers do to preach, until I had any call. However, if a call were necessary, I have the same plea to molest your eyes that they have to fatigue God Almighty's ears, which is to beg you would never forsake or neglect me; and though you have often promised me you never would, yet a Court has taught me among many other things that we must sometimes run the risk of being troublesome, even where one wishes to be least so, or one shall run the risk of being forgot even by those who are most willing to remember one.

This being the case, do not wonder if I send you now and then an insignificant letter, as I would change your ring or tie a knot in your handkerchief, merely as a memorandum that I exist: and not as a thing that I propose should give you either pleasure or pain, or have any other consequence than barely that of bringing the idea of bringing me into your mind. But that my letters may be of some use to you, you may sign the dead warrant for Maddington partridges upon them, if you please, by ramming your gun with them. It will be one way of giving them some fire; and the kindest thing you can do to a friend is certainly supplying his wants where he is most defective and most indigent. Do not think that I say this by way of soliciting a compliment to my parts; for without any affectation, if ever I had any, it is quite spent. But this I must say for myself, that if the head of Mount Vesuvius was in the thick fogs and heavy damps that every day surround me, I believe there would no more signs of fire upon that hill than there is upon any in the High-lands of Scotland. The tops of most of those in which I am at present situated, are like Zembla's rocks covered with eternal snows and impenetrable ice; and the present fashion of icing their perukes (as pastry cooks do christening cakes) most typically in colour sets forth on the outside that coldness which

[1] Holland House.

every candid jury will find on the in. A recent example of these icy heads occurs to my mind in the person of my frozen Ld Onslow.[1] He went into France sometime ago to settle his son in a warmer climate, in order, as I suppose, to see what could be done towards thawing the hereditary snows in which his parentage had congealed him. But the Miracle of St. Januarius has not been performed on the father or the son. They are come back unliquified, and were some days ago presented to the Queen. The Father-Bear kiss'd her hand first, and then presented his Cub. When the Queen asked his Lordship how he had been entertained at Paris, he told her he had had a perpetual cascade upwards and downwards most part of the time he had been there ; which polite phrase he explained to Ld Godolphin, who stood next him, in a voice loud enough for the Queen to hear, that the water of the Seine had purged and vomited him almost to a skeleton. This was as to his health : and as to his pleasure, he said, the women were so impudent and the men so ignorant, that he was scandalised all day with the conduct of the one, and tired to death with the trifling and frivolous conversation of the other. " One sees nothing (says he), Madam, but eating and gaming and making love among the ladies, and one hears of nothing talked about by the men but places and pensions, which you know, Madam, coming over and over again must make one weary of one's life. They talk of nothing but their fine eating, Madam ; but I saw nothing to brag of. Their bread has no taste, all their meat stinks, and for wine there is absolutely none." " That is," says the Queen, " no claret " ? " No, Madam," replied the Peer, " no wine at all : No. Madam, not a drop. So, Madam, after I had seen enough of the French to know them and to despise them, I brought my son back again ; and thought I would sooner cut my son's throat than leave him to be educated among such a pack of w—— and rogues and fools."

You will not wonder, dear Count, when I see these farces gratis every day, that I have not yet been at Bartholomew Fair,[2] though it is this year in great request. You know I love comedies in

[1] Thomas, 2nd Lord Onslow, who died in 1740. His son succeeded as 3rd Baron, and was father of the 1st Earl.

[2] Held in Smithfield from the reign of Henry I until 1853.

high life ; therefore Bullock, Harper and Lee [1] shall never be the better for my custom, whilst I can be so well entertained in our own booth, where Nature writes and Ld Onslow performs. At the other drolls, the dress makes the Harlequin, the Merry Andrew and the Scaramouch. But here it is the reverse. It is not the trappings that make the men ridiculous, but the men the trappings ; and as a red and yellow coat there debases the wearer, here a wearer debases a blue or red ribbon ; whilst wealth, titles, and power and honours can no more give sense to the D. of N[ewcastle], than paint, patches and brocade can give beauty to the Duchess of Rutland.

Adieu. I am called in a hurry to Council.

TO HENRY FOX *Kensington, September 19, 1732* [2]

~~Dear Count~~—(" Scratched out, because it looked kind ").

I send you this scrap of paper, only to let you know I have this moment finished a long letter designed for you, that I will never send you. To speak truth, I dare not venture it by the post. I wrote it to divert myself, and since that diversion is over, I am glad I had prudence enough not to send it, because I believe it would have diverted you ; and you deserve no diversion at my hands. Spietato ed ingrato ! Adieu. I hope it is very bad weather, that you seldom see a bird to shoot at, and that whenever you do that your gun flashes in the pan. In short, I hope que tout vous est contraire comme le vent au Roi, and that you fret and ennuyez at Maddington as much as he does at Helvoetsluys.[3] What manner of King is this, that the winds and the seas will not obey him ? We talk of nothing here but the wind, and look at the weather-cock five hundred times a day. Lady Charlotte [4] said today—, but I forget myself, and will not tell you anything to make you laugh. Go and pout, and be

[1] Three well-known actors of the period.

[2] Holland House.

[3] The King had spent the summer in Hanover.

[4] " Lady Charlotte de Roucy, an old Protestant refugee French lady, always with Queen Caroline." [Note in Horace, Earl of Orford's writing.] (*See ante*, p. 112.)

gloomy and sour and miserable as the country, easterly winds, spleen and indigestion can make you.

My services to Ste. . . .

TO STEPHEN FOX *Kensington, Sept. 26, 1732*[1]

The King is at last arrived at Kensington. He came this afternoon about five a clock in perfect health and spirits. He landed at Gravesend; and after all the rout you have heard me make about meeting him there with the barges, I was a quarter of an hour too late. I met him a mile on this side the town, and rode up to his coach, desiring his leave to show my joy for his arrival by hollowing with the mob. He, like a very gracious master to a very negligent servant, stopped his coach, which was going full gallop, and asked me to come in. So that I have already had a conversation of three hours with him, in which he ask'd me incessant questions, and seem'd so glad to see England again that it was impossible not to be glad to see him. At Greenwich, his Master of the Horse, his Lord in Waiting, and the Gold Stick met him in the body coach, into which he went, and passed through the City hither. I have been near threescore miles to day, and have not yet dined; so you will not wonder, when I tell you I have not spirits to add anything more than an Adieu.

TO STEPHEN FOX *Kensington, October 7, 1732*[1]

I know you love a little dab of history, and for that reason I send you the enclosed. It was new yesterday. I read it this morning, and as I am never shy of telling you my opinion upon any occasion, I freely own to you, if I had had it sent me as a fragment of historical controversy written in King Charles the 2nd's days, I believe I should have liked it.[2] But there is something which I feel but cannot define in the style, the manner of expressing himself, and the way of thinking, so old-fashioned, and qui sent si furieusement la vieille Cour, that, though I should like a picture of one of my ancestors thus dressed in the stiff cravat-strings and feathers of those days, yet a modern author

[1] Melbury.

[2] We have no clue to the book in question.

in *such* accoutrements has not the same effect. Beginning a paragraph with " Good Gods " ! and ending it with " Alas ! " is what I cannot bear. An author who is capable of it, I should expect to be as formal and as soporiferous as any of the black gentlemen who begin their discourses with, " Let us pray ", and end them with " Amen ". Besides these *peccadillos*, there is such an exploded, obsolete reverence for Majesty, merely for being Majesty : such a leaning to divine hereditary Right : and such a partiality to a monarchical form of Government, besides little compliments thrown in to the Church and the clergy, that he very often turns my stomach, and seems as many years behind his countrymen in his notions upon Government, as the Germans are behind the rest of Europe in their notions of philosophy. *His beholding a King, with a guilty people prostrate at his feet, and taking them by the hand as if they never had been offended*, is like Descartes's [1] *subtil matter* [*sic*]. It would have done very well a hundred years ago ; but, as Horace says upon another occasion, " non est hic locus ", so I say upon this, " non est hic tempus ". In short, the book is old-fashioned ; and as I designed only to send it to you for half an hour's amusement, without playing commentator upon it, I shall not endeavour to justify or explain my position any farther, but leave it here.

The D. of Richmond goes to Goodwood on Monday se'nnight, and writes to you tonight to know when you design coming to him. He is going to pull down and rebuild his house in town,[2] and intends staying in the country all winter. If I do not see Redlynch this autumn, I shall be miserable. When you go to Goodwood I shall go with you : and if you were to go to the ice of Greenland or the hottest furnace in Africa I would, if I could, do so too. . . .

TO HENRY FOX *Kensington, October 10, 1732* [3]

Dear Count,

You may well stare to see my hand upon paper in two days after my receiving a letter which you had owed me two months.

[1] Renée Descartes (1596–1650).

[2] Richmond House, in Whitehall, with its gardens running down to the River.

[3] Holland House.

It is being much better than you deserve; and perhaps instead of making you fear, will encourage you for the future to offend. If it convinces you that I will rather have you on your own terms than not have you at all, it will state the case very fairly. Be generous then, give us good measure as you can, let me have as much of you as you can afford, and name your own price.

The days your gun snapped oftener than it went off, I fancy your mouth did the same, as often as it opened; and by the description you give of yourself, your luck and the weather, it is very natural to conclude your temper was as bad as the one and your countenance as gloomy as the other. As for Punto (though as you observe I have not the honour to know him), yet I hate you for abusing your acquaintance. How can you maliciously compare him to Lord Onslow, when the poor dog never said a word in his life, whilst the other puppy never meets one's eyes without invading one's ears, and proves himself so much inferior to poor Punto, that, whereas Punto by many signs and tokens evidently shows he has reason without speech, the other brute full as often demonstrates that he has speech without reason. . . .

I send you enclosed a book that was just now sent to me with this recommendation, "There is so much wit and so much wickedness in this paper, that I conclude your Lordship will find it seasoned to your taste"; And as these two ingredients will, I believe, make it full as palatable to you, I send it to you without having read it. But as I am to dine in town, I can get one. Adieu. I am in a great hurry. . . .

TO STEPHEN FOX *Ickworth, October 21, 1732*[1]

I went by moon-light on Wednesday to Hockrill, and arrived here by midnight on Thursday. One reason of my being so late, was staying to get Maran[2] out of the round-house where he had lain all night. The story is too long for a letter, but Ragotin[3] never met with a more terrible distress. I can laugh at it now, but I was excessively peevish then, and had like to have

[1] Melbury. [2] His servant.

[3] A character in *le Roman Comique*, by Scarron.

been worse than peevish ; for never any body was nearer being shot through the head. The second cause that occasioned my late arrival here, was the natural incapacity of trotting that attends Lord Bristol's coach-horses, from the accumulate causes of disuse, fat, age and repletion. Since I came here we have often spoke of you, and clubbed our praises whenever the subject came on. Lord Bristol admired your parts ; I commended your heart ; my lady (qui ne loue pas volontiers) threw in an encomium on your temper ; Lady Hervey extolled your complaisance ; Lady Ann put us in mind of your good-breeding ; and Felly flattered your jokes. I had a great mind to sum up the whole with a line out of Ovid,

"Singula quid referam ? Nil non laudabile vidi. . . ".

The next letter, and also one on November 11, were published by Lord March in *A Duke and his Friends* (i, 222 etc.). A copy of the second is at Ickworth. They fit in so well in the series, that we reproduce them, by kind permission of the present Duke of Richmond.

TO THE DUKE OF RICHMOND

St. James's, October 31st, 1732 [1]

I obeyed the commands your Grace honoured me with from Godalming the moment I received them, by directing and forwarding your letter to Mr. Fox. I wish I could as easily obey the more obliging orders you were so good to lay upon me at the same time, and that it was as much in my power as I am sure it is in my inclination, to wait on your Grace soon at Goodwood ; but my Lord Chamberlain's absence, and the King's declaring he will not miss one Opera all the time he is at Richmond, will prevent my being the better for His Majesty's journey thither, which is fixed for next week.

You will think me most incomparably dull for not having picked up anything worth relating from the occurrences of a Birthday,[2] but one Birthday is so like another, that excepting the colours of people's clothes, your Grace may tell yourself the history of the day full as well as anybody that made a part

[1] Printed in *A Duke and his friends*, by Lord March (i, 222).
[2] The King's Birthday.

of it. The Spanish Ambassadress [1] was there dressed in the English fashion, and stared at in the English fashion; for wherever she turned there was a ring of spectators, whisperers and laughers, which put me (who am concerned for the reputation of England) as much out of countenance as did her.

It is no news to you that Mr. Poyntz's match with Miss Mordaunt is all settled; [2] but Lady Deloraine's behaviour upon it is a particular that you may not have been informed of. As she looked on the two Governors as part of the perquisites of her employment, so she considers Miss Mordaunt as one who has picked her pocket. However as there is no remedy for this loss, no Jonathan Wild that can get her her trinket again, she is forced to give it up, and comforts herself with thinking that since the junior Governor will be the junior husband too, she shall not have the worst of the bargain. . . . This is the last new comedy my Lady has obliged the Court with, in which her Ladyship, like Molière, is the principal performer as well as the composer.

The letters that came in yesterday brought the news of the old King of Sardinia's death. I conclude people will say he was poisoned, but I have not yet heard they do. What a catastrophe, and what an exit for the greatest prince and ablest politician of his time. Adieu, my dear Lord, I am going to Lady Pembroke's to hear the new Opera-woman, Celestina. The Operas begin on Saturday.

TO STEPHEN FOX *St. James's, November 4th, 1732* [3]

I am just come from a long, dull, and consequently tiresome Opera of Handel's, whose genius seems quite exhausted. The

[1] Madame de Montijo, wife of Count de Montijo (1693–1763). *Carlisle*, pp. 92, 99 (Lady Irvine to Lord Carlisle, February 1733) speaks of her as "an ugly little woman; can speak nothing but Spanish". Her husband was a handsome little man. He gave most splendid and costly entertainments at his Queen's command "at which no person is pleased, and he has the least reason of all to be so."

[2] We have already referred to Miss Anna Maria Mordaunt, "the fair Circassian" and Maid of Honour (*see ante*, pp. 49, 75 *n*.). Stephen Poyntz (1665–1750), diplomatist, was Governor to the Duke of Cumberland, and remained his trusted adviser until the end of his life.

[3] Melbury.

bride's recommendation of being the first night, could not make this supportable. The only thing I liked in it was our Naples acquaintance, Celestina; who is not so pretty as she was, but sings better than she did. She seemed to take mightily, which I was glad of. I have a sort of friendship for her, without knowing why. Tout chose qui me fait resouvenir ce temps m'attendrit; et je suis sûr que ce soir à l'Opera j'ai soupiré cent fois. Mais parlons d'autre chose. . . .

I must tell you a story of Mademoiselle Maloze, Myrmont's [1] sister, which I know to be fact, and that I wish may divert you as well as it did me. When Mon^r^ and Mad^ame^ Montijo came to England, she, because they were an Ambassador and Ambassadress, without knowing any thing more of them, sent them a message to welcome them to England, to let them know that she had been lame several years and not made any visits, and therefore hoped they would accept the compliment of that message instead of a visit. The very next day Monsieur and Madame Montijo, from their great civility and great idleness, went to Somerset House [2] to thank her for this favour, and desiring her porter to go in and ask if they should not trouble her in case they came in to make her a visit. The porter to their great astonishment made a low bow and said, 'Madame est morte ce matin.' Was not this dying in character, and like the sister of Myrmont, who in his last dose of laudanum, when he had not spoke in several hours before, drank it off, "À la santé du Roi et de la Reine", and never spoke after? Adieu. The clock strikes eleven, and my letter will be too late. Adio, caro & carissimo.

TO STEPHEN FOX *St. James's, Nov. 7, 1732* [3]

. . . If I go to the D. of Richmond's at all (which is not sure), it shall certainly be at the time you go; the greatest inducement (upon my honour and truth) that I can have to go or stay anywhere. But pray tell me why you do not come up with Mrs.

[1] Armand de Bourbon, Marquis de Miremont, a Huguenot refugee, who had a pension on the Irish Civil list.

[2] Old Somerset House was turned into apartments after 1692 for the nobility and the poorer courtiers. [3] Melbury.

Digby ? Can the following a poor woodcock four hours in the four and twenty afford you pleasure enough to compensate for the solitary ennui in which you must pass the other sixteen ; or what other amusement do you propose ? The slope and the piece of water I conclude are finished.[1] There will be no wheel-barrows to follow nor any pick-axes to watch. The Count will have the spleen ; the gloom of November, and the frowardness of easterly winds will take possession of him, so that you must expect no entertainment from that quarter. Whilst you are talking to him, he will be reading ; and whilst he is reading, he will be thinking of something else ; by which means you will know nothing of him, nor he of his book. Hill will have the gout ; so between his corporal and the Count's mental maladies you will have no body to laugh with, nor anybody to laugh at. Come to London then for a fortnight before you go to Sussex ; and instead of seeking pleasure where it is not to be found, bring one to me in whom it is never to be missed.

Tell the Count my wrath is so much slackened, if not quite extinguished, that if that dilatory monster, Jackson, had yet got me *The Difficulties and Discouragements* of Bishop Hare[2] that I would have sent it, and writ to him at the same time, " For Count Cassius is yoked with a lamb who beareth anger as the flint does fire, that much enforced sends forth a hasty spark, and straight is cool again."

Adieu, I expect the King every moment to go to the Opera. Lady Russell is brought to bed of a son, which they are afraid will not live. . . . It is thought in the City that the ship the Duke of Bedford was in is lost. They have no account at all of it.

TO THE DUKE OF RICHMOND

St. James's, November 11th, 1732[3]

I am extremely thankful to your Grace for the honour of your remembrance, for the letter I received yesterday, and the obliging

[1] At Redlynch.

[2] Francis Hare, Bishop of Chichester (1671–1740) produced in 1714 a tract under this name, which was censured by Convocation. The subsequent quotation is from Shakespeare's *Julius Cæsar*, though not in the exact words.

[3] Printed in *A Duke and his Friends* (i, 224). A copy at Ickworth.

manner in which you tell me I should not have been an unwelcome guest at Goodwood. Your complaining in such a letter for want of matter to fill it, puts me a little in mind of some people's hospitality, who set you down to a table of twenty dishes of meat and tell you at the same time they are afraid there is nothing you can eat.

As to the account of the loves, courtship and marriages of your beasts, it seems to me not so much a literal description of Goodwood dens as an allegorical epitome of the whole matrimonial world.[1] If you would follow the example of Æsop and write fables upon your birds and beasts, I have a notion that without going out of your own park you might characterise the persons, tempers and occupations of all your acquaintance. The marriages of your bears, tigers, wolves and monkeys would certainly do for a representation of half the conjugal performances in England. But now and then you would, I confess, be a little puzzled to represent some matches one sees between brutes of a different species, which is a privilege I believe peculiar to human brutes, and consequently would be difficult to be well couched in fable and allegory.

For example, if you were to talk of a marriage between a great she-bear and an old baboon, in order figuratively to describe the sweet union of my Lord and Lady St. John ; or if you told us in delineating the Duke and Duchess of M[anchester] that one of your she-tigers was mated with a jackass, people would immediately see that the account was feigned in order to satirise these people : and the beauty of the parallel would be quite lost for want of beasts that are guilty of those daily absurdities which we find among men. Your monkeys would do admirably for my dear Lord and Lady Carn[arvon] ; but if the Countess of Del[orai]ne's wise match had taken effect,[2] under the denomination of what bird or beast would you have been able to describe a little animal that has all the simplicity of a dove without its tenderness, and all the venom of a serpent without its cunning ? The subject I have *entaméd* is so inexhaustible, that if I was to take up Lady Hervey's visiting book I am sure I could, by that assistance to

[1] The Duke maintained a menagerie at this time in the park at Goodwood.
[2] She married Mr. William Wyndham, of Ersham, Norfolk, in 1734.

my memory, humanise as many beasts as *Snyder* ever painted, or as you and Noah ever protected. . . . Adieu, my dear Lord ; voilà bien des fadaises ; and if after this galimatias you should rank me in a triumvirate with Bowen and Misaubin,[1] I think I should have no reason to complain of your justice. . . .

TO STEPHEN FOX *St. James's, November 11, 1732*[2]

. . . I breakfasted this morning with the Bishop of Salisbury,[3] who would not own he knew any thing of a story I heard last night at Lady Albemarle's ; which was that they were so afraid of telling Lady Russell her son was dead, and so embarrassed how to conceal it, that, after a grand consultation where Old Ætna was Speaker, it was determined a child be bought to represent the defunct, till she was strong enough to hear the truth and be told that it was only a Pretender. I have forgot whether or no I sent you word that Lady Deloraine had asked the Queen's leave to marry Mr. Windham, and that the Queen told her she had no objection to her marrying, though she had an insurmountable one to any married woman being Governess to her daughters. Upon which my Lady has prudently resolved to keep her own employment, and give Mr. Windham no new one.

I had a long letter yesterday from his Grace of Richmond, wherein he says you have promised to be at Goodwood the middle of next month. Ld. Albemarle went yesterday tête à tête with the D. of Newcastle into Norfolk. I dined with him the day before, and never saw any body [so] reluctantly punctual to an appointment. I could not have suffered more in his situation. I advised him to play sleeping, and to shut his eyes in order to shut his ears. . . .

TO STEPHEN FOX *St. James's, November 14, 1732*[4]

Excepting the agreeable days I have pass'd alone with you, I never spent one in a more pleasant male tête à tête than I did

[1] John Misaubin, born in France, M.D., Cahors, and L.R.C.P. He died in 1734.

[2] Melbury.

[3] Benjamin Hoadly (1676–1761).

[4] Melbury.

yesterday. Ld. Chesterfield came early in the morning to breakfast with me. We went together to make our court at Richmond, came back together, and dined together alone afterwards *à petit couvert* in his library.[1] I have not known him in so good humour and spirits of several years. He was incessantly entertaining; and though naturally I know your taste is not turned to romances, but that truths and facts are your search, yet the historical, political, amorous, familiar, foreign and domestic novels which he told, were related in so compendious a manner and so lively a style, that I am sure you would have been infinitely pleased to have been an invisible auditor. I always listen to him as I read poetry, without hoping for a word of truth; and no more consider any thing he says in the light of truth or falsehood than I do any thing that Ariosto writes. If ever I do think of it upon that foot, it is only to admire the fertility of his imagination and the luxuriancy of his invention; and, as one values other people in proportion to their adherence to truth, one admires him most when he deviates most from it. With all this he is positively no liar; a liar, if I understand the definition of one, being a man that tells things as true, which he knows to be false in order to deceive. Now his Lordship never thinks of the things he tells being either true or false, and [as] for deceiving you, provided he is sure you like his manner of telling them, he concerns himself no more about the credit you give to his narrations than he does about the authority he has for them. He is a most wonderful composition.

I concluded the day at Miss Skeritt's.[2] Our Naples friend Celestina sung and supped there with her husband, Mr. Hempson, another of our Naples friends, who used to live with the Consul and play upon the flute. There was no body there besides, excepting Lady Susan Hamilton [3] and our Florence acquaintance, Sir Robert Morton, who is just come over, and, moyennant

[1] Lord Chesterfield had a house in Bloomsbury Square at this time. It was his boast that his library was the finest room in London. Chesterfield House was not built till 1749.

[2] Maria Skerrett, Sir Robert Walpole's mistress after about 1728. His first wife died in 1737, and he then married Miss Skerrett in March 1738. She died in the following June of a miscarriage.

[3] Sister of James, 5th Duke of Hamilton.

Lady Susan Hamilton by a Scotch nationality, was brought thither under her wing. Voilà la Gazette de hier. Adio, caro & carissimo & sempre caro. Pray tell the Count that I hear by a letter the Duke of Richmond wrote to me last post, that he had written that day to invite his Countship to Goodwood. I hope he intends to accept the invitation ; and since we could not be all together in Somersetshire, that we shall be so at least in Sussex, though that will not be half so well.

I desire you would always put your letters in covers, for at best they are not very legible ; and when they are nudities, I tear them all to pieces in opening, which makes the deciphering of them so infinitely difficult and laborious, that I am sure it would pose Mr. Wills himself.

The last letter in 1732 is addressed to his physician Dr. Cheyne. It can be compared with Hervey's long statement on his own health, printed by Mr. Sedgwick in the Appendix to the *Memoirs*, vol. iii.

TO DR. CHEYNE *St. James's Palace, December 9th, 1732*[1]

Dear Doctor,[2]

I am prodigiously scandalised at what you say of me in your letter to Lord Bateman. If you were as just to *my* practice as I am to *your* doctrine, it would be impossible for you, whilst I always acknowledge and revere you as the great Æsculapius of this age and country, to speak of me as an apostate, a heretic or even a schismatic in your medicinal religion. In order therefore to set you right, and let you know who is one of your most pious votaries, I write this letter to tell you the method I am in. In the first place, I never taste wine or malt-drink or any liquid but water and milk tea. In the next, I eat no meat but the whitest, youngest and tenderest ; nine times in ten, nothing but chicken ; and never more than the quantity of a small one at a meal. I seldom eat any supper ; but, if any, absolutely nothing but bread and water. Two days in the week I eat no flesh. My breakfast is dry biscuit not sweet, and green tea. I have left off butter as bilious. I eat no salt, nor any sauce but bread-

[1] Ickworth.

[2] *See ante*, p. 12.

sauce. I take a Scotch pill once or twice a week, and thirty grains of Indian root, when my stomach is loaded, my head giddy and my appetite gone. I have been ill lately ; but it was by an accident, and such a one as would have made a coach-horse sick. I bled, vomited, purged and sweated by my own prescription, and by these means in four days got rid of a sore throat, cough and fever, that would have stuck by a true beef and pork-eater as many months. After this account of myself, I expect you should compare me no more to *Mahomet's Tomb*, because I think my rigid perseverance in this faith entitles me, in the Heaven of Health, to the place immediately next to the Angel Gabriel. Dear Doctor, Adieu, and believe you have not in the world a greater admirer and more sincere wellwisher than

Your most obliged and most grateful humble servant.

I have not bragged of the persecutions I have suffered in this cause ; but the attacks made upon me by ignorance, impertinence and gluttony, are innumerable and incredible.

CHAPTER VII

1733

With the year 1733, the *Memoirs* recommence. Hervey's letters are to the Fox brothers, chiefly to Henry. The latter had spent Christmas at Goodwood, and Stephen especially had made great steps in the Duke's affection and approbation. Probably Hervey was there too. The mention of Pope in the first letter, that of January 16, addressed to Henry at Redlynch, seems to indicate that he was sending verses written by the poet.

TO HENRY FOX *Digby House, Tuesday night,* *[January 16] 1732/33*[1]

I am just come from the Opera, and forgo entertaining and being entertained by the good company here, in order to obey your commands and give you an account of the various occurrences of this day. Imprimis, the first occurrence of this day is that the D. of Richmond and your brother came to town last night. In the next place, our Sovereign Liege went to the House of Peers and made the enclosed Speech. The Lords' Address was moved and seconded by Ld Lothian and Ld Lovelace, scrub-doings; that of the Commons by Bromley and Knight.[2] The first of these said nothing in very good words; and the last had as little eloquence as matter. Barnard and Sandys proposed taking no notice in the Address of *avoiding animosities, etc.*; but nobody took notice enough of *them* to bring their objections to a question. Shippen had a mind to give us an anniversary, florid philippic against the Administration, but was rather pompously dull than animating or smart: and proposed adding some words which, instead of producing any altercation, were seconded by Sir Robert Walpole. Sir *thing* [*sic*] Bernard[3] tried to kindle a little flame by way of episode about trade; but his speech *hung fire*, or rather flashed in the pan. In short, the whole was languid. I know no other news,

[1] Holland House. [2] For the debate, *see Egmont*, i, 307.
[3] No doubt Sir John Barnard (*see above*), M.P. for London.

but that Pope has put out another Satire which he calls the *Use of Riches*,[1] and dedicates to Lord Bathurst. He is so abusive in it, and in so much plainer terms than in his Chandois-performance of impertinent memory,[2] that it is very probable some of those to whom he pretends to teach the proper use of riches may teach him the proper use of cudgels. The disagreeable people here (where your brother plays first mob) are so noisy, and make such a bustle, some twitching my letter, and others reading over my shoulder, that I must bid you Adieu.

TO HENRY FOX *Jan. 18, 1732/33* [3]

Dear Count. I am just going to the masquerade, so shall leave your entertainment by this post entirely to Mr. Pope. Ld Torrington [4] died yesterday; and Ld Pembroke is dying tonight, though he sent the Queen word this morning that he was very well, and only lay in bed because the weather was cold. The newspapers say the D. of Bolton is dead; but they lie. The whole world, high and low, rich and poor, are ill of this epidemical cold. Ld Sunderland keeps his bed for a rheumatism. The Speaker [5] has been ill, but is better. The Ld Chancellor [6] is so ill as to be confined to his house; and Ld Raymond [7] officiates in the House of Lords for him. This is just such a letter as Garney or Graham would write; but no body talks of anything but fevers and excises. Adieu.

[1] *Moral Essay* III. [2] *Moral Essay* IV. (*See ante*, p. 124 and *n.*)

[3] Holland House.

[4] George Byng, 1st Viscount (1663–1733), Admiral. First Lord o the Admiralty.

[5] Arthur Onslow (1691–1768). Speaker of the House of Commons from 1728–61.

[6] Peter, 1st Baron King of Ockham (1664–1734), Lord Chancellor 1725–33. Lord Hervey gives an account of him in the *Memoirs*, p. 243. "He was made Chancellor as much by the voice of the public as by the hand of power." Had he retired in time he would have gone down to posterity as a great lawyer, but (Lord Hervey tells us) apoplectic fits warped his intellect, and "he had such diffidence of himself that he did not dare to do right, for fear of doing wrong".

[7] Lord Chief Justice.

TO HENRY FOX *St. James's, January 23, 1733*[1]

Dear Count,

I have received and thank you for your letter. I had anticipated your commands of sending the Satire, which ought to have been at Redlynch before your letter got to Salisbury. I now send you des fadaises; but in the country anything is better than nothing. You may make Hill sing them; and then light his pipe with them. Old Pem. is at last departed. He died in character just as he lived, lying, positive, absurd, and humorous. The old Duchess of Rutland[2] followed him to-night; so that the most remarkable throat and back in England are now no more. They say Lord Peterborough can not recover; so that of the veteran nobility there is now only his Grace (or rather Highness) of Somerset remaining. Lord Foley died yesterday morning, and has left (as people say) an immense estate. I know nothing yet of the disposition of Lord Pembroke's affairs. You see, as to private occurrences, one is entertained with nothing but deaths and diseases; and all public topics run on Standing Armies and Excises. The Presbyterian affair is quite over,[3] which is not unlucky for the Administration. It would have embarrassed and distressed many people if it had gone on. Duke Hamilton is dismissed from the King's Bedchamber, though it is not yet declared. The newspapers have given him Lord Cathcart for a successor; ma non lo credo. I have a notion it will be Lord Cowper, though I have heard nobody name him. I saw a letter yesterday from Mrs. Horner from Naples, giving a terrible account of the earthquake; and of poor Lord Binning's death. Adieu. I hope you like facts, or else my letter will be very unwelcome; for as to imagination, I have no more to-night than my Lord Grantham or Sir John Rushout. I have no more ideas than the last, and no more words than the former.

[1] Holland House.

[2] Catherine, daughter of Baptist Noel, 3rd Viscount Campden, and third wife of John, 1st Duke.

[3] *See Egmont*, i, 303, etc.

TO HENRY FOX *St. James's, January 25, 1733* [1]

You tell me, my dear Count, you like to have me write to you, and for that reason I do it. But if you are not literally pleased with seeing my hand upon paper, you have but little chance for any other entertainment from my letter.

I have nothing to recount but a journal of the day, which consists of several theatres I have been in, several dull farces I have seen played, and several dull players I have seen act. The first Theatre I was in was in company with your brother at Sir Robert Walpole's, where we saw the farce of a full Levee. Kissing, whispering, bowing, squeezing hands, etc., were all acted there as usual by the political pantomimes who officiate at those weekly performances, where several boons are asked which are not so much as promised, and several promised which will never be granted.

From thence I went to the Grand Theatre in St. Stephen's Chapel, where no farces have yet been played worthy of note. The actors are all assembled, and the parts cast; but the best pieces are not to come on till next week. Sr. John Rushout [2] spoke a dull prologue to day, and Sir Aston made a flourish; but it was only an imperfect rehearsal and ended in nothing.

From hence I went to the Theatre at St. James's, where the tragedy of a Cabinet Council was acted, to the sorrow of sixteen poor malefactors: and the comedy of a Privy Council, to the joy of Sr. Charles Wager who was sworn in today, as successor to Ld. Torrington defunct.[3] Ld. President [4] performed his part in this scene with a great deal of dull dignity and becoming formality, his hands full of papers, his nose full of snuff, and his mouth full of nonsense. A Drawing Room followed by way of petite-pièce. Who acted, or what was acted here, I choose to pass over in silence.

In the evening I attended His Majesty to the Theatre in Drury Lane, where Mrs. Porter [5] play'd Queen Elizabeth most excel-

[1] Holland House and Ickworth.

[2] 4th Bart. (1684–1775), M.P. for Malmesbury and Evesham; a leading follower of Pulteney.

[3] First Lord of the Admiralty.

[4] Lord Wilmington.

[5] Mary Porter, d. 1765. Owing to an accident, she was not acting 1731–3.

lently (with a cane) for her own Benefit, and to the fullest audience that ever was seen. The Dowager Dss of Marlborough was there with the Dss of Bedford [1] and the Dss of Manchester. The Alpha and Omega of these three wept at the moving scenes. Tender creatures ! And in one part of the play where Essex says,

> " Abhor all Courts, if thou art brave and wise,
> For there thou never shalt be sure to rise.
> Think not by doing well, a fame to get,
> But be a villain, and thou shalt be great,"

her Grace of Marlborough cried charmingly, and clapt her hands so loud that we heard her cross the theatre into the King's box.

This play being done by nine a clock, I went to my fifth and last Theatre at my Lady Strafford's,[2] to see that medley farce called a Modern Assembly ; where I saw the Master of the House play man of quality and his talkative Lady affability. My Ld Tyrconnel play'd fine-gentleman, and Mrs. Vernon fine-lady. Mr. Warren played wit, and my Lady Keys [3] played beauty. In short, every body played something, and most people played the fool. Tired of this, I came home a little after ten, and sat down to write you the occurrences of this day and night. I must now finish it, or it will be too late for the post. . . . Encore, mon cher et très cher, Adieu.

The next letter to Henry Fox, written on February 6, introduces the thorny question of Excise, upon which Walpole had decided to introduce a Bill, to make up for the shilling in the pound taken off the Land Tax, believing that it would be a popular move, as indeed it was with the landed proprietors. But for once he did not foresee the consequences of his action ; as the Opposition were able to raise such a storm in the country, that the measure had to be withdrawn in April, useful and well-thought out as it was. Hervey gave Henry Fox a dissertation on the whole question.

[1] Lord John Russell had become Duke of Bedford.

[2] Thomas Wentworth, Baron Raby (d. 1739), created Earl of Strafford in 1711, married Anne, daughter of Sir Henry Johnson, of Brodenham, Kent.

[3] Lady Kaye, an old widow, mother of Lady North, was fond of Beau Warren, a gamester. [Note in Horace, Earl of Orford's writing.]

TO HENRY FOX *St. James's, Feb. 6, 1733*[1]

. . . As to what you enquire about the diminution of the Land-Forces this year, my answer is there is to be none. 17,700 men were voted in this Committee, and that Resolution agreed to yesterday in the House. There were very long debates on these days, that lasted till seven a clock ; the first the dullest, and the last one of them the liveliest you can imagine. Tom Windham[2] made the finest historical rant you ever heard, and called troops, "those new-fangled trappings of English Majesty." He abused Horace Walpole[3] without any disguise ; and with very little disguise said the King loved nothing but an army, and his Parliament nothing but money. But upon the whole, I do not think there were so many bold things said as last year, nor any thing so strong as what was said by Jack How and Norris.

As to the Excise Bill, I will tell you what it is, at least what I understand it to be, in as few words as I can. You know that to supply one shilling in the pound taken off of land for one year, the Salt duty was given for three years ; so that to keep that shilling still off the land, some fund must be found to answer the other two-thirds, the Salt duty at this computation raising but one third of that shilling. The expedient to raise this sum without making any new tax, is to change the duties on two commodities only (which are wine and tobacco) from duties on importation into inland-duties, that is to turn the customs into excises. The principal objections made to this scheme are these : first, that it will increase the number of officers, and consequently the power of the Crown, as well as the expense of collection to the public. Secondly, that it will be a clog on trade. Thirdly, that it will increase the revenue of the Civil List (one penny per pound on Tobacco being part of that revenue) ; and fourthly, that the excise officers being creatures of the Crown will always determine in any disputes for the Crown, because part of the advantage of carrying those suits will accrue to the Crown.

As to the first of these objections, which is the increase of

[1] Holland House and Ickworth.

[2] Thomas Wyndham (1681–1743), Lord Chancellor of Ireland, created Baron Wyndham of Finglass.

[3] Horatio Walpole.

officers, mum,[1] cider, ale, beer and perry being already excised, and wine and tobacco being generally sold by those people who sell the other, it will be little more trouble for the officers who overlook the one to take cognisance of the other. So that, with a very small augmentation of their salaries, and proportionably speaking a much smaller augmentation of their number, it is proposed this duty should be thus collected with very little additional charge to the public [2] and few additional officers.[2]

As to the second objection, that it will be a clog on trade,—those who support this project say that it can not be. For what you mean or ought to mean, when you talk of clogging [2] the trade of this Kingdom is either obstructing [2] or burdening [2] the commerce and navigation, or increasing the price of goods to the consumer. As to the first, the taking off the duty on importation will evidently be an ease, not a burden, to the original importing merchant; as it will hinder him from being pressed for so much ready money in order to carry on his dealings as was necessary before; and as to the last, as no new duty is proposed to be laid on these commodities, the price of them to the consumer will stand just as it did.

The third objection is, that this project will increase the revenue of the Civil-List, the duties on Tobacco being six pence and ⅓ of a penny per pound, and one penny of this belonging to the Civil-List. To obviate, or at least to weaken this objection, it is proposed that the one penny pr pound payable to the King should still remain in the form it now stands, and be paid at the Custom-House; whilst only the other 5 pence and third of a penny, which is appropriated to public uses, shall be converted into excises.

The fourth objection is partly answer'd by the answer to this last objection; for though the excise-officers and judges are creatures of the Crown and nominated by the Crown, yet when no trial that comes before them shall be for money disputed between the Crown and the subject, but all between the subject and the public, so the excise-officers will have no temptation to be biassed by the Crown; nor the Crown no reason to attempt to bias them, because the Crown can be in no way advantaged

[1] A kind of beer brewed in Brunswick. [2–2] Added by Lord Hervey.

by their determination. For as the penny payable to the King is to remain still a duty on importation and to be paid at the custom-House, so if any dispute arises with regard to that penny, it must be tried, not by the laws of excise, but by the laws of the customs: and the appeal from the first decision will be not to the judges of the excise, but to the Court of Exchequer.

These are my notions of the state of the scheme, not very clearly set forth I believe; but the quickness of your apprehension will I hope supply the defects of my representation [1] and make you,[1] conceive what I mean better than I can express it.

I was at the masquerade last night till 4 this morning, [and] was well diverted. I was at the Westminster Feast today, and not diverted at all: was at the Opera with the King to night; and as soon as I came from thence I sat down to write to you. I am now sleepy, tired and half-blind; besides which it strikes eleven, and my letter will be too late. Adieu, therefore, my dear Count, *aimable et aimé*.

I forgot to tell you that yesterday Duke Hamilton wrote the King a letter of resignation of his employment; and this day Sr Robt Walpole received the King's orders to let Ld Hinton, Ld Pawlet's son,[2] know that the King had appointed him Duke Hamilton's successor.

We offer no explanation of the next letter. There appears to be some connection with Hervey's letter of February 17 (p. 162) and that some work of Voltaire is involved.

TO HENRY FOX *St. James's, February 8, 1733* [3]

Dear Count,

I send you the enclosed, because I am sure it will entertain you, and that you cannot help having some compassion for a silly Christian, as well as the greatest regard, esteem and affection for a noble, good, tender and charming Mahometan.

I think the Dedication bad, false and impertinent. It is dedicated by a superficial Frenchman to an Englishman, and the

[1] Added by Lord Hervey.

[2] John, 1st Earl Poulett (1663–1743). His son was created a Baron in 1733/4, and later succeeded as 2nd Earl.

[3] Holland House.

dedicator pretends to be better acquainted with our country, our manners, our laws, and even our language than the dedicatee. Adieu. I am in a great hurry.

TO HENRY FOX *February 13, 1732/33*[1]

Dear Count. The enclosed are mightily liked, and therefore I send them to you. *The Advice to a Lady* is written by Mr. Littleton.[2] The other by Westly, and spoken after the play acted last Westminster Feast, when Dr. Friend[3] took his leave of the school. Send me word how you like them all; that is the tax I expect for every thing I send you. I am now at the Dss of Marlborough's,[4] with her Grace, Mr. Littleton and Mr. Hammond: the first squeezing out sentiments, the second talking good, sound common-sense; and the third laughing *dessous sa coïffe*, comme dit Madame de Sévigné, à tout ce que debite la Princesse, dont il encense en apparence les autels superbes et sacrés. Adieu.

The next letters, both written on February 17, one to Henry Fox, the other to the Duke of Richmond and printed in *The Duke and his Friends* (i, 237), speak of Pope's *Imitation of the First Satire of the Second Book of Horace*, which was published just at this time in February 1733, and largely occasioned the fracas between Pope and Hervey. For in it the poet made a most poisonous attack on Lady Mary Wortley-Montagu, as Sappho, and also originated the title of "Lord Fanny", which has stuck to him ever since, although in neither case were the references authenticated. In *The Letter to a Noble Lord*, referred to in Hervey's letter to Henry Fox of January 31/February 11, 1734, and reserved from publication (see p. 189) until after the writer's death, in 1751, Pope explained the name *Fanny*, which he said that Lord Hervey gratuitously took to be a reference to himself, "Fanny is the plain English for Fannius, a real person, who was a foolish critic and

[1] Holland House.

[2] George Lyttelton, M.P. (1709–73), who later became one of the Prince of Wales's most intimate advisers. Many of his verses have been published, with a number of his other writings. His friend, James Hammond (1710–42), a member of the Prince of Wales's entourage, was also a writer of poetry.

[3] Robert Freind (1667–1751), Headmaster of Westminster School (1711–33), brother of Hervey's former physician.

[4] Henrietta, 2nd Duchess of Marlborough. [Note in Horace, Earl of Orford's writing.]

an enemy of Horace, perhaps a noble one. . . . This Fannius was, it seems, fond both of his poetry and his person. . . . He was, moreover, of a delicate or effeminate complexion. . . ."

TO HENRY FOX *Feb. 17, 1733* [1]

I liked your criticisms upon Voltaire of all things ; and could not help communicating them to some who tasted them as much as I did. I will not give you my opinion of this last production which I send you of Mr. Pope's, because I am determined to indulge my vanity so far as to believe it would hinder my having your opinion without prejudice, and that either from your particular partiality to me, or your general propensity to contradiction, you would certainly be warped one way or the other. I am excessively sorry to hear poor Hill is so ill. . . . Ste. went yesterday morning for a week to Goodwood. I know no news. As for the Excises, I feel upon that head, as the Emperor in *Auren-Zebe* does to his wife, " If I but hear them named, I'm sick that day ". From whence you must logically conclude I am in a constant state of very bad health, for it is the physic I am forced to take from morning to night.

TO THE DUKE OF RICHMOND

St. James's, February 17, 1733 [2]

I sent your Grace Mr. Pope's new Satire by the last post, but as I have pride enough to desire to be minded whenever I write, so I had wit enough to find out that would not be my fate if I sent my prose in the same packet with his verse, for which reason I postponed this letter till to-night.

I would have done myself the honour to epistolise your Grace long ago, but as I had only leave to trouble you when I had any thing to communicate worth your attention, I should have exceeded my commission, if you had seen me in manuscript one moment before Mr. Pope appeared in print. Gay's work afforded nothing worth repeating ; his *Achilles* [3] is a hero as much

[1] Holland House. [2] Printed in *A Duke and his Friends*, i, 237.
[3] Acted at Covent Garden in February. Gay had come to London at the end of 1732 to arrange for its production, and died there.

inferior to Macheath, as to Homer's Achilles, and talks no more in the spirit of the *Beggars' Opera* than he talks Greek. For my part, I know not what to make of it; it is not a tragedy, nor it is not a comedy; it is not heroic, nor it is not burlesque; but it has all the phlegm of the first without the dignity, and all the ridicule of the last without the pleasantry. The only part that has the least pretence to humour is that of Ajax, and to do the living Mr. Hall, and the defunct Mr. Gay justice, one must own that the entertainment of that part is more in what he looks than what he says, and the effect of his belly rather than his lips.

News I know none; politics you hate, and so do I. Yet I hear nothing else all day long, the worst of politics too, which are mercantile politics. Excises, Wine and tobacco are the three words on which all my male companions ring the changes from morning to night; till I am sick of the two last, as if I had been drinking the one and smoking the other with my Bury Aldermen.

Again a gap in the letters; but in the interval, Hervey was called to the House of Lords on June 12, where there was a dearth of speakers on Walpole's side, as Lord Hervey of Ickworth, and was given a Barony. Consequently, amongst the Ickworth papers, we find a copy of a letter from him to the King, of date June 18, expressing the greatest gratitude for the great honour done to him, but asking for leave to go into Suffolk for a few days. His next brother, Thomas Hervey, an Equerry to the Queen, was to take over the family seat at Bury St. Edmunds, and he felt that he should be there. This was clearly necessary; for Hervey had accepted this promotion without any word to his father, who, as we have seen, was always opposed to the Walpole régime. Indeed, Lord Bristol heard the news with some annoyance.

TO THE KING *June 18, 1733*[1]

. . . My brother not being opposed, my sole reason for taking this journey, is in order (in and about Bury at least) to obey the commands of your Majesty's Speech to your Parliament, and as far as my capacity will assist my zeal, *to undeceive the deluded*, and point out *the force of Truth* with regard to every misrepresented measure of this last winter, as well as the arts and designs of those invidious commentators who have endeavoured to set

[1] Ickworth.

all persons and all things in a bad and false light. And as the whole country will be assembled at this election of my brother's, I shall now have an opportunity of executing this purpose more effectually than I could at any other time. . . .

We also find among the Ickworth papers a copy of a letter written to "My dear Cousin", and in Hervey's writing, "To Mrs. D.", referring to congratulations gratefully received. It will be remembered that the only surviving sister of the Fox brothers, Charlotte, had married Hon. Edward Digby in 1729; and we may clearly assume that she was the recipient of the following letter, as well as from certain local references in the text. There seems to have been no relationship between the Digby Earls of Bristol, and the Hervey family, but the fact that Charlotte Fox, for whom Hervey always expressed the deepest admiration, had married a Digby was perhaps sufficient reason for Hervey to invent the "cousinship."

TO MRS. DIGBY *St. James's, July 5th, 1733*[1]

I received my dear Cousin's kind congratulations and agreeable remembrance at Ickworth, where I went to attend my successor at his election, and to take leave (for my father's life at least) of all Corporation solicitation, hypocrisy, flattery and nonsense. I know the reflection you will make upon this last line immediately, and that you will want to tell me that, whilst I live in a Court, I have only changed the scene and taken leave of persons but not of things: that I shall still pass my time in the same round of employments though in a more splendid circle: and be as much the slave of such offices at St. James's as at Bury. All this may be true, but you must allow the difference of actors makes a great difference in every farce, and that the same drama and characters that entertain and keep up one's spirits in Drury Lane might lay one to sleep acted by strollers in a country fair.

I wish you may be as well pleased with changing your scene, and that all your joy may not be barely the getting rid of Dorchester brutes. Not that I have a contempt for negative pleasures, or desire to have, when actual ones are so[2] rare; but I would have you taste of all sorts.[2] Would to God it were in my power

[1] Ickworth.

[2-2] In Hervey's writing.

By Jon. Richardson

CHARLOTTE FOX, WIFE OF HON. EDWARD DIGBY

to make your return to London easy to you ; it would really be a sensible pleasure to me in other lights besides that of doing you service, though that alone would be no small one.

Mrs. Clayton [1] is gone into Bedfordshire for the summer. If her situation enabled her to do all the good her heart inclines her to, there are many people of merit who would not want any ingredient towards happiness that Courts can give. But she, like many other people, seems perhaps to want a will, when in reality she only wants power.

Your Countess-friend, my next neighbour at St. James's, is so sweet upon me of late, that her words, temper and looks are like the Land of Canaan, flowing with milk and honey.

Lord Carteret's daughter was married on Tuesday to Lord Weymouth.[2] I suppose you have written or will write to wish joy. He spoke of you to me this winter in the House of Lords, with great justice and seeming kindness ; and if statesmen have kindness in words it is all one can expect, at least out of power. When in power they should seem to have it in their actions, and do at least as they would do if they had it in their hearts ; but really to have it there, is not in their nature, or their vocation, or their character, and not always for their interests. And as they are so seldom served from kindness, it is indeed [3] no wonder (as they are generally men of discernment) that they no oftener bestow from that motive. Adieu, my dear Cousin. You asked so kindly how things went with me, that I cannot help telling you, never better. The clouds that gathered round me [4] last year [4] are dispelled, though I was in so disagreeable a situation, that to justify myself (which I could have done) did not dare to speak ; for *that* would have put me in the wrong, though I was not so before, and have led me into the commission of one fault whilst I was clearing myself of another.

[1] Charlotte Dyves, wife of William Clayton, who was later created Lord Sundon. She was Woman of the Bedchamber to Queen Caroline, favourite of Sarah, Duchess of Marlborough, and a close friend of Mrs. Strangways-Horner. She became Mistress of the Robes, and died in 1742.

[2] Thomas, 2nd Viscount Weymouth's second marriage, to Lady Louisa Carteret.

[3] In Hervey's writing.

[4–4] In Hervey's writing.

TO STEPHEN FOX *July 7, 1733*[1]

. . . The day you went to Goodwood, your brother and I went to Totteridge[2] through much dust and much conversation. We found her Ladyship as usual in great spirits and good humour; and his Lordship (as usual too) in neither. She was talkative and merry; he silent and gloomy. She glad when we came and sorry when we went; and he neither glad of the one nor sorry for the other, any more than if his make was incapable of any fluctuation in those two sensations. . . .

We next come to a letter addressed, on July 18, to the Duke of Richmond.

TO THE DUKE OF RICHMOND

Hampton Court, July 18th, 1733[3]

All you untaken rogues are so careless, notwithstanding the daily danger you are in of the gallows, that it is to no purpose your friends give you either advice or warning. Otherwise I should desire you to take some little thought how to extricate yourself out of many difficulties that surround you and may chance to fall upon you before you are aware of them. For though you may escape the *Certiorari* you talk of for your removal to Newgate, yet I am credibly informed there is a writ of *Habeas Corpus* now issuing from the Royal Bedchamber Office, for the removal of your's and my Lady Duchess's body forthwith to your respective waiting prisons in Hampton Court, where you are to suffer several weeks' imprisonment for diverse and sundry crimes of Omission towards the Lords and Ladies of Their Gracious Majesties' Bedchamber; by whom you both stand indicted of the said sins of Omission, and for which, as the allegation of the said indictment runs, you have not yet commuted. Whereupon you are to be forthwith cited into *the Court*, and if you do

[1] Ickworth.

[2] The home of Lord and Lady Bateman. Hervey wrote to Henry Fox at the end of 1738: "The D. of M. brought her from Totteridge last Tuesday, and she is now in a lodging in London. The reason given for their parting is, their humours being so very different, that it makes them mutually unhappy to live together. If there is any other, it is the one at least they do not give."

[3] Ickworth. Not in *A Duke and his Friends.*

not appear, a writ of contumacy will be immediately issued against you both, in the names of our Sovereign Lord the King, and our Sovereign Lady the Queen. I suppose Lord Albemarle, your Attorney in this affair, has already given you notice of this process commenced against you, and that the consequence of it will be our seeing you soon here. Without joking, you are both expected: and though you may pass your time more pleasantly where you are, I cannot but own that, as I shall pass mine so much more pleasantly for your being here, I am not sorry to think you will be forced to come. But do not be angry with me for saying this, since I can assure you I do not know any other thing in the world that could be disagreeable to you, that would not be so to me.

I know no news. At London I neither left people enough to furnish, relate, or invent any: and at Court your Grace knows, that, between the people who can't say anything worth repeating, and the people who wont, one seldom hears anything one cares to hear, seldomer anything one cares to retain, and seldomest of all anything one should care to have said, or cares to repeat.

According to the signs and tokens mentioned in the Scripture to notify the approach of the Last Day, one should imagine it were not far off; for, if I remember right the words of our Blessed Saviour, they are these, "And in the latter days there shall come scoffers, and there shall be wars and rumours of wars." What follows I shall leave the *Craftsman* to quote. But if these are the signs of a general dissolution, Lord have mercy on us; for that the scoffers at our wise and good religion abound and swarm, nobody I suppose will deny; and for wars and rumours of wars, both foreign and domestic, I hear of nothing else—the foreign, in Poland for King Augustus's successor; [1] the domestic, in Scotland for the Earl of Sutherland's.[2] The Stanislaus we maintain at the latter is the D. of Atholl you know, and his competitor, Lord Aberdeen; but, if I have any skill, the Court of England will as surely carry its point at the Diet of Edinburgh,

[1] Stanislaus Lecszinski returned to Poland as King, after Augustus the Strong's death: but again waived his claims in 1738.

[2] John, 16th Earl of Sutherland died in 1733. This no doubt refers to a contest for the election of a Scottish representative peer. The Duke won the day.

as the Court of France at that of Warsaw; though the old Duchess of Marlborough says not. And if she was as willing to bribe at one election as she's able, or the Emperor as able to bribe at the other as he's willing, perhaps both might go in a different manner from the way they will do now. But as long as she only writes letters, and he memorials, the Duke of Atholl and poor snorting, stupid Stanislaus *ont beau jeu.*

Adieu, mon cher, mon aimable, mon beau & mon noble Seigneur.

A letter to Henry Fox, in London, follows, seemingly written on July 31, the same day as he wrote a letter to Mrs. Clayton, of which a copy survives at Ickworth. Henry Fox apparently was just starting abroad, and after a preliminary skirmish in Paris, and a subsequent return home, remained on the Continent until the summer of 1735. He spent a large portion of these two years in the South of France, chiefly at Nice with Mrs. Strangways-Horner, who was living in a villa there, with her young daughter Elizabeth, her only child, born in 1723. Henry Fox seems to have supervised the education of what proved to be his future sister-in-law, then in her teens, and extracts of his letters to her are printed in *Henry Fox, First Lord Holland.*

TO HENRY FOX *July 31?, 1733*[1]

Dear Count. Ld Cowper not coming to relieve the D. of Richmond, we[2] could not leave this place till today. I propose being back by dinner on Tuesday; but for fear any accident should happen to keep me longer, or any other way to prevent my seeing you, I send you the enclosed, which the Duke of Richmond chooses to send by you rather than by the post, as it gives him an opportunity of recommending you to those to whom they are addressed.

As to the clothes, he will write to a friend of his at Paris, to bring them to you when you are there; and all the trouble you will have will only be to perjure yourself and swear you've worn them, and bring them over. Adieu. I am this moment stepping into the calash for Goodwood. Remember the threat, ou que le grand Dieu vous damne.

[1] Holland House.

[2] Lords of the Bedchamber.

TO MRS. CLAYTON *Hampton Court, July 31, 1733*[1]

Madame,

. . . I will not trouble you with any account of our occupations at Hampton Court. No mill-horses ever went in a more constant, true or a more unchanging circle, so that by the assistance of an almanack for the day of the week and a watch for the hour of the day, you may inform yourself fully, without any other intelligence but your memory, of every transaction within the verge of the Court. Walking, chaises, levees and audiences fill the morning. At night the King plays commerce and backgammon, and the Queen at quadrille, where poor Lady Charlotte runs her usual nightly gauntlet—the Queen pulling her hood, Mr. Schutz sputtering in her face, and the Princess Royal rapping her knuckles all at a time. It was in vain she fled from persecution for her religion : she suffers for her pride what she escaped for her faith, undergoes in a Drawing Room what she dreaded from the Inquisition, and will die a martyr to a Court though not to a Church.

The Duke of Grafton takes his nightly opiate of lottery, and sleeps as usual between the Princesses Amelie and Caroline ; Lord Grantham [2] strolls from one room to another (as Dryden says), " Like some discontented ghost, that oft appears, and is forbid to talk " : and stirs himself about, as people stir a fire not with any design [3] in the placing,[3] but in hopes to make it burn a little brisker, which His Lordship constantly does to no purpose, and yet tries it as constantly as if it had ever once succeeded. At last the King comes up ; the pool finishes, and everybody has their dismission. Their Majesties retire to Lady Charlotte and my Lord Lifford ; the Princesses to Bilderbec and Lony ; my Lord Grantham to Lady Frances and Mr. Clark ; some to supper and some to bed : and thus (to speak in the Scripture style) the evening and the morning make the day.

[1] Ickworth. The original is printed in Mrs. Thomson's *Memoirs of Lady Sundon*, 1847, with two other of his letters.

[2] Frederick Nassau, 3rd Earl of Grantham (d. 1738), Lord Chamberlain to the Queen. Hervey said that he was for ever in doubt what he should do, and for ever at last determined to do what he should not. *Memoirs*, p. 288.

[3–3] Added in Hervey's writing.

Adieu, dear Madam, and believe me without the formality of a conclusion,

Most sincerely yours.

TO STEPHEN FOX *Sunday* [1]

I send you back the Dedication you lent me here enclosed; and since you ask and I have promised you my opinion of it, I make a conscientious resolution to give it you very sincerely. Of all sorts of Epistles, I hate Epistles dedicatory; and of all Epistles dedicatory, I should most hate this to be addressed to me. There is not anything I had not rather have my name put to than the top of such a performance, except it were the bottom of it. There is a stiffness, a pedantry, an obscurity, a pumping for something and a displaying of nothing, that runs through the whole; and as people who praise adroitly can commend without [2] seeming to flatter,[2] so he from an awkwardness peculiar to his own pen seems to flatter without commending. As for correcting and altering, it would be loss of time; let him burn it and try again. Or do you write a Dedication to yourself, as Petulant does love-letters, and send it him, to send it you. Adieu.

I left the King at Chapel as soon as I had made my confession and received absolution, and must now return to take my quota of the Pope of London's benediction.

A portion of a letter written in August to the Bishop of Salisbury, with a dissertation on the Duke of Newcastle is worth publishing; and also Hervey's views on "puns". A number of by-elections seem to have taken place that autumn, which were a source of worry at the time to the Court. But in the end Walpole outstayed everything and everybody; and all came right in the end.

[1] Ickworth. No date. It is placed in the volume of copies early in 1733, but the sequence of the letters is by no means dependable. We have printed it, as it may possibly refer to some document which we cannot trace. It can hardly in any case, be connected with the *Dedication* which led to Hervey's duel. (*See ante*, pp. 68, 69.)

[2–2] Substituted by Hervey for "flattering".

TO THE BISHOP OF SALISBURY[1]

Hampton Court, August 14th, 1733

. . . I hear of nothing but elections, and of no elections without oppositions. Those in Sussex to the D. of Newcastle, both for the county and for Lewes, were very unexpected, are vigorously pushed, and will I believe be very ineffectually pursued. But as he was born to be in a fidget, a fright and a bustle, the usual alacrity of his restless machine has doubled all its movements upon this occasion; and as other people by application work their blood sometimes into a fever, he seems to have given his limbs that distemper, by quickening the pace of the one as much the ordinary effects of that disease quicken the course of the other. To know therefore when this new sort of fever of his abates, instead of feeling his pulse one must look at his legs and arms; there is but one symptom that his limb-fever and a blood-fever have in common, which is that of being very *light-headed.* I hope you will not call this a pun; in the first place because I hate a pun upon any occasion, and in the next place because I am sure upon this, it would be more improper than any other; for as one's words should always be adapted to one's subject, so the giving them too many senses, when one speaks of a man who seldom gives any to the words he makes use of, will admit of no excuse; unless one can say (as of puns, I believe one generally can) that as two negatives makes an affirmative, so two senses often make nonsense. If you want to have this point settled, I advise you to apply to your friend, countryman and neighbour, Mr. Dodington. I know nobody so likely to settle and clear any point relating to punning; though his partiality to punning perhaps will no more let him allow that one's words can have too many senses, than that one's bow can

[1] Ickworth. Benjamin Hoadly (1676–1761), Bishop successively of Bangor, Hereford, Salisbury, and Winchester. A great friend and ally of Lord Hervey, and a prolific writer on religious controversies. He was never a *persona grata* at Court, although Hervey thought that he was treated unfairly, and did his best to assist him. A later letter to the Bishop on September 6, spoke of his reply. "I am very angry with you for what you say about me and puns and Christians; and think, when you was blotting and blurring, as you call it (unless you were infected by one day's conversation with Sherwin), that you had much better have blurred your paper a little more, and my reputation a little less, by blotting out the whole paragraph."

have too many strings. Yet the one he has often let his company find out; and the other perhaps he may one day find out himself. . . .

Trouble on the Continent had resulted from the death of Augustus II (" the Strong "), King of Poland, on February 1, 1733. The Elector of Saxony, son of the late King, who finally took the throne, was one competitor, and Stanislaus Lecszinski, who had already worn the Crown and had been deposed, was the other. The Emperor (Charles VI) supported the former, and was joined by the Czarina of Russia. The French, on the other hand, naturally supported Stanislaus, and carried his election early in September; for the Poles were divided in their opinions. In England, the pretensions of Stanislaus were at first supported, as the best chance of a struggle being avoided upon the Continent. Walpole, as usual, was anxious to keep out of any entanglement which might involve England in war: but the Emperor and Russia continued their opposition, forced Stanislaus to retire, and a new election placed the Elector of Saxony on the Polish throne as Augustus III. At this moment France struck back, and her movements were detailed in the following letter to Stephen Fox, much on the same lines as in the *Memoirs*. He spoke, however, in the *Memoirs* (p. 219, etc.) most scathingly of the character and talents of the young King of Sardinia, from personal intercourse when staying at Turin in 1729, a judgment with which Croker in his edition of the *Memoirs* most profoundly disagreed.

TO THE BISHOP OF SALISBURY

Hampton Court, September 6th, 1733 [1]

We are still in expectation of news from Poland: and it is thought, though the dispute has hitherto lain in all appearance between Stanislaus and the Elector of Saxony, that neither of them will be chosen; but that the Primate, having all along underhand, by the help of French money received for the interest of Stanislaus, promoted that of his nephew, he will at the time of election get his nephew chosen, by representing to the electors the dangers to be apprehended from choosing either of the other two great competitors, and saying that the only way to avoid those dangers is to take a third person. That that third person ought to be one of the first quality among themselves; and of

[1] Ickworth.

that class, if they know of any more fit or more worthy than his nephew, that he desires they would choose him. But if not, though the honour of being their King is one he never sought for his nephew; yet for the peace of his dear Country, and for the peace of all Europe, he is willing to give him to his countrymen to do what they will with, [1] and sacrifice him to the throne.[1] . . .

TO HENRY FOX *Hampton Court, September 13, 1733* [2]

Dear Count, Though I am so angry with you for never having writ to me, that I would not contribute anything to your pleasure, but as I never can be so angry with you as to neglect your interest, I must inform you that Mr. Andrews has written to Sir Robert Walpole, upon reviewing his troops at Hindon, to say he is ready to make them join your's, and fight against the common enemy, that is Ld Weymouth, who has declared he will set up two members there, but desires to be excused naming them till Ld. Carteret (whom he expects every day at Longleat) shall come to give him his advice in this important affair.[3] Mr. Andrews's letter to Sir Robt. I have sent to your brother; and Sr. Robt. has promised to make Andrews do any thing you would have him. But I very much suspect that Andrews will only have a seeming merit in giving up what he would have had no benefit from keeping, and what I fear you will receive little by his transferring. In my last conference with Sir Robt. I insisted on nothing but the returning officer being secured to you; and what farther I am to say I expect directions for from your brother and you.

The Progress is at an end. Ste. was left at Redlynch. The Duchess of Richmond and Lady H. are coming here, and the Duke is going to Sussex. I received a letter yesterday from

[1]–[1] Added in Hervey's writing.

[2] Holland House and Ickworth.

[3] This refers to Henry Fox's abortive election at Hindon in Wilts, which is referred to earlier in these letters. (*See ante*, pp. 20, 21, and *n*.), and his further attempt to secure the seat. He had gone abroad, however, in July, leaving his brother to fight his battles for him when the time came. We shall see the result later on.

Voltaire.[1] He is charmed with you, and by the sort of commendations he gives you he must be sincere: for had he only had a mind to flatter you, it would have been impossible he should just have pitched on those good qualities which you really possess. Pray bid him send me a direction for my letters to him, written in a hand I can read; for the date of his (which I suppose was to serve me for a direction) I can not decipher.

My compliments to Mr. and Mrs. Digby, Mrs. Horner, etc., etc. It is public day; consequently you know I am in a hurry. Ld. and Lady Chesterfield [2] are to come here to day for the first time. Does not that wedding surprise you a little? He has been marry'd these four months.

TO STEPHEN FOX *Hampton Court, October 9, 1733* [3]

At my return to this place this afternoon I found a letter from you; and the Duke of Richmond sending this night to London, I have an opportunity of answering it.

But among many things I have to say to you, you must forgive me if I begin with what is most material to me, though perhaps least so to yourself, I mean our meeting. I long to see you, and to see you at Redlynch, because there I shall see most of you.

The wedding [4] is to be on the Birthday; and in a week after,

[1] Henry Fox had evidently been calling on Voltaire about this time. That he had visited him was clear; for years later, in 1760, when his son, Stephen (2nd Lord Holland) was staying in Geneva the latter saw Voltaire constantly. Voltaire wrote to his father, "'Tis for me a good fortune to receive the son of the amiable and honour'd Mr. Fox, who was formerly so kind to me." This passage effectively dates the occasion.

[2] Lord Chesterfield married Melusina de Schulenburg, daughter of George I's mistress, the Duchess of Kendal. We find in a letter from Hervey to Lady Sundon on September 11, 1733; "I think this match the wisest thing the man could do, and the silliest the woman. I want to know if you are of my mind; for few people agree with me here, when I say I think he was in the right to marry her, and will be so much in the right, now he has married her, as to make her a very uncommon good husband." (*Memoirs of Lady Sundon*, ii, 233.)

[3] Melbury.

[4] The Princess Royal's marriage to William Charles Henry, Prince of Orange, did not actually take place until March 14, 1734, as the Prince became very seriously ill shortly after his arrival in England. Hervey in his *Memoirs* wrote of him at this time in a most uncomplimentary strain. "A miserable match," he called it, "both in point of man and fortune, his figure being

the King goes to Richmond, and the bride to Holland. As soon as they do so, I am free, *from* my duty and *for* my pleasure. If therefore your time is so carved out that you design to be then at Redlynch, I will attend you there. So much for what I have at heart. As to your brother's affairs, I know too well how much you hate trouble ; and am always too much concerned that any thing you hate should happen to you, not to be sorry that every thing relating to his election (as matters now stand) is to be transacted by you.

Now for the affairs of the Nation. There came two expresses within these two days from France. The first inform'd us that the French had pass'd the Rhine and besieged Fort Kehl, a place in Suabia belonging to the Emperor, over against Strasbourg. Fifteen thousand more of the French troops have enter'd Lorraine ; and at the same time the King of France sent a message to the Duchess Dowager of Lorraine, to tell her that the reasons of State obliged him to send her these visitors ; yet as he had the greatest regard and affection imaginable for his dear Cousin, so if she pleased to take shelter from the storm in Paris, or any other place in his Dominions, she should be welcome and received with all the honours due to a grand-daughter of France.[1]

The second express brought advice of the French army in Dauphiné having left their quarters there and march'd into Savoy, in order to pass the Alps before the passage became more difficult, and to get into Italy, to attack the Emperor immediately there. This march through the King of Sardinia's territories is pursuant to the Treaty lately concluded between the Courts of Turin and France, by which that King obliges himself to give the French army free passage, on what terms is not known ; but some fat morsel in Italy to be sure is promised him for this civility, a morsel which perhaps the French may not be able to

deformed and his estate not clear £12,000 a year." Better acquaintance with the Prince, however, led the writer to modify his opinion, and induced much kinder conclusions later on.

[1] Elizabeth Charlotte, sister of the Regent Duke of Orleans. The *Memoirs* give her reply, that, according to Hervey, of a " Spartan heroine ". " She did not think it at all proper for the mother to take sanctuary in the dominions of a man who had so inequitably seized the son's, and that she should never hope to receive favours where she had not found justice."

get, or, if they do get it, which perhaps they may not be willing to part with. This policy of the King of Sardinia's I own to me appears to be but ill-judg'd. However I will make no comments, but only tell you facts.

The discontented party in Poland have proceeded to another election; and this day the Elector of Saxony's Minister had an audience of the King, to notify his Master's being chosen King of Poland. Stanislaus is at Dantzic.

Chavignie [1] yesterday was here to present a Memorial from his Master to our Court, containing the reasons of France for the steps she has lately taken and the hostilities committed against the Emperor.

Adieu, my dear, dear Ste; and believe me, whatever public or private changes or chances, friendships or enmities you may hear of in the world, that the heart of your present gazetteer is ever faithfully and unalterably,

Yours.

On October 15, 1733, Hervey made further allusions to the wedding, and to the confusion on the Continent, in a letter to Dr. Middleton.[2]

. . . We are extremely busy in our preparations for the wedding, which the King has this day declared shall be kept on the Birthday, and at St. James's. The foreign affairs grow every day more and more embroiled; and first or last I fear the two Kings of Poland will put all Europe in arms. It will be very odd to have all the great Powers engaged in settling a point that naturally should have been of great indifference to them, and in behalf of the two disputants, who neither of them at first had a mind to solicit the Crown for which they are now contesting; but both at present are engaged in honour to pursue what neither by inclination at first undertook. Adieu. Are you to pass the winter among your books and your enemies at Cambridge; or do you intend to give part of it to conversation and your friends in London?

[1] Théodore de Chavigny (1687–1771), French Ambassador.

[2] Ickworth. The Rev. Conyers Middleton, D.D. (1688–1750), a constant correspondent of Lord Hervey's, especially on controversial subjects. He was a Fellow of Trinity College, Cambridge.

A few days later Hervey wrote to Henry, then abroad, from Hampton Court:[1] "Send me your opinion", he said in the last paragraph, "of the enclosed. They were written to Dr. Sherwin, to entertain the Richmond-Caravan in their later progress." These verses were clearly, *The Epistle from a Nobleman to a Doctor of Divinity: in answer to a Latin letter in verse: written from H . . . n C . . . t*, which put the final touch on Pope's indignation and fury at the attacks made upon him in the earlier months of the year, reputedly by Hervey and Lady Mary Wortley-Montagu (and doubtless the attribution was correct).

Pope certainly started the trouble, with a few scattered aspersions on Hervey, and followed them up towards the end of 1732, as we have seen, in the *Imitation of the First Satire of the Second Book of Horace*, by his attack on Lady Mary Wortley-Montagu and on Lord Hervey. Both foolishly hit back before long, probably in conjunction, with *Verses addressed to the Imitator of Horace*, published in March; without measuring the cost, or realising the relentless malignity to which they were exposing themselves. No direct mention of these passages-at-arms appear in Hervey's letters, nor are they referred to in the *Memoirs*. But shortly afterwards, while Pope's wrath was still simmering, Hervey added fuel to the flames with the above-mentioned *Epistle to a Doctor of Divinity*, in which he castigated and chastised the poet.

Dr. Sherwin was a Canon of Chichester, and was well-known to the Richmond family at Goodwood, in the character of a useful butt for their wit and pleasantries. Even a bogus highway-robbery had been recently staged by members of the house-party to upset and alarm him, a story related in Lord March's *A Duke and his Friends* (i, 264, etc.). But Hervey's attentions to the Canon did not end there. Annoyed that the latter had allowed the *Epistle* to get into the hands of the printers of the *Craftsman*, and again wishing to amuse the Richmond family, he next wrote a *Character*, and not a very edifying one, of which we shall hear more a few months later, when that too got to the printer, who tried to blackmail him in consequence. The copy of the *Character*, when sent out abroad to Henry Fox, is headed "*Dr. Sherwyn's Character, designed for his Epitaph.*"

The references to Horatio Walpole's trip to the Continent, show clearly that he had many other political fish to fry besides bringing over the "Bridegroom-Highness."

[1] Holland House and Ickworth. October 20, 1733.

TO HENRY FOX *Hampton Court, October 20, 1733* [1]

At my return from hunting half an hour ago, I found a letter from you written in a damned, splenetic humour, a hand scarce legible, and a style that bespeaks neither a healthful body or mind. I wonder not at either of them being distempered. For the first, a sedentary life, the water of the Seine (which never agreed with you), and the vineyards of Champain [*sic*] (which never agree with any body), easily account. And for the latter, the prospect of a Carnival to be kept at Nice would put most minds, even without the self-tormenting, black propensity of your's, upon a manner of reflecting that would not be apt to make them very lively company. You need not have cautioned me against blaming on to your brother this sudden resolution you have taken to stay abroad this winter. In the first place, to determine anybody to be in the wrong for anything, without knowing all the reasons they have for acting, is always unreasonable ; in the next, though I thought *you* in the wrong I should not be very ready to allow it, and especially where you would least like perhaps to appear so. Everything that I can do to secure your election at Hindon shall be done with as much diligence as if you were here to forward it yourself ; and I dare answer for it your brother will act the same part in his province.

We talk of nothing here at present but the marriage, which is to be kept at St. James's on the King's Birthday, if (as Ben says) "Winds and tides serve". The yachts are already sail'd. Horace Walpole is gone to fetch his Bridegroom-Highness over : that is, he is gone to Holland, and *that* the reason given for his going. Mais le fil blanc dont cette raison est conçu is so plain, that the coarse stitches of it are seen by the most purblind eyes in all Europe. I hear the Cardinals discovered them at fourscore without spectacles. I am brimful of politics, but dare not tap myself at this distance, because I know my letter, that is to go through as many countries and as many hands as the Fiancée du Roi de Garbe, will also, like her, show all that it has to everybody that lays hold of it.

[1] Holland House and Ickworth. ("To Mr. H. Fox, in the South of France", in Lord Hervey's writing.)

The law-preferments are at last adjusted. All that is to appear of the manner of adjusting them is that the Attorney is to be a Peer and Chancellor.[1] Mr. Dodington [2] is gone to Ireland. Great geniuses never do anything like other people ; so that, as it is usual to pun in England and bull in Ireland, he reverses that ordinary conduct, and after *bulling* here, is now *punning* there. Lord Scarborough [3] is returned hither at last out of the North. The Opposition brag of their hold there, but if I have any skill, he'll be a Joseph. Lord Chesterfield has not stirred from Twitenham [*sic*] since the declaration of his marriage. He talks, my Lady Chesterfield kisses, and the Duchess of Kendal spins all day long—" How like a dog looked Hercules, thus to a distaff chained." Now and then, by way of digression and relief, Lady Torrington and Lady William Pawlet drop in ; which makes his Lordship's situation just as desirable as their's, to whom crying is an ease, since he has no resources to dissipate his ennui, but such as are the types and symbols of ennui in every other company they come into.

I thank you for Voltaire's verses, and like them extremely. Send me your opinion of the enclosed. They were written to Dr. Sherwin to entertain the Richmond-Caravan in their late progress.

TO HENRY FOX *St. James's, November 19, 1733* [4]

I was in hopes by this time, dear Count, that I should have been in a capacity to send you an account of our long-expected royal wedding. But the Prince of Orange, falling ill the very day before *that* appointed for the ceremony, and, though recovered from danger, continuing still too weak for marrying plight, consummation is now deferred for three weeks ; and all the Courtiers dispersed to their respective sports or business in their several countries. Sir Robert set out yesterday for Houghton, with the usual members of the Norfolk-Congress, who are to hunt, be noisy, jolly, drunk, comical, and pure merry during this

[1] Charles Talbot, Baron Talbot of Hensol (1685–1737), succeeded Peter, 1st Baron King of Ockham (1669–1734), who had had a stroke.

[2] Dodington held a sinecure in Ireland, the Clerkship of the Pells.

[3] *See ante*, p. 67 and *n.*

[4] Holland House.

recess ; and then to re-assemble here in order to solemnise the conjugal-affairs, and methodize the Parliamentary ones.

Your friend, Lord Sunderland, now Duke of Marlborough, will certainly be ruined by his succession to his new title.[1] For as he thinks he must increase his expenses with his grandeur, and the éclat of his way of living with that of his appellations, he is, without the addition of one thousand pounds a year to his income, doubling the charges of his disbursements, which were before so extravagant that, without these supplemental new drains, he was the beginning of this year threescore thousand pounds in debt. So that, as paradoxical as it may sound to have the ruin of a man completed by becoming Duke of Marlborough, it will, if his grandmother lives seven years, certainly be his case. By the bye, he is reconciled to her ; he and his Duchess have both been at Marlborough House. The Batemans are now the only people that remain in disgrace at that Court ; and there is even a flying report that secret orders are given for Lady Bateman's picture to be whitewashed.[2] But this wants confirmation.

I send you the enclosed ; though perhaps you may not think them worth sending. But as one goes under the name of Lord Chesterfield, and the other under Lord H—y's, people here have read, criticised and talk'd of them a good deal.

Adieu, dear Count, I spend my time chiefly, now you and your brother have abandoned me, with the D. and D^ss^ of Richmond ; and following the advice of Madame Barnevil,[3] I could tell you a thousand stories that would entertain you if you were here, and that would bear black and white if I dared to venture them. But the misfortune of Court-anecdotes are that the things that tell best are generally least fit to be told. You

[1] Henrietta, Duchess of Marlborough died unexpectedly on October 24 ; and Lord Sunderland succeeded as 3rd Duke.

[2] Lady Louisa Stuart wrote in her *Introductionary Anecdotes* (*Letters of Lady Mary Wortley-Montagu*), " the Duchess had the face of Lady Bateman's picture blackened over, and the sentence, ' She is blacker within ', inscribed in large characters on the frame ; and thus, placed in her usual sitting-room, it was exhibited to all beholders."

[3] This seems to refer to the play by Lillo, *George Barnwell*, which took the town by storm at this time. Lord Perceval spoke of it in December, 1733, as, " the famous moving tragedy, acted at the Haymarket Playhouse." (*Egmont*, i, 472.)

may think I say this to lay a trap to make you wish yourself with me, which I should be glad to have you do : but should have no pleasure even in those wishes if I thought I cheated you of them, and had not merit enough towards you to claim them as a debt.

TO STEPHEN FOX *November 29, 1733*[1]

I intended to write to you by the last post, but was prevented ; and for fear of the same accident, if I should defer it till night, I now sit down, in a detestable humour, a good deal of company, and consequently a good deal of noise—bad concomitants with a pen and ink, but no great impediments to the little use I have at present for them, since all I have to say is to answer two or three odd things you say in your last letter. As I must begin with the oddest, I must ask what you mean by talking to me of your living alone, till you apprehended your being unfit for my company in London, and if you are now to learn that I should like you rusty better than any other body polish'd. In the next place, you are quite as unintelligible when you talk of the Duke of Marlborough's losing five thousand pounds a year by being so ; unless you mean to insinuate that to keep up the éclat of the title, he will make at least that increase in his expenses. And if that was your meaning (which I believe it was not), you would be as much in the right, as, if you mean anything else, you are in the wrong.

Your notions (or the notions of those demi-human, demi-brutal boobys, your country-neighbours) of there being any finesse in the Prince of Orange's illness, are to the full as ill-founded as those of the Duke of Marlborough. He is really and bonâ-fide in a very bad way, has had a violent fever, has now a cough, and is, for the little time he has been ill, incredibly weak.

I thought I had sent you word that Mount Ætna *non conta piu*, at least for the D. of Marlborough or his Duchess ; but Lady Bateman is not yet admitted to her presence. Lord Bateman has let me into the whole Radnor affair ; but I am apt to think, he will not carry his point here, and am sure he ought not. For

[1] Melbury.

what Minister in his senses would disoblige a man that serves him, to serve a man he can't oblige.

The new Ld. Chancellor Talbot had the Seals given him in Council half an hour ago. The late Lord Chancellor was not well enough to come and resign them ; they were sent for this morning by warrant. The poor devil is speechless, and so ill, that I believe his breath will soon follow them. Adieu, I am now in the Bedchamber Woman's room ; and the King's dinner being just over, mine is just going to begin. His Majesty goes to the play, so that I shall not have time to add any thing more by this post tonight, if any thing should occur that I should want to say.

TO STEPHEN FOX *St. James's, December 6, 1733* [1]

I am sorry to hear, my dear Ste., that the journey hither is put off for a fortnight longer than you once designed. How can you prefer making your constituents drunk to making your friends happy ; and stay loitering at Hindon or Shaftesbury, whilst I am wishing for you in town ?

You continue to make a most horrid peaupouris [*sic*] about the Duke of Marlborough's affairs ; but neither you nor I are enough concern'd about them for me to take or give the trouble of explaining and setting them right.

The Queen has got the gout, and is rolled in and out of the Drawing Room every day in that chair given her by the King of Poland, in which Lady Deloraine played " Sea-Goddess " last year at Kensington. The Prince of Orange mends very slowly ; I have given (though I have not received) orders to fit up an apartment for him at Kensington, against he is well enough to go there.

It is not to be imagined how pleased my Lord Chancellor seems with his new promotion ; nor is it to be wonder'd at that he should find so much pleasure in having his finger at last on those Seals, on which he has all his life had his eye.

I heard it was said by a great man in the Opposition the other day, that the Court need not be so elate on their acquisitions in

[1] Melbury.

the House of Lords; for that they would not find that Court-volubility, with a little Westminster-Hall chicanery, would ever be able to make a stand against the true and noble spirit that seemed to spread itself of late through that body.

I send you enclosed some verses, which you have already seen in manuscript, and which were printed without my knowledge.[1] The advertisement you saw was, I fear, for the publication of genuine things; and all the trouble and bustle I have had to prevent their coming out, I shall adjourn the recital of till I see you. Pope is in a most violent fury; and j'en suis ravi. Adieu.

The Emperor has lost every thing in Italy on this side the Ecclesiastical State, except Mantua and the Castle of Milan.

TO THE DUKE OF RICHMOND

St. James's, December 27th, 1733 [2]

My dear Lord. I did last week fully intend to be at this moment by a good fire at Goodwood; but Lady Hervey, without being in direct labour, having been these four or five days enough in pain to apprehend it every moment and keep her room, has desired me not to leave her; which I, like a good husband, as in duty bound, have complied with.

Ste. is come to town, but so fine a gentleman, that when I asked him to accompany me to Goodwood, I found it was as impossible to get a direct answer from him, as it would have been to have got a direct answer from his Grace of Newcastle, if I had asked him anything relating to the present state of Europe, or the particulars of a manifesto that was to be in print in three days.

À propos to the affairs of Europe, I hear your Grace talks of being in Holland at the meeting of the Parliament here; which I don't approve, and which perhaps you do not care whether I do or no. However I shall *shoot my bolt* [3](as the ordinary people call it),[3] and tell you I think one may be as outré in one's negligence as in one's affectation of importance. So now go or stay, and say I am a very impertinent fellow or not. I shall, like the

[1] *The Epistle to a Doctor of Divinity*, to Dr. Sherwin.

[2] Ickworth. Not in *A Duke and his Friends*.

[3–3] Added in Hervey's writing.

Spanish Friar, declare *liberari animam meam*, and leave you to your own determinations.

It is at last resolved [1] that the Prince of Orange shall go to the Bath. He is to set out next week: he looks very ill, but everybody agrees in his not being in danger. . . .

I hear your friend, my Lord Lovel, who is gone into Norfolk to make votes by his hospitality for his brother, entertains all the freeholders with cursing English blockheads, descanting on the impossibility of living like a gentleman if one is served by them, telling them the progress he has made in garbling his family of the uncouth, awkward dogs, and that in another year he hopes not to have one of them under his roof. But whilst His Lordship, by his superfine gentility, proves himself perfectly free from being a John-Trot [2] in his taste, one cannot but own, that on this occasion and in the place and the company he now is, that the being so very French is being a little Irish too. Adieu.

[1] Altered by Hervey from *determined*. [2] A bumpkin.

CHAPTER VIII

1734

In 1734 the Ickworth MSS. provide no material, with the exception of four or five copies of letters in the Holland House series. The contribution, however, from the latter source is fairly substantial, and mostly to Henry Fox, who was still abroad. Clearly from the opening sentences of the next letter, Hervey was beginning to feel that he had gone too far in his attack on Pope. His efforts were the attempts of a gnat to penetrate the hide of the rhinoceros. He had also to some extent realised that he was likely to come out second-best with the poet, in what proved to be an unequal contest of wits.

TO HENRY FOX *St. James's House, Jan. 12, 1734*[1]

I have now two letters, my dear Count, to thank you for. As to the first, without the least flattery to you, I approve of the additional verses you have made to the letter prodigiously, & like some of the corrections, but not all. But I am so tired of hearing, seeing & talking of these odious verses, that I shall not launch anew into a subject which nothing but your writing upon it could have induced me to behold mention'd again with common patience. Parlons donc d'autre chose.

How could you be such a mole as not to see that the reason of H. W's[2] going to Holland (though the pretence was to fetch over the P. of O.) could be no other than to concert measures with the Dutch on the present conjuncture, & to persuade them to remain in inaction like us, without hampering themselves with an obligation of neutrality. When a very great person (not a man) told me that Hor. was to go & fetch the P. of O., I burst out laughing her face, & asked if they thought anybody would believe that Hor. was sent by his friends as a Show-Officer, & pick'd out of

[1] Holland House and Ickworth.

[2] Horatio Walpole. Hervey (*Memoirs*, p. 230) wrote that he was sent "to concert measures with the Ministers of the States, and agree what part England and Holland should take at this very conjuncture of affairs. But this finesse was as coarse as it was ridiculous and unnecessary ; everybody, the moment he was nominated for this voyage, discerning the reason of it . . ."

the Court as a proper figure for a Bride-man? As to the marriage, the Lord knows when it will be perfected. His Highness is gone to Bath, & not at all in consummation plight.

You ask me what countryman a Samoïade [*sic*] is. He is of a people that inhabit the North-East side of Russia, a short, ugly species, hardly humanised in their form & not more civilised in their manners: but of such warm constitutions, that, notwithstanding they live in a chilled climate where light & warmth are as great strangers as in a house of Ld Burlington's building, yet they find the poor little [1] warmer-season [1] they call Summer so much too hot for them, that those who can afford it always pass that part of the year at their villas in Nova-Zembla. I never see Lord Tyrconnel [2] but I think of these people, who sweat in frost, stink with health, and are as much inferior to many brutes in understanding as they are to human-kind in their figure.

The Parliament (do not be malicious & abusive upon the transition) is to meet on Thursday. Your brother & Mr Campbell [3] are to move the Address in the House of Commons, & your humble Servant in the House of Lords.[4] I'll send you the King's Speech as soon as he has spoke it. You will find a great many good words in it, & several very well turned paragraphs. But modern Kings, like the ancient Oracles, should never deliver their meaning too plain, that the ambiguity of their sense may leave a possibility of different expositions according as future events require.

I am against your selling stock at present, & have told your brother so. I am likewise extremely against your being out of England at the time of the Elections, but have not told your brother so.

The reconciliation of the Duke of Marlborough to his grandmother happened naturally, & without being negociated, upon the death of his aunt; but I hear it is not likely to last. The

[1–1] Altered in the copy, in Hervey's writing, to "faint, pale sunshine."

[2] John Brownlow, 1st Viscount, d. 1754. The King described him as "a puppy that never votes twice on the same side." (*Memoirs.*)

[3] John Campbell, of Cawdor, M.P. for Pembrokeshire, and a close friend of Henry Fox in later life. *The Parliamentary History* gives Campbell as moving, and Fox as seconding.

[4] The *Memoirs* state that Newcastle bitterly opposed this selection.

Batemans are as bad as ever. It is certain that he is, by his own confession, 30,000 £ in debt ; & others say much more. However he is retrenching his expenses, & has begun by putting off his hounds. His wife is grown tall, fat, coarse and proud.

Adieu. You will easily imagine after all I have told you and that the Parliament is to meet on Wednesday, that I have business enough upon my hands. How can you be so stupid as to ask what Lady W. goes abroad for ? For her *health*, to be sure. What does *every body* go abroad for ? Poor Count, your parts are sadly impaired. I wish you would come to England and oil them ; or the rust will eat into them in a little while irretrievably.

TO HENRY FOX *January 20, 1734* [1]

My dear Count. I send you inclosed the King's Speech and the Addresses of the two Houses, entertainment enough for one post, for which reason I am less sorry that I have neither time nor matter to give you more.

Your brother and I (as fame reports, and friends and foes allow) behaved well. I hope you will like the Lords' Address, because every word of it is my own. The King told me in the most obliging manner that it was the best he had ever seen, but that my having said too much in it of him, was the reason he could not say so much as he would upon it to me.

To day is the Prince's Birthday.[2] The Queen is ill, and cannot appear ; but the King will be in the great Drawing Room as usual in the morning, though there will be no ball at night.

Mrs. Digby is in labour ; so that I'll keep my letter open to the last minute to let you know how she does.

Jack Spencer is to be married next week to Ld Carteret's third daughter.[3] The Dss of Bedford made the match. What luck that man has in disposing of his female nursery !

[1] Holland House.

[2] The Prince of Wales had been persuaded by Dodington to go to Court on New Year's Day, and by the Queen's influence the King decided to speak to him, which was well commented on by the Courtiers.

[3] John Spencer, the Duke of Marlborough's brother.

Adieu. Carestini[1] dines with me, and is to sing here all the afternoon. The company is to be the Princess Royal, Lady Murray and the Bishop of Salisbury. You do not wonder at the two last.

I can not help bragging to you of a present the Queen made me about a fortnight ago of the finest gold snuff-box I ever saw, with all the Arts and Sciences, by her own bespeaking, carv'd upon it.[2] Encore, mon cher et très cher, Adieu.

Again Hervey returned to the subject of his wordy-warfare with Pope. He would seem to have been ill-advised in entrusting any business of this kind to Newcastle, considering that both men loathed one another. Hervey was clearly not prepared to stick at trifles in order to get himself out of a bad hole, and seems to have brought off the coup which he describes, very successfully. Copies of the *Character*, and another copy embodying the alterations intended to turn the paper into "*Parson F—d's Epitaph*,"[3] are amongst the Holland House MSS. but hardly merit publication. Hervey's unhesitating and immediate action is the chief point especially to be emphasised.

TO HENRY FOX[4] *January 31st, 1734. St. James's House*
February 11

Eccomi in folio; from whence you may conclude I design to write abundantly, and give you a great many words, how sparing soever I may be (in prudence) of some intelligence you ask; and how costive soever I may appear (from impotence) in sense and entertainment.

In the first place, since you will have me talk again of these detestable verses, that proved me imprudent and Sherwin—himself, I must let you know that I have been the [lo]ad[5] of every press, and the song of every hawker for these last six

[1] Cajo Fabrizio, known as Carestini, the male contralto, who first appeared in London in the previous December.

[2] The gift of this snuff-box was picked out by the Prince, as "an insult and an outrage". He complained at the same time that "it was extremely hard a man whom the whole time had been so impertinent to him, should be the Queen's constant companion and her most distinguished favourite." (*Memoirs*, p. 274.)

[3] The identity of Parson Ford, as he appears in Hervey's letter, is nowhere explained. The alterations only affect 12 lines; and while modifying the asperity of the *Character* of Sherwin, are of no special importance or interest.

[4] Holland House. Henry Fox was in Paris.

[5] Torn by a seal.

weeks ; though Pope has not written one word but a manuscript in prose never printed, which he has shown to several of his friends, but which I have never seen, and which, I have heard from those who did see it is very low and poor, ridiculing only my person, and my being vain of over-rated parts and the undeserved favour of a Court.[1]

The jumble of the advertisements in the *Daily Courier* is too long a story for me to enter into the particulars of it. The first of them was owing to a mistake of the Duke of Newcastle, whom I desired to order the printer to say that nothing promised by a former advertisement to be published should come out ; and instead of that they said what was come out was not mine, though I had own'd it to every mortal, and to Arbuthnot,[2] who came to me from Pope about it. And my answer to Arbuthnot, when he asked me why I had been so very severe on Pope, was, " Because he was a rascal, had begun with me, and deserved it ; and that my only reason for being sorry the verses were printed, which I did not design they should be, was because I thought it below me to enter into a paper-war with one that had made himself by his late works as contemptible as he was odious."

What vexed me was the printer's having got a copy of Sherwin's " Character ", written by me, which they threatened to print. However I warded this blow, by turning the verses immediately into an " Epitaph on Ford ", and pretending they were written two years ago. This, by the Duke of Richmond's good management, passed on Sherwin ; and he is now boasting of being abused with me by the *Craftsman* and says it is because he and I are known to be such useful and firm friends to the Government.

The best things that have been written against me (though God knows, without prejudice, bad is the best) I will send you by the

[1] This was the *Letter to a Noble Lord*. It was dated Nov. 30, 1733, but was not printed until 1751, after Pope's death, when published by Warburton, *Works*, Vol. viii, 253 etc. Horatio Walpole, at the request of Sir Robert, stopped the earlier publication of it, by getting an Abbey in France from Cardinal Fleury for Pope's friend, Mr. Southcote. (*See H. Walpole's letters*, ed. Toynbee, iii, 57.)

[2] Dr. John Arbuthnot, Hervey's physician before he consulted Dr. Cheyne : and a close friend of Pope.

next post. Sherwin denies having sold the copy of my verses; though I know he gave a copy, if not, to a printer.

I shall not tell you how I think I spoke in the House of Lords, it was above half an hour. Those who had a mind to depreciate, did it the old way, by saying it was all studied, wrote down, and got by heart. The first is true; the two last false; and if I find I can speak off-hand, I am easy whether people think I do or no. I had but 48 hours given me to draw the Question and the Address and to consider what I would say, and was ill-used; though that is another long and now old story.

The debates hitherto in both Houses have been very bad; and, notwithstanding all the menaces thrown out before the Parliament met, I believe it will prove a short and easy session. The Triennial Bill, the Debt of the Navy, the Pension Bill, the new modelling the Army, and a Domestic-family proposal which I dare not mention plainer, are the things at present chiefly talked of as the bones of Parliamentary contention for this year. . . .

Lady Hervey is brought to bed of a nasty, shabby girl. Princesses Emily and Caroline are to be her god-mothers; and last post I wrote to the Prince of Orange to be god-father.[1] This little domestic paragraph came in oddly enough by way of parenthesis. I now return to more public matters.

There has yet been but one division in the House of Lords, which was on a Question moved by Lord Bathurst, for the King to lay an account before the Lords of the good offices he had employed for an accommodation of the present disputes. They were so beaten in this debate, that they only desired to withdraw their Question, which was refused; and, Lord Carteret moving to adjourn, the division was on the question of adjournment, the numbers 57 and 33. Nobody left us but Lord Willoughby,[2] who has thrown up his pension; and Lord Falmouth, who I believe will be saved the trouble of doing the same thing by his employment. Lord Willoughby told Sir Robert W. that the

[1] The letter is among the Ickworth copies. This daughter, from her names, was clearly Emily Caroline Nassau. Miss Stuart puts her birth a year later.

[2] Richard, 13th Lord Willoughby de Broke (d. 1752). His brother, John Verney (1699–1741), was Attorney-General to Queen Caroline; and was nominated Master of the Rolls in 1738.

reason of his quitting him was Sir Robert's having given an employment to that rascal, his brother, Varny. Sir Robert said he did not know his brother was so. "Yes," replied my Lord, "that you did; for I wrote you word of it last year." I send you enclosed a copy of verses of Swift's on the Dissenters, very nasty and not very pretty, my own verses on Sherwin, and the alteration of them to Ford. The cargo upon me, you shall have next week. Adieu, my dear Count. I leave Signor Stephano to give an account of myself. I forgot to tell you that the printer of the *Craftsman* wrote to Sherwin, and sent him enclosed his own "Character" as written by me, desiring him to sign a certificate, that a *Letter from the Nobleman* was written by me. Sherwin sent me the printer's letter, and part of his letter to me was this, "You see, my Ld., the way that rascal, the *Craftsman*, has taken to pique me into setting my hand to a most notorious untruth. I know nothing at all of the whole matter. Let him print if he dares."

In the next letter, February 8, Hervey sent four copies of verses to Henry Fox. They are as follows, and are among the Holland House MSS.

(*a*) "The Lord H—r—y's first Speech in the House of Lords."
(*b*) "*Horace to Barine*, imitated to Lord Hervey, Book 2, Ode 8."
(*c*) "An apology for printing *The Nobleman's Epistle*."
(*d*) "To Ld Hervey and Lady Mary Wortley by Mr. Pope."

(*a*), (*b*), and (*c*) are probably by some hack-writer connected with the *Craftsman*, and are disallowed by the experts for various reasons from being part of the output of Pope's own pen. They appear in the Appendix (C), for they are almost unknown. They are written in the hand of a secretary.

(*d*) A short set of verses, two stanzas, are in Hervey's own writing, and are recognised as being by the poet himself. They run as follows:

To Lord Hervey and Lady Mary Wortley,
by Mr. Pope.[1]

When I but call a flagrant Whore unsound,
Or have a Pimp or Flaterer in the Wind,

[1] Holland House. Entirely in Hervey's writing. The spelling, etc. is unaltered.

Sapho enrag'd crys out your Back is round,
Adonis screams—Ah! Foe to all Mankind!

Thanks, dirty Pair! You teach me what to say,
When you attack my Morals, Sense, or Truth.
I answer thus,—poor Sapho you grow grey,
And sweet Adonis you have lost a Tooth.

TO HENRY FOX *February 8, 1734* [1]

Here are the things, dear Count, which I promised to send you. Here is one poem more on the same subject, called *Tit for Tat*,[2] too large to be sent in the packet which you shall have soon, it being the best of them all, the most abusive with regard to me, and the most impudent as regard to other people.

There is a fourth *Essay on Man*, as much too big to be comprehended in a letter, as it in many parts too obscure to be comprehended by any understanding. All that is to be understood shows the author to be as much in the dark with regard to the subject he treats of, as his readers are left by his manner of treating it. It is a series of contradictions upon that great contradiction, his text that *Whatever is, is right*. It is inscribed to Ld Bolingbroke in 20 or so very fine verses. I will not enter into a criticism upon a thing you have not seen, because it would be as great an absurdity as any this writer is guilty of, in pretending to demonstrate that all we call bad is conducive to what God calls good. Pope is certainly the author of them. Adieu. I am at present at the Council table, hearing press warrants read, and reports from the Plantations, qui m'embrouillent l'esprit autant que la Philosophie embrouille la cervelle de Monsr. Pope.

The next letter (February 14) deals with the debate in the Lords on making commissions of officers for life, introduced by the new Duke of Marlborough in opposition to the Court, an action which King George took very ill. Hervey spoke, in the *Memoirs*, of the King's dislike for the Duke being only equalled by his hatred for the

[1] Holland House.

[2] *See* p. 195; and Appendix D. This is a printed broadsheet.

Duke of Bedford, who took the same line in politics, and acted against Walpole. He, as we have seen, had recently married Marlborough's sister, Lady Di. "The two Dukes", Hervey wrote, "were as much alike in pride, violence of temper, and their public conduct, as they were different in their ways of thinking and acting in private life. The Duke of Marlborough was profuse and never looked into his affairs; the Duke of Bedford covetous, and the best economist in the world. The Duke of Bedford was of such a turn as to have been able to live within his fortune, if it had been fifty times less; and the Duke of Marlborough to have run his out, had it been fifty times greater. . . ."[1] The real reason why the Opposition pressed this matter, futilely as it turned out, was to take the opportunity of bringing up again the case of Lord Cobham, who had been dismissed his regiment for his vote on the Excise Bill, and also in the hopes of bringing Lord Scarborough over their side. In this they also failed, though the debate drove him to resign his Mastership of the Horse.[2] Hervey gave his reasons in a subsequent letter. He did not mention Lord Carteret's subsequent motion in the *Memoirs*, so this is probably the only account of the debate.

TO HENRY FOX *February 14, 1734*[3]

Dear Count,

This is the fifth letter I have sent to you since I have received one; but I give you fair warning for the future I will write no more than I read: and for your silly excuse of having nothing to say, I shall not allow it. Say your thoughts on everything I say, which will be text enough for you, and will be bribe sufficient for me.

We had yesterday a great debate in both Houses on the same Questions. The first was a Bill to make all commissions in the Army for life, which was moved in the House of Lords by your friend the Duke of Marlborough, who was extremely frightened, said but little, and what he did say was neither remarkably well or ill. He was seconded by Lord Winchilsea, who did better than usual; his words flowing easier, though his matter did not at all strengthen the stream. Lord Anglesey[4] spoke, whom I

[1] *Memoirs*, p. 246.
[2] Lord Scarborough's punctilio is fully discussed in *Egmont*, ii, 32.
[3] Holland House and Ickworth.
[4] Arthur Annesley, 5th Earl of Anglesey, who died in 1737.

had never heard before, and in whom I was extremely disappointed. It was just such a sort of speech as Lord Gower has made a hundred times, and did make again yesterday. Lord Chesterfield spoke much the best on that side, and much the longest. He answered your humble servant, who, though not the best, spoke longest of any body on our side. The Dukes of Newcastle and Argyll, Lord Ilay and Lord Cholmondeley and Lord Scarborough were the only persons, except 3 or 4 words said by Lord Delaware [de la Warr], who debated against the Bill. *For* the Bill, every Opposer spoke that had ever opened his lips in Parliament, except Lord Carteret, which I took for prudence and judgment in him. But the sequel of this relation will show you, as the sequel of the debate showed me, that I was in the wrong, and refined more for him than he did for himself. The division on the Bill was $\frac{78 \text{ Votes}}{22 \text{ Proxies}}$ in all 100, against it. $\frac{49 \text{ V.}}{13 \text{ P.}}$, in all 62, for it. Lord Foley and I were tellers. After this was over, Lord Carteret moved for *an Address to the King to know who advised him to cashier the Duke of Bolton and Lord Viscount Cobham, and of what crimes they were accused.* This Question passed in the negative by the same numbers as the former, except 2, there being one less on each side. The Duke of Argyll on this question abused the Duke of Bolton (who sat facing him on the wool-sack) most excessively. He said, when Lords talked of soldiers being broke without reasons given by the Crown, he could not but fancy they had put it in the plural by mistake ; for though it was true there had been two Colonels broke, he knew but one soldier. It is true, said he, there was a soldier broke to make way for a Colonel who was no soldier ; and that Colonel was now again broke to make way for one that was. Nothing else very material passed in this debate ; and with regard to anything that happened in the House of Commons I am totally ignorant, excepting that there was but one division, and in that the majority for the Court was 100. The occasion of this profound ignorance is that the King and Queen sent for me the moment they came from the play, and I from His Grace of Richmond's where I dined, and kept me with them till 12 a clock. It is now ten in the morning. I am but just up, and shall be so busy all this day, though not about business (for the House does not sit), that I shall not be able to sit down again to write. Adieu.

I send you enclosed *Tit for Tat*,[1] which is suppressed on account of the eight lines on the Q., and reprinted without them. This copy is therefore very precious ; keep it. It was brought me in manuscript by the printer. My answer to him, who offered me not to print it, was that I did not care to take the trouble of reading it ; but if it was very abusive upon me, the best thing he could do would be to print it forthwith : for that he would certainly get a great deal of money, and should have no trouble given him by me, let it be what it would ; since a rotten egg more or less, after so many being thrown, was of no consequence to me at all.

Mr. Spencer is married tonight.

TO HENRY FOX *St. James's, Feb. 25, 1734*[2]

My dear Count,

I am just going to the masquerade, and the post-bell it's last round, so you will easily imagine I can not trouble you long, and should not have troubled you at all, but that I always love to give the first intelligence of extraordinary news to curious people. It makes them pleased with one's letter ; and they are apt to impute that to writing well which is only the effect of writing first. My news is this. Lord Scarborough last Friday quitted his employment of Master of the Horse. His reason for it was that, as he had formerly declared himself to be for making the commissions of the officers for life and had now voted

[1] *Tit for Tat*, described in Hervey's writing on the Holland House copy of the broadsheet as, "An Answer to the Nobleman's Epistle", is printed. Another copy of this early edition, but in a slightly different format, is at the British Museum (11631.K.3). There is also a further copy there in long-hand. *Tit for Tat* is not accepted as from Pope's pen. We have placed the passages referred to by Hervey in Appendix D, but have omitted four unpublishable lines on the last page, as well as a number of other small and unimportant alterations, all cut out of the re-issued sheet.

[2] Holland House.

against it, he determined, lest people should imagine he had voted so, not upon changing his mind, but for fear of losing his employment, to quit that employment: and so demonstrate that conviction of having been in an error was his only motive for his manner of acting on this occasion. He declares he takes nothing ill of the King, that he approves all his measures, wishes his Ministers well, will act in concert with them as much as ever, be as often at Court, assist them as much in Parliament, and act as zealously for the support of the King and the Administration as if he were still in all his employments. His regiment he keeps, and is still of the Cabinet.[1] At this distance plain narratives of facts is all you can expect from me; conjectures, comments and reflections I leave you to make for yourself. For nobody that could be fool enough to send their thoughts upon such things twelve hundred miles and through twelve hundred hands, could have sense enough to have their thoughts upon any subject worth communicating. Adieu.

Ste. says he'll write to you on Saturday. I told him that was not post-day. He said it would go when post-day came as well as if it were writ upon it.

The next letter, a very short one, on April 12,[2] spoke of the writer as, "lately very sick and very much out of humour." He said that he was going to Somersetshire as soon as the King went to Richmond. "We have many and long debates in the House of Lords."

On April 25, he wrote:

The opposition at Shaftesbury makes Ste. fret, but I hope that will have no other ill effect. Hindon is safe. Charles Stanhope, bro. to Lord Chesterfield, is thrown out at Ailesbury, and Lord Limerick at Wendover; so that neither of them will be in Parliament.[3] The Princess Royal set sail yesterday. I went and

[1] Croker mentions that the Great Officers of the Household were usually at that time members of what was called the Cabinet Council.

[2] Both this, and that of April 25 are Holland House.

[3] The General Election was in progress. Stephen had sat for Shaftesbury since 1727. But as there was a doubt there, he also stood for Hindon, in Wilts. At Shaftesbury he failed; but his opponent, Philip Bennett, was unseated on petition, and Fox took the seat in February, 1734/35, giving up Hindon, for which he had been elected. Henry Fox took his place there, and thus at last became a Member of Parliament.

stayed a day with her at Gravesend whilst she was wind-bound. I am in great favour there. Her eldest brother was so afraid of giving her concern, that he took no leave of her—the vicissitudes of this world.

Hervey left for Bath in May, as the next letter on May 11 tells us. The unsettled state of affairs in Europe is also referred to, the direct result of the King of Poland's death as we have already seen. Some of the repercussions in Italy also have already been mentioned. Walpole managed to keep England out of the embroglio, notwithstanding the attempts of King George, backed by Lord Harrington, to take a hand on the Continent. At this moment Stanislaus had taken refuge in Dantzig, where he was besieged by Russian troops. " Madam ", said Walpole to the Queen late in 1734, " there are fifty thousand men slain this year in Europe, and not one Englishman."

TO HENRY FOX *Redlynch, May 11, 1734*[1]

I have not heard from you my dear Count ! time out of mind. Reflect then on my goodness in continuing, notwithstanding such usage, to write to you.

I will not talk to you one word on elections ; I have talked and heard of them till I am sick of the sound ; besides Mrs. Digby has already put you au fait of every particular.

I leave this place to-morrow morning for the Bath, where I have promised to make Princess Emily a visit of two days : and from thence I go to Richmond, not to attend *His* but *Her* Majesty. Whilst I have been here I have taken up my habitation in your new alcove-room, which has a thousand beauties and agrèmens, and nothing unpleasant belonging to it but the colour, of which by your order it was painted. It was a detestable fancy ; and throws a gloom over it as bad as that of your own temper in an easterly wind, after dinner, or in a coach. Au reste Redlynch is extremely improved.

Lady Frances Pierpoint[2] is at last married to Mr. Meadows.

[1] Holland House.

[2] Lady Frances Pierrepont was the 2nd Duke of Kingston's sister. She married Philip Meadows. Their son was created Earl Manvers. Lady Frances's sister was Lady Mary Wortley Montague.

He is welcome to her for me. She has a sly, and at the same time a determined look, that would have made me dislike her more for a wife than any woman I know.

The Duke of Dorset[1] is come back from Ireland. What they will do with him God knows; for the Duke of Richmond, I believe, will, and I am sure ought to be, Master of the Horse. There is a thousand embarras and tracasseries about the Kentish election. Lord Catherlough,[2] who has acted very oddly in several things this year, is playing the devil there, roars against the Duke of Dorset, and does all he can against Lord Middlesex, and his best to boulverser tout dans ce quartier.

People talk, conjecture and speculate much on the French fleet.[3] That it was never designed for the relief of the imprisoned, persecuted Stanislaus and the miserable bombarded Dantzicans, is pretty evident; but what it was design'd for is more obscure.

Most of the Princes of Europe seem to me to be run mad. France s'épuise, as I am told, and for what? The King of Sardinia is weaving fetters for himself; the Queen of Spain is turning Heaven and Hell for the Prince of Asturias, and rejecting the most advantageous proposition for Don Carlos that ever was or ever will be made to her. The Emperor is huffing and bullying everybody at Vienna, and banged and buffetted in effigy in every part of the world; whilst the Elector of Saxony, like a fool, entered into a quarrel when he should have kept out of it, and like a coward drew himself out of it when he should have prosecuted it. Voilà bien des politiques.

Lord Hinton[4] is here with us, who diverts Mrs. Digby and me prodigiously. There is a young Shaftesbury Captain, Seymour, here too; mais il est de cette espèce de sottise qui nous ennuit à mourir. He made the pen I am writing with, so perhaps

[1] *See ante*, p. 67. Lord Scarborough was offered the Lord-Lieutenancy in 1735, in succession to Dorset, but he declined the post. Stephen Fox had been offered the post of Secretary under him and had accepted, but was disappointed. Dorset therefore returned to Ireland until 1737.

[2] John Fane, younger son of Vere, Earl of Westmoreland (d. 1762). Created an Irish Baron in October 1733.

[3] The *Memoirs* speak of a fleet of about 90 sail lying in the Channel.

[4] Lord Poulett's eldest son and a peer. (*See ante*, p. 160 *n.*)

he may tire you as much by proxy, as he does us in person. Adieu. When do you come over?

The election furore had come to an end before the next letter to Henry Fox, on June 9. The results had proved satisfactory to Sir Robert, though his majority in the Commons was slightly decreased. The outstanding success of the Court was the manipulation of the election of Scottish peers, which was entirely due to Lord Ilay. The Queen had a special dislike to both him and his brother, the Duke of Argyll, whom he succeeded in the Dukedom in 1743, having received his Earldom of Ilay in 1706. But such was his triumph on this occasion, that the Queen's views were considerably moderated; though he could never eradicate a long-standing resentment against him for his earlier support of Lady Suffolk. We shall hear more of this trial of strength in the Lords.

TO HENRY FOX *Richmond Lodge, June 9, 1734*[1]

. . . I have been here this three weeks, which is ever since I came from Redlynch. Mrs. Clayton invited me to the house the Queen gave her at Kew, but she going into waiting last week, I decamped, went to London, and designed to return hither no more. But before I had been in town six hours, I received by a messenger a letter, dictated by the King and written by a page, to command me to return immediately to stay here as long as he did, and to tell me he had ordered a house to be taken for me and one of his coaches to attend me. These are great honours; the Queen has given me another fine snuff-box, and I am with him or her or both all day long. They furnish themselves so much to the conversation, that it never languishes nor tires one; and I never saw them in better health, humour, or spirits in my life. There is something I long to tell you, but I dare not. We all remove tomorrow to Kensington. They say the Parliament is to sit in October. We like it in it's cradle extremely, and hope it will prove a very good child. If it is as like it's father that went before, when it is grown up, as it seems to be now it is in it's swaddling clothes, it is all we desire.

The express that brought the names of the Election for the 16 Scotch Peers being over arrived last night. My Lord Ilay has carried all before him. The highest of our side was 60, of

[1] Holland House.

their's 25 : the lowest of ours 54. The 7 that are left out of the former 16 are, Montrose, Marchmont, Tweeddale, Stair, Haddington, Rothes, Buchan. Their successors are Bocleugh [*sic*], Portmore, Findlater, Balcarres, Cathcart, Sutherland and Leven. The Dukes of Queensberry and Hamilton both stood. Were you not surprised to hear of Sir William Windham being married to Lady Blandford, or rather of her being married to him.[1] Lady Bolingbroke made the match. How she prevailed with the bride, God knows ; for he is neither young enough to be married for love, nor rich enough to be married for interest. He has but an eye and a half . . .

There are no new Peers to be made ; and if I can guess at the way of thinking of those where the power of creation lies, it is one that will be long dormant and very sparingly used. Our strength now in the House of Lords will leave the natural reluctance to the exercise of that power undisturbed.

I say nothing to you of Foreign affairs. You are as much au fait of all those transactions as I am. Horace is returned from Holland ; he laughs as loud, but not so heartily, as before he went. You know the Prince of Orange is going to the Rhine in a fortnight. Whilst he is there, the Princess Royal will be here. Adieu. I have left the King at church ; and am afraid Maddocks knows how to make his court too well to let his sermon allow me to write longer.

TO STEPHEN FOX *Kensington, August 10, 1734*[2]

Dear Ste. I am extreme full of business to day, having a long letter and of no small consequence, to write by order of my great friend and Patroness. But no business can ever make me neglect what you desire, or prevent my finding time to do any thing that you say would give you a moment's pleasure ; for absent or present I love you most unfeignedly, and uninterruptedly.

[1] Maria Catherina de Jong, Marchioness of Blandford, and widow of Henrietta, Duchess of Marlborough's son. Sir William Wyndham (1687–1740) was a friend of Lord Bolingbroke. Lord Perceval wrote that she had made Lord Blandford a good wife, though somewhat older than him ; but was left very badly off.

[2] Melbury.

In the first place, I must tell you I have executed all your's and my friend Winnington's commissions. I have given the plan to Bridgman,[1] sent the warrant to Nanny, and wrote about the mole-hill engine to Ickworth. Employ me often in things more material, when my good fortune will enable me to be of service to you in such, and in trifles when it will not.

The weather was so bad that the King did not hunt to day. I hope it will be no impediment to your sport; and if it is so very convenient as to keep us at home at Kensington, and to suffer you to go out at Maddington, the putting a stop to what plagues me and none to what recreates you, is all I can wish: and more than I can reasonably or frequently expect from it. The Queen has bought me the prettiest and the agreeablest new horse you ever saw.[2] He has infinite spirit, and never makes a false step—two qualities that rarely go together. And being, what the grooms call vicious without any other fault, Montesquieu might properly say of him, what he so improperly says of Cæsar;[3] and what you and Winnington would not give up for no other reason than because I condemned it.

I can not conclude my letter without letting you know that the King yesterday made me a present of a thousand pounds a year, and said so many obliging things to me in his Closet when he did it, that I should be in as much confusion and as much ashamed to repeat them, as I was to hear them. Praises one is

[1] Charles Bridgeman (d. 1738), gardener to George I and II. He laid out the Kensington Palace grounds, and many other royal gardens.

[2] Hervey wrote in the *Memoirs* in 1733: "Wednesdays and Saturdays which were the King's days for hunting, he had her [the Queen] to himself for four or five hours, Her Majesty always hunting in a chaise, and as she neither saw nor cared to see much of the chase, she had undertaken to mount Lord Hervey the whole summer (who loved hunting as little as she did), so that he might ride constantly by the side of her chaise, and entertain her whilst other people were entertaining themselves with hearing dogs bark and seeing crowds gallop." (*Memoirs*, p. 221.)

[3] In his *Considérations sur les causes de la Grandeur et la Décadence des Romains*. The passage to which Hervey seems to refer (ii, 281) runs as follows: "On parle beaucoup de la fortune de César; mais cet homme extraordinaire avait tant de grandes qualités, sans pas un défaut, quoi qu'il eût bien des vices, qu'il eût été bien difficile que, quelque armée qu'il eût commandée, il n'eût été vainqueur; et qu'en quelque republique qu'il fût, il ne l'eût gouvernée." (*Compare* p. 287.)

conscious one does not deserve, puts one almost as much out of countenance as reproaches that one does.

I have a mind to direct this letter, as one does a note to one's goldsmith, to you and Company. But you know so well what you may show; and have such an unlimited discretionary power always lodged in you to make what use you please of my letters, that such a particular authority on this occasion is unnecessary. Adieu. I am to be this afternoon with Carestini in the Princess Royal's apartment. I told him that he had in half an hour made Mr. Winnington, who had all his life been an atheist to the power of music, a bigot to it.

TO HENRY FOX *Kensington, August 15, 1734*[1]

I own, my dear Count, it is a great while since I wrote last. But I have had a great deal of business, been in many little distresses, and execrably out of humour. In this situation, what could I do?—my time and my thoughts taken up, and during the little relaxation I had in either, not daring to tell you what engrossed them. For you must know I am grown more cautious than ever about letters, and never send anything even in an anonymous manuscript that I would not print with my name. What pleasure then can I have in writing to you just in the same style that I would speak to Grantham? Or how can you in that case read *me* with more pleasure than I hear or talk to *him*? You told me in your last I took too much snuff. When I tell you the Queen has given me a very pretty horse, and that I hunt twice a week by the side of her chaise, you will say perhaps I ride too much. But I must tell you too that last week the King ordered a thousand pounds a year to be added to my salary: but told Sir Rob. Walpole he would not have it put on the Establishment, because he meant to give that to Lord Hervey which he had not given to his predecessor, and would not give to his successor. When I went to His Majesty to thank him for this favour, he was so gracious and so kind that he confirmed by another instance what I have often said of him, which is that, as nobody can disoblige more formidably, so nobody can oblige more agreeably.

[1] Holland House.

The Bishop of Winchester is dead. Hoadly I believe will succeed him, and Sherlock, Hoadly. The Archbishop of York has had one foot in the grave, but chose rather to pull it out again than to let the other follow. The other Archbishop still remains Prince Prettyman with regard to that nasty journey which we must all take: and the Bishopric of Gloucester is still dormant.

The opponents threaten to make a great fracas next winter in Parliament upon the election of the Scotch peers. But as there must always be some topic given out for the subalterns of a faction to clamour upon, so I believe this text is only preached from till some other is found, and that, like the Debt of the Navy last year, it will be discussed in Coffee houses and pamphlets, and never debated in Parliament.

Another thing of much more consequence has been talked of for the deliberation of Parliament next winter, and several steps both privately and publicly taken to prepare the way for it.[1] But this is a subject I can not explain or expatiate upon; nor is it enough a secret for you not to know what I mean, though it is too delicate to admit of a farther disquisition. Ld. Ches[terfield] is said to have laid the corner stone of the building, whilst Mr. Dodington contents himself with the care of the offices and the attic, when the other has had the sole direction of the principal story. Adieu, my dear Count. If I could write to you with the same safety that I flatter myself I can speak to you, my pen would be as flippant in your absence as you always find my tongue in your presence. . . .

Have you read Montesquieu's book upon the Roman Government? I like it; though he has three faults that I hate. He is sometimes obscure, sometimes contradicts himself, and sometimes, in order to say things which no body ever said before him, says things which no body will ever say after him.

TO STEPHEN FOX *Kensington, August 16, 1734*[2]

. . . Since I wrote this letter I received your's, and return you a thousand thanks for the kind part you always take in every thing

[1] No doubt the Prince of Wales's affairs.

[2] Melbury.

that relates to my pleasure, interest or character : for I think the last as much concerned in this as the other two. I know not what I said in my last letter, but I meant to say there was nothing in it you might not show to any body. Nor dare I, indeed, ever write otherwise, even to you ; for such odd things have come round to me again that I am sure were never circulated by those to whom they were written, that I could never be easy if I ever sent upon paper any thing I would not send to the press with my name to it. There is nothing improves so fast in people in power as curiosity and suspicion, except the means of indulging those qualities ; and they keep pace with them, till their suspicion and intelligence grow almost universal. But of the King's favour to me, I am so far from making any secret, that there is no body I know enough to speak to, to whom I do not tell it. You insist upon knowing what the King said to him [? me] ; and for that reason I hope you will impute my telling it not to my vanity but to my obedience. He said he knew the affection with which I served him, and every body knew my abilities to serve him : and assured me that he should be as ready on any future occasion to do any thing to please me, as he was glad to oblige me upon this. I told him I was extremely sensible of all his goodness to me ; but that it was so easy for any body to be grateful in words, that I begged he would measure my gratitude only by my actions ; and whenever they fell short of my power to serve him, to withdraw that favour to which I pretended no other merit than my assiduity and my affection. A great many more handsome, proper and kind things pass'd between us, but I perceive they do not look so well as they sounded, and so I shall cut my narrative short. Adieu.

TO HENRY FOX *Kensington, September 1st, 1734* [1]

I received the verses, my dear Count, the day after my last letter to you, and think them without the least flattery extremely pretty and perfectly classical. As to asking Mr. Hammond's [2]

[1] Holland House.

[2] *See ante*, p. 161. He was a member of the Prince of Wales's suite, and therefore had been alienated from Hervey.

opinion of them, it must be by letter if I do ; for he has never been near me these six months. Not that our friendship dies any violent death. It was a chronical case. It begun to languish in the autumn, continued weak all winter, and is now in the very last stage of a consumption. I believe I may say of him, as Anthony does of Dolabella, " He was once my friend " ; *but time and other views have bound him fast to Chesterfield.*

Our Court will soon be extremely thinned, by so many people belonging to it repairing to the Bath. Princess Emily set out this morning. The Duke of Grafton,[1] who eats an ox a day, is going there, to enable himself to eat two. Lord Grantham[2] goes to cure himself of what he calls vapours, which are in reality nothing but the common effects of gluttony and idleness, of a good stomach and a bad head, that is stupidity and ennui. For poor Princess E——, the hot spring that would cure her might be found nearer than Bath. . . .

I told Granny very gravely that, as the Bath waters were never reckoned good for the head, and that as I took his chief

[1] Charles, 2nd Duke (1680–1757), Lord Chamberlain. He was reputed to be intimately connected with Princess Emily, who was also courted by the Duke of Newcastle.

Court and Society, by 7th Duke of Manchester (ii, 334), quotes from lines on him from Hervey's pen :—

So your friends, booby Grafton, I'll e'en let you keep,
Awake he can't hurt, and he's still half asleep ;
Nor ever was dangerous, but to womankind,
And his body's as impotent now as his mind.

Hervey wrote of the Princess (*Memoirs*, p. 275) : " She had much the least sense of the whole family (except her brother), but had for two years much the prettiest person. She was lively, false, and a great liar : did many ill offices to people and no good ones : and for want of prudence said almost as many shocking things to their faces as for want of a good nature or truth she said disagreeable ones to their backs. . . ."

[2] Lord Grantham, Lord Chamberlain to the Queen. (*See ante*, p. 169.) Elsewhere Lord Hervey wrote, " I have received your Grantham packet, and delivered that part of it which was ostensible into his hand, to be explained by his own *Reader*, concluding he has such an officer in the family, though not at the head of it. For the future, I join with you in desiring we may never name him." For his difficulty in writing an official letter, *see Memoirs*, p. 823. " Lord Hervey said that as this was the first example, and he believed would be the last, of Grantham's literary correspondence, that ever would appear in history and be transmitted to posterity, it would be a pity not to have it perfect."

complaint to be there, I wondered at his trying them. He has made noises with his mouth in several people's ears, and to very little purpose, about the request he made to you with regard to Wales. All that he can make anybody understand about it is, "dat as de shilling is more as de ninepence, Mayster, how you call my Ld. Hervey's friend is vary unreasonable". I have set it in a clear light to everybody here, have shown the substance of his demand as unreasonable as it really is, and described his manner of making it as ridiculous as I could; but nothing can come up to the original. Adieu, my dear Count.

TO STEPHEN FOX *Kensington, October 3, 1734*[1]

The head-ache I complain'd of in my last, has continued upon me till this afternoon; but I hunted yesterday notwithstanding, partly medicinally, partly politically: hoping the exercise would do me good, and to follow Madame Barnwell's advice to her daughter of—"Faites bien votre cour." I hope it answered the last end better than it did the first; for I was so ill after it, that at my return I was forced to go immediately to bed, and after lying sleepless till five o'clock in the morning, I took one of Ward's pills, which has removed all pain. Mais je trouve les flots, apres la tempête, encore bien agités. . . .

Not to trouble you longer with telling you what you are as well acquainted with as I am, I shall hasten to answer the other parts of your letter. The Duke of Richmond has been in England about a week, and returns this next to Holland, to fetch his Duchess, who is now past the danger of miscarrying, but not at all well in other respects. She is extremely vapour'd and, it is fear'd, inclining to a dropsy. His Grace carry'd with him from France to Holland, and brought from Holland hither, one Monsieur de Feyie,[2] a sensible, well-behaved man, a great favorite of Monsieur le Duc's, a virtuoso, a mechanic, and a Botonic-Royal-Society [*sic*] man. I dined with his Grace on Monday at Chelsea. The master of the house[3] was a little absent, which

[1] Melbury.

[2] This may be Charles de la Faye (d. 1762), F.R.S. 1725, one of the clerks of the Signet office. On the other hand, the context seems to point to a foreigner.

[3] Sir Robert Walpole.

he seldom is ; and the Duke of Richmond was cheerful and entertaining which he always is. The Duke of Newcastle talk'd without thinking ; and Lord Lonsdale [1] thought without talking, as usual. Lord Albemarle was well-bred, and talk'd neither more nor less than came to his share. Sir Charles Wager say'd two or three good things, with maritime roughness and Spartan brevity. And this was all our company.

With regard to the last affair in Italy, both sides call themselves victors ; and I believe the truth is they are both losers.[2] Koningsegg is not kill'd. P. Lewis of Wirtemberg is. It is impossible for me to speak by letter my sentiments on the present state of affairs, but I write every day *for* you, though not *to* you. Adieu.

I wish people who read history in search of truth, were to hear Kinski and Loos [3] talk on our side upon these facts, and Montijo and Chavigny on the other : that they were to read the different accounts of the most recent, and what one should imagine the most known occurrences ; and when they see how well the letters coming by Germany or France from Italy tally with each other, the ease with which one comes at truth, even in one's own times, must certainly make those history-bigots well satisfied with the exactness it must ever come to one by tradition.

A few days later another letter to Henry Fox on October 7. The reference to the Princess Royal in this letter, seemingly so simple, though coarsely worded, has significance ; but the position is fully set out in the *Memoirs* (pp. 367–72). Shortly, when the Prince of Orange went to the Rhine to visit the armies, the Princess Royal returned to England, and there for the first time announced that she was pregnant, secretly fearing that she might not be allowed to leave Holland, and hoping that she would be allowed to have her baby in England. But this was not to be ; though she, the Queen and everyone else, were dissolved in tears on every occasion when her departure

[1] Henry, 3rd Viscount Lonsdale (d. unm. 1752), Lord Privy Seal 1733–5. Hervey wrote in the *Memoirs*, " He was certainly an honest and a sensible man, but his integrity inclined him now and then to being whimsical, and his understanding to be rather too disputative."

[2] The battle of Guastalla. Köningsegg had shortly before taken over the command of the Imperial Army. P. Lewis of Würtemburg was a relation of Queen Caroline.

[3] Baron Loos, the Prussian Envoy.

was mooted. Horatio Walpole, the British Envoy to Holland, rightly in this case (but from Hervey's account of him surely a most tactless diplomat), insisted that she must return home for the great event; although he did not improve his position in Court circles, by so doing. Her return to London from Colchester, related in the next letter, although received with delight by her family, was a bad slip on her part; for the Prince had taken special steps to arrange for his arrival to time to meet her at Helvoetsluys, had she gone straight on.

TO HENRY FOX *St. James's, October 7, 1734*[1]

If the climate you are in has cured you (as you brag) of suspicion, I have a reason more than I had, and one stronger than all the rest, to be satisfied with your absence; since it has removed the only thing I wish alter'd in one who had before good qualities enough to make even that supportable. But if you only brag, or if the cause taken away the effect should cease, and upon your return I should find you either uncured or relapsed, you have done very injudiciously to lay yourself such a foundation for disappointment; since the knowledge of mankind should speculatively have taught you, as the knowledge of Courts has practically every day taught me, that the failing to possess one thing one expects, overturns the merits of many things that ought to oblige, & are often more than one deserves.

As to my communicative conduct when I see you, you need have no apprehension of it's being as open as you can desire. For as my prudence is continually stopping up some little rivulet of confidence, so you may be sure the channel where I permit the main stream to flow, will of course be swell'd; and when you return to open the sluice, you have more reason to fear it's rapidity should overwhelm you than that there will be any want of water, draw what you please.

I know not how coolly I express'd myself on the B. of Winchester's[2] promotion, but I neither felt nor acted coolly whilst

[1] Holland House.

[2] Benjamin Hoadly (1676–1761), whom we have met before as Bishop of Salisbury, a friend and correspondent of Hervey. The whole story is told in *Memoirs*, p. 395 etc. It would appear that it was largely owing to Hervey's activities that Hoadly obtained the fulfilment of a promise made many years before. Neither the King nor Queen were favourable to the Bishop; but his claims were strongly supported by Walpole.

A. Pond, pinxit

HENRY FOX, 1st LORD HOLLAND (pastel) 1737

it was in *dispute*. I know that word surprises you, but I did not use it at random, though the story is too long for a letter.

As to the two affairs that are to come into Parliament, those who ought to know better than me, those who are better informed of facts & are much better able to make judgments upon these facts, think the Scotch affair will come under consideration & the Welsh one not. I think just the reverse, at least that the one will be much stronger push'd, when the time for pushing comes; though the other is now the only topic of conversation. Dodington has certainly managed his matters so ill, that he is in disgrace on both sides. Two stools never make a wider gap for a poor broken rump than upon this occasion. He has indeed followed his nose, for he has fallen quite flat.[1]

You have by this time read Montesquieu's book. I expect every day a long letter with your remarks upon it. It has faults & beauties enough to bear folios of criticism.

How the devil can you read philosophy? No body ever wrote upon the subject that was not mad himself, or did not do all he could to make other people so. The sum total of all the philosophers' doctrine is, to persuade you, you are a very miserable being: that few pleasures are in your power: that those which are, you should forego: and because you cannot possess every thing you wish, that therefore you should enjoy nothing you possess. There is one way of arguing all philosophers have, which is such a satire upon one's good nature, that I can not bear such an indirect manner of being told, "Sr, you are the most malevolent being in the Creation," which is comforting you in your own miserable circumstances by bidding you reflect on the much more miserable lot of some other poor creatures. As if it would comfort me for breaking my leg that my companion had broke his neck; and that I should be less solicitous to have my leg set again, because his neck could not. In short, philoso-

[1] Dodington's position in the Prince of Wales's household was disclosed to Hervey by Miss Vane, to whom he had become reconciled, and with whom he was secretly on the same intimate terms as before she had left him for the Prince. Indeed Hervey was able to warn Sir Robert in the early summer that Dodington had quite lost caste. He was shortly afterwards supplanted in the Prince's favour by George Lyttelton, whom we have seen as a writer of verse (*see ante*, p. 161).

phers provoke me more than parsons. For parsons talk nonsense because they are paid for it, & many of them have the grace to be ashamed of it. But philosophers talk nonsense, because they hope to be admired for it, & are fools enough to be proud of it.

I hope I have followed your advice, or more properly and politely speaking obeyed your orders, en laissant courir ma plume sufficiently. One thing that has contributed to my obedience to you is my being a good husband, and coming from Kensington to this place to nurse Lady Hervey, who miscarried last night. Her aunt is now with her; & rather than let her inflict herself upon me, I chose to force my self on you.

The Princess Royal is to go to Holland next week. Her big belly grows very prominent.

TO HENRY FOX *St. James's, November 2, 1734* [1]

I intended writing to you, my dear Count, these ten days, but in the hurry of removing to London, the bustle of the Birth-day, & being perpetually with the Queen, who has been ill enough to keep her room these three days, I have not had one hour of leisure. The Queen this morning is much better, notwithstanding the disorder occasioned by her concern for parting with the Princess Royal, whom I put into her coach drowned in tears about an hour ago. She is to lie this night at Colchester, and, if the wind is fair, which is now directly contrary, she is to embark tomorrow-noon at Harwich for Holland.

The Prince of Orange is already at the Hague expecting her. Ten days ago she was got as far as Colchester, & returned to Kensington the next day, upon meeting letters that told her the Prince of Orange could not be in Holland by some few days so soon as he had designed.

Ld Falmouth [2] died of an apoplexy last week, which is of no great consequence to any body but his ugly, wrong-headed son. I dined yesterday at the D. of Richmond's with Ld Harcourt,[3]

[1] Holland House.

[2] Hugh Boscawen, 1st Viscount (1680–1734). His son, Hugh (1706–82), M.P. for Truro, was opposed to Sir Robert.

[3] Simon, 2nd Viscount (1714–77).

who is just of age, and, as the newspapers say, "just return'd from his travels". He is a pretty figure, well-bred, I believe sensible, & they say admirably well-disposed to the Government & the Administration. This being the time of the Norfolk Congress, the Palace & town are both thin. No place is full but the Opera; and Farinelli [1] is so universally liked, that the crowds there are immense. By way of public spectacles this winter, there are no less than two Italian Operas, one French play house, and three English ones. Heidegger has computed the expense of these shows, and proves in black & white that the undertakers must receive seventy-six thousand odd hundred pounds to bear their charges, before they begin to become gainers.

We have had a fine trial of interest between Montijo and Kinski on St. Charles's day, when each of them made feasts, one for the Emperor, & the other for Don Carlos, & both insisted on being attended by all their acquaintance; but no body caring to divide themselves like Solomon's child, you know that was impossible. Sr Robt Walpole promised Kinski, but had the gout, & could not go. The D. of Newcastle was terribly embarrassed; Spain is in his province,[2] & Vienna at his heart. So his Grace, like the philosopher's ass between the two bundles of hay, attracted by both, went to neither; and thus our English Cicero, retiring to his Tusculum at Claremont, shut himself from public care, was lost to the world, & enjoyed in private the equally instructive & agreeable converse of his Atticus, Mr. Tyrrel.

The King gave colours in the Guards last week to Ld Dursley, Ld Ossulston & Ld Charles Fitzroy. I suppose your sister has wrote you word of Ld Chesterfield having had the weakness at Bath to return to gaming, & the same success at it as usual.

You see the Pss Royal is to lie in Holland, though you would not believe it. That her sister was to lie in any where by the D. of H., nobody ever thought of but the journalists. Ld King [3] is going to marry a sister of Ld Aylesford's, & is to be against us. He was last spring to have been married to a daughter of Sr

[1] Carlo Broschi (1705–82), the famous singer known as Farinelli. He made his first appearance late in October, and at once put Carestini in the shade.

[2] As Secretary of State for the Southern Department.

[3] John, 2nd Baron (1706–40), son of the Lord Chancellor.

William Wyndham's, who died of the small pox whilst the writings were drawing. Lady Blandford, they say, is with child ; & the Duchess of Marlborough is reported too to be five months gone of that desirable pregnancy, that every body is so proud of at first & so peevish with at last. But Mrs. Spencer [1] says this report is entirely without foundation ; & at the same time flirts her fan over her own great belly, with an air of sufficiency & satisfaction, as if she had obtained a grant from Heaven of the monopoly of making children for the Marlborough family, & that no body could breed where she came, any more than they can speak.

Ld Cardigan [2] is come to town, thoroughly changed, as fame reports, in his taste, his politics & his person. As to the last, I can answer for it myself, for instead of being, as formerly, a good likeness of his handsome mother, he is now a bad likeness of his ugly father. But whether he is as fond of his wife, and as tired of his mistress, and as out of humour with the Opposition and attach'd to the Court, as is currently talk'd of, is what I can only repeat without being able to affirm. Voilà une longue Gazette, qui sent la ruelle d'une vieille femme, dont je m'ennuie moi-même, et dont vous vous ennuyerez, j'ai peur, aussi, mème à Nice. Adieu.

Several allusions in Hervey's letter to Henry, at Nice, of December 9, require explanation. Lady Suffolk's final retirement from the Court, after a reign of some twenty years, was there announced. It is discussed at some length in the *Memoirs* (pp. 380–5). She seems to have literally faded away from the Palace, resigning her office of Mistress of the Robes in a long private interview with the Queen, but without having taken leave of the King at all. Hervey thus summed up the situation :

" The true reasons of her disgrace were, the King's being thoroughly tired of her : her constant opposition to all his measures : her wearying him with her perpetual contradiction : her intimacy with Mr. Pope, who had published several Satires with his name to them, in which the King and all his family were rather more than obliquely sneered at : the acquaintance she was known to have with many of the

[1] Wife of John Spencer, the Duke of Marlborough's younger brother. (*See ante*, p. 187.)

[2] George Brudenell, 4th Earl (1712–90). He married Mary Montagu, granddaughter of John, Duke of Marlborough, and was created Duke of Montagu in 1766.

opposing party, and the correspondence she was suspected to have with many more of them. . . ."

It was not long, however, before she surprised the world by the announcement of her marriage with George Berkeley, son of the 1st Earl of Berkeley, who was much younger than herself, and had neither health nor any very special attraction to commend him.

Another item of interest in the letter, is the removal of Bubb Dodington from the Prince of Wales's counsels. But Hervey is so vitriolic against both men, that he no doubt makes the worst of the episode, to which we have already referred, and to the medium by which he obtained early information of what was afoot. (*Memoirs*, p. 385 etc.)

TO HENRY FOX *St. James's, Dec. 9, 1734* [1]

My dear Count,

. . . Lady Suffolk's having quitted the Court I dare say surprised you. I can not talk on the subject. Few Court occurrences will bear a narrative, but fewer still admit of a comment.

As to the downfall of Mr. D.,[2] the particulars of which you are so curious to hear, as well as the confirmation of the fact, I can only tell you with regard to the last there is not room to lodge a doubt. With regard to the first, the reasons are variously reported ; that his Patron has planted many trees before his house, in order to prevent D.'s seeing more of what passes in his garden than he knows of what's doing in his cabinet, the whole town is acquainted with, by going to peruse the plantation, and having ocular proof, moyennant un shilling au jardinier. That every lock in the P.'s house to which D. had a key is chang'd, nobody knows, but the 70 or 80 bosom-friends to whom *the Changer* told it, and the 70 or 80 bosom friends of each of those. The disgracié is in the country, has been so some time, and it is said (but I do not believe it) will continue there all winter.

Mrs. Spencer was yesterday brought to bed of a son ; and the Dss of Marlborough is certainly with child. Poor Lady M.

[1] Holland House.

[2] Mr. Dodington losing the favour of the Prince of Wales. The trees in the garden of Carlton House hid his windows. [Note in Horace, Earl of Orford's writing.] Dodington's garden adjoined the Prince's.

Wortley is dying. I am very sorry; I shall hear her talk no more, but I shall see her posthumous works.[1]

I pass more hours than ever with a great man, who (as Monsieur Masson says) is *not* like that Ennius described by Horace, qui, nunquam nisi potus ad *arma* prosiluit dicenda.[2]

As to the Parlt, I can tell you nothing about it; any more than that the Opposition look elate, talk big, and menace in general, without telling where, or whom, or how, they will attack.

I hope you do not brag, when you say you have got rid of your suspicion, your gloom, your spleen, and all the other concomitants of a foggy day and a beef diet. Take care you do not relapse, and that you come not back to England as you went from it, *Homo basilicus*; which, if you will consult Littleton's Dictionary, you will find signifies a *surly Count.*

Ste. is in the country ennuyé, and by his own account of himself *dull.* Adieu. On m'appelle.

In the letter of December 18 to Henry Fox, we find an exceedingly long dissertation on Montesquieu's book already alluded to, in answer to a critical exposition from his correspondent. This is omitted.

TO HENRY FOX *St. James's, December 18, 1734*[3]

. . . I like most of your reflections on Montesquieu's book extremely, but when you say you found no obscurity in him, I think you compliment your own apprehension more than his perspicuity. At least for my own sake I am determined to think so, since there are many things in him too dark for me to discover; and therefore I will believe you understand him much quicker than most other people, and not that I understand him much slower. . . .

With the quantity I have written, and the number of books I have been forced to look over whilst I have been writing, I find I have sat up about three hours beyond my usual time. Therefore reserving a thousand things more that I have to say

[1] Lady Mary Wortley-Montagu lived till 1762, nearly twenty years after Hervey's death, so the latter was disappointed!

[2] Horace, *Ep.* 19.

[3] Holland House and Ickworth.

to another opportunity, I shall release myself and you, and go to bed—but before I go I must tell you I am so pleased with all you say of Lord B., and your remarks on the *Craftsman*, that if ever I write against the first and comment on the last, I will do by you as Montesquieu does by Rollin, use your words and sink your name.

Rundle[1] is put by. Benson, Master of Bennet Coll. in Camb. is Bishop of Gloucester; and Secker, B. of Bristol. The Duke of Richmond is Duke of Aubigny. He gets about 8000£ in all by old Portsmouth's death.[2] How old she was I know not, and am astonished you care to know. He is not yet Master of the Horse. Lord Chesterfield lost a good deal at Bath; but says to everybody he lost nothing, and to the Dss of Kendal that he did not play. I know no news of your brother, but that he come to town yesterday, and that I dined with him and Nanny. Your question about my Lord Cardigan I cannot answer. 'Tis a thousand a clock, and I no more sleepy than if I was but just up. I could write all night long, if I did not fear making you tired and myself sick.

[1] Thomas Rundle (1688?–1743) was appointed Bishop of Derry in 1735. He had been suggested for the see of Gloucester; but owing to a contest of strength between Gibson, Bishop of London, and Lord Chancellor Talbot, who was backing Rundle, his chaplain and former tutor, in which neither would give way, Walpole thought it wiser to compromise, and to give the latter the Irish Bishopric. Rundle was a friend of Whiston, the lecturer, who was said to favour Arianism. (*Memoirs*, pp. 399–405.)

[2] Louise de Kéroualle, Duchess of Portsmouth, Charles II's mistress, died in Paris on November 14, 1734, at the age of 89. (*A Duke and his Friends*, i, 291.) She was also Duchesse d'Aubigny, the property where she lived in France: and to that the Duke of Richmond, her grandson, succeeded with the title.

CHAPTER IX

1735

In the New Year, 1735, we find among the Ickworth copies a letter purporting to be written by Mrs. Digby to her brother Henry on January 13. From the style, however, it was clearly written by Lord Hervey.

WRITTEN FOR MRS. DIGBY TO HENRY FOX AT NICE

Clarges Street, January 13th, 1735[1]

. . . Now for my news. The Duke of Richmond is at last declared Master of the Horse, and Lord Pembroke[2] Groom of the Stole, each of them with a salary of £3,000 a year. Lord Godolphin upon his resignation, instead of a salary of £5,000, has a pension of three ; and to make up this reduction has a Peerage in reversion after his death given to his cousin Godolphin. It is said that the Duke of Portland, upon a negotiation undertaken in his name by the Duke of Kent, had the employment of Lord of the Bedchamber, in the room of the D. of Richmond, offered to him ; and that his answer from Bulstrode (where this offer was sent) was, that the Duke of Kent had bartered for him without authority, that he was very well affected to the Government, wished the Administration well, and approved of all their measures, and was very thankful for the honour the King intended him : but that as to the employment, the attendance was not convenient for him, and the salary he did not want. Lord Hervey, who was with me yesterday, says there is not one word of truth in all this story ; but he, you know, is too good a courtier for his word to go for anything upon this occasion. They talk of Ld Harcourt too for the Bedchamber. He is for the Court, I hear ; and people commend him.

I expected when I came to town to hear a great deal about Lady Suffolk ; but they talk of her no more than if she did not

[1] Ickworth.

[2] This was Henry, 9th Earl (1693–1751), son of "old Pem.", whom he succeeded in 1733. He was known as "the Architect Earl". (*See ante*, p. 114, as Lord Herbert.)

exist, or than if she never had existed. One might as well ask questions about Henry II and Fair Rosamond ; it would hardly seem a story more out of date.

The Parliament meets to-morrow. There will be no opposition for the Speaker, and for what I can learn, not much bustle about the Scotch. If so, notwithstanding all the mountains the Opposition have been raising, the plagues of the Administration (like one of Pharaoh's) will be nothing but mice, which these great mountains bring forth.

As for peace and war, I hear little about it, and understand less ; but it is rumoured that the Dutch say nothing but, *No, No, No,* to everything that Horace proposes. Lord Waldegrave and Lord Essex [1] arrived yesterday. Lord Essex, in the infinite leisure of a Foreign Minister (in which character he has had nothing to do, but to eat, sleep, fiddle, and order his Secretaries to transcribe Gazettes) is grown, they say, so fat that he is hardly knowable.

My Lord Chesterfield is Dodington's successor, and Mr. Lyttelton his vice-minister : his Lordship and his proxy live in great harmony and intimacy, and do not only co-operate at the ear of a Prince, but join their labours also, as I am informed, for the press in a work called the *Persian Letters* [2] or *Usbeck at London,* a sequel to Montesquieu, which work is to be published next week. I hope my Lord will succeed better in his politics and his belles-lettres than he has done in his marriage, or he never will be Lord Steward again,[3] nor write anything worth reading. For, as I hear, he is no more likely to get money than children by his wife ; the Duchess of Kendal being as angry with him for his playing at the Bath, as his Countess is for his flirting. Adieu.

Hervey made no mention in the *Memoirs* of the debates on the Address, when Parliament was opened on January 14 ; but these doings are shortly referred to in subsequent letters.

[1] William, 3rd Earl. (*See ante*, p. 39.) He was Envoy to Turin, 1731–7.

[2] *Letters from a Persian in England to a friend at Ispahan.* Montesquieu's work was *Lettres Persanes.*

[3] Lord Perceval (*Egmont*, i, 369) related that when the Duke of Grafton acquainted Chesterfield with the King's demand for his wand (on account of his vote on the Excise question), he replied, " I insist that you tell His Majesty my place and all that I have in the world is at His Majesty's disposal, except my honour."

TO HENRY FOX *Thursday night, 8 o'clock. Jan. 23* [*1735*]

I am just come from the House of Lords, extremely tired as you may imagine from the length of the attendance: but more so from the heaviness of the debate on the Address to be made in answer to the K.'s Speech, which, with the *Craftsman* of Nov. 16 which you desired, I here send you enclosed.

The Address was moved and seconded by the D. of Devonshire and Lord Hinton. Lord Carteret and Lord Chesterfield objected to it, upon the old Shippen-anniversary argument, of not tying the House down by general words to approve everything that had been done, or grant every thing that should be asked. Adieu. Dinner is come; and the moment I have swallowed it, I am ordered to go up stairs. The Address in the House of Cs. is not to be moved till Monday, and then by Hedges and Campbell. The D. of Argyll and Lord Ilay are both so ill, they were not at the House. Sir Robert Walpole is ill too of the gout, and confined.

The next letter, January 24, 1735, is addressed to the Princess of Orange at The Hague, where she had at last arrived safely via Calais and Flanders. Bad weather and illness, feigned or real, made her turn back again to Harwich after her second start; but this time the King and Queen refused to see her, and she was ignominiously forced to pass over London Bridge, on her way to Dover, without any stay in London.

One of the chief topics in the letter is the Scottish Petition, a complicated and troublesome affair, as the writer tells us, for Court and Opposition alike. The dispute went back to the election of Scottish peers after the General Election, when subsequently Lord Ilay was accused of wholesale bribery in carrying the whole sixteen vacancies in the Walpole interest. A Petition from the Scottish peers resulted, but was only lukewarmly supported by the Opposition; indeed Lord Carteret refused to help at all, feeling that he might find himself in an awkward situation. The Duke of Bedford presented the Petition about the middle of February, but it was negatived after prolonged debates in which Lord Hervey took part. His speech is reported *in extenso* in the *Memoirs* (pp. 425, etc.). Hervey and Fox started a correspondence on the subject in Latin, but with this we shall not delay the reader, as the copies of Lord Hervey's letter of February 20, at Holland House and at Ickworth vary considerably; and anyhow the subject is of little importance. It is noteworthy, however, that an excerpt in Horace, Earl of Orford's handwriting, stuck on to the page, reads, " This is the famous epistle which occasioned Pope's hatred of Lord Hervey." It seems impossible, however, to connect this note with the letter in question, and it seems probable that it has been attached to the wrong document.

TO THE PRINCESS ROYAL, AT THE HAGUE

St. James's, January 24th, 1735[1]

. . . I shall now by way of appendix to this manifesto acquaint Your Royal Highness supplementary with what is passing here in the political world without doors; and for the anecdotes of the Palace continue to refer you, Madam, to the mediating power, the Pss Caroline.

We had an excellent Speech yesterday from the Throne; but it is unnecessary to send it, because it is reported here that your R.H. saw it in Holland before we heard in England, and that the reason why we had it not sooner was, that you were not, like David, *the pen of a ready writer.*

There was a debate on the Address, which was excellently moved by his Grace of Devonshire, and seconded by my friend Lord Hinton, whose speech was extremely well composed, though the fatness of his tongue hindered it from being equally well uttered. Lord Carteret declaimed against these two champions, and Lord Chesterfield joked. The D. of Newcastle took upon him to answer them both, but Your R.H^ss. knows the proverb says two heads are better than one. Lord Hardwick spoke incomparably; Lord Str—d and Lord B—st[2] à leur ordinaire: it is difficult for such great genius to improve.

The D. of Argyll and Lord Ilay were both of them sick and absent, as well as several Bishops; notwithstanding which, the majority on our side was so great that the division was 89 against 37.

I am told that the opponents are all broken with one another, and like Alexander's captains, even before their Alexander, Sir Robert, [3]whom they design to succeed, is dead, that they[3] are tearing one another to pieces in dividing a reversion, and

[1] Ickworth.
[2] Strafford and Bathurst.
[3–3] Added in Lord Hervey's writing.

scrambling for acquisition which all of them covet and perhaps none of them will ever possess.

The Scotch opponents rail at the English opponents, and say they have thrust them like the forlorn-hope in the front of a battle; and now they see their poor dupes cut off, are for making their own retreat as fast as they can, leaving the bodies of their fellow soldiers to be torn by dogs and vultures,—without the common humanity of giving their miserable poor carcasses the decent ceremony of an honourable internment or revenging their fall.

On the other hand, the English tell the Scotch that they embarked, it is true, together, and were to run equal risks as far as they could. But if the seat of an English peer in Parliament was held by a different tenure than that of a Scotch peer, the Scotch knew that before they engaged; and the English say they are very sorry they have lost such honest, wise and zealous friends out of the House of Lords, but know not how to help it. They add too that the Scotch Petition is an affair which can come to nothing, when they have so many other points to go upon in which they have the strongest probability of distressing the Court and overturning the Administration. However, the Scotch Petition is to be (they say) presented, though it is likely to be so ill supported.

TO HENRY FOX (AT NICE)

Clarges Street, February 10, 1735[1]

You see I take your advice, for with wisk[2] in the room, I desired to be left out, and a pen and ink to be brought to write to the Count.

Your long letter gave me much pleasure, and I have not only read your remarks on Montesquieu through, but have transcribed all those I approve (which are almost every one of them) into my own book. . . .[3]

I will take care to lay by for you everything, both verse and prose, that comes out this winter.

[1] Holland House and Ickworth. [2] i.e. whist.

[3] Another long notice of Montesquieu's book is here omitted.

They talk still of bringing in the Scotch Petition. The English Opponents are heartily sick of it, knowing there is nothing to be made of it; and yet they know not how to drop it. They talk of addressing the Petition only to the temporal peers, which will be an effectual way of getting rid of entering into the allegations of it, because in that case the Petition so addressed will certainly not be received. I hear Ld. Carteret was much against pushing this thing at all; in the first place, I believe, because the Scotch malcontents having elected Ld. Che[sterfield ?] their General in Chief, his Lordship did not care to fight as a Lieutenant only to that Commander. In the next, as there is no hope of vacating the seats of the present sixteen, his Lordship would not readily, I fancy, come into any measures that should clog the wheels of Government in future Administrations; few successors, how exasperated so ever they may be against the present possessors, caring to hurt the possession, though they might be glad to hurt the person possessed.

30,000 men are voted for the sea-service this year by a majority of 73. I was present at the debate, which was a very long, a very decent and a very good one. Your brother's election comes on to-morrow sen'night.[1] Lady Delaware died last week. Adieu. . . .

. . . Though I begun this letter at Mrs. Digby's on Monday, yet I finished it, at least thus far, this morning (Thursday, 13) at home. I am now going to the House, and will keep my letter open to tell you what we do with the Scotch Petition, that is to come in for certain this day.

The Scotch Petition has been presented this day by the D. of Bedford. It sets forth only in general undue methods and illegal practices for gaining votes, and does not seem to aim at vacating the seats of the sitting 16: but prays leave to lay these facts before the House. It is signed only by 6 Lords, namely, the Dukes of Hamilton, Queensberry, Montrose, and the Earls Stair, Marchmont and Dundonald. It is to be taken into consideration on this day sen'night.

[1] Stephen Fox's petition against Mr. Bennett at Shaftesbury, in which the latter was unseated for corruption.

TO HENRY FOX *St. James's, April 7, 1735* [1]

I can never thank you enough, my dear Count, for the delightful letter I received from you yesterday in Latin. Had I met with it in *Pliny* or *Tully*, to a *Tacitus* or an *Atticus*, I should have been pleased with it. But when I consider'd it as from you to me, I was charmed with it; flattering myself that the sentiments of it were as much the growth of your own heart, as the style and spirit seemed to be the growth of Rome: and of course receiving as much satisfaction in thinking I was not deceived in the one as I did entertainment in finding myself so agreeably deceived in the other. . . .

The Duke of Bedford could not help presenting the Scotch Petition; it being so natural for him, who had last year moved the Questions previous to the Scotch Elections (that were rejected) to take this subsequent step, which was designed to prove the necessity there was of proposing those precautionary measures for the security of a free Election, and the impropriety of having rejected those proposals.

The Duchess of Bedford is very ill, and going to the Bath. She is thought to be in a bad way. . . .

. . . The D. of Richmond is out of town, so I cannot yet make your compliments to him. He is gone to pass the holidays at Ditton as usual with seven or eight schoolboys, who are within ten or twelve years of their grand climacteric.

I will be sure to execute your commission to Winnington. He is at present in Hertfordshire. If Sr W. Y[onge] is made Secretary at War (which I believe there is [2] not much [2] doubt of), the vacancy which that promotion will make in the Treasury, will, it is thought, a little cool a friendship that has long subsisted between one I have just spoken of, and one who could speak for himself and seldom does. Adieu.

I am at present up to the neck in Acts of Parliament relating to the *Sinking Fund*. It is taken this year for the current service, and (as the opponents *have* said in the H. of Commons, and *are* next week to say in the H. of Lords) in breach and violation of public and Parliamentary faith; which I hope is maintainable and demonstrable not to be true. . . .

[1] Holland House. [2–2] In Hervey's writing. Altered from *little*.

. . . Mr. Cook[1] yesterday resigned his Gold-key. Ld Lovel, who dined with me today, knew nothing of it, and abused his brother for an hour together. Mr. Woodhouse[2] being dead of the smallpox, Mordent [*sic*] is to petition against the dead man, and to come in for Norfolk by compromise, to save both parties the expense and fatigue of a new election. Tack these 2 things together. Once more, Adieu. . . .

My Lord Vane is to be married tomorrow to Ld William Hamilton's widow ;[3] and Mr. Bloodworth in a very little time to Lady Louisa Bertie. He, who the malicious say (very unjustly, I believe), is the occasion[4] of this marriage, is going to be married himself. I dare explain no further, if you do not understand me ; but this is an answer to the question you asked in your last letter but one in these words—" How does the other affair, which Ld C—— was likewise at the head of, go on " ? To the question you asked just preceeding this, whether the Dukes of Hamilton & Queensberry have not, by standing candidates as Scotch peers, given up their claim to their English peerages ?—I answer, *No.*

I have taken my leave of you in this letter as often as Anthony does of Dolabella.

Before May 19, when Hervey wrote again, the King had departed for his triennial visit to Hanover. This visit had far-reaching consequences, from the fact that he fell in love with an extremely good-looking married woman, high in Hanoverian society, Madame Walmoden. Consequently his return to England at one time seemed likely to be indefinitely postponed, so passionate was his attachment : the details of which were minutely described to the Queen in his own letters to her, much to her annoyance. Actually he arrived back at the end of October, having faithfully promised his new lady-love to be back in Hanover before May 29, 1736.

[1] Robert Coke, of Langford, brother of Lord Lovel (created Earl of Leicester). Originally Vice-Chamberlain to Queen Anne. He died in 1750.

[2] W. Wodehouse, M.P. for Norfolk. He was succeeded in the representation by his brother Armine, who died three years later.

[3] Lady William Hamilton, *née* Hewes, married William, 2nd Viscount Vane, on May 19, 1735.

[4] " The occasion " : the Prince of Wales, who was supposed to have liked Lady Louisa Bertie. [Note by Horace, Earl of Orford.] The Prince married in 1736.

TO HENRY FOX *Kew, May 19, 1735*[1]

At my return to London last Saturday from Gravesend, I found a letter from you after a silence of two months; and for the sake of the one, I forbear chiding you for the other.

The King set sail about nine in the morning; and during the interregnum, that is, till the news comes of his being landed in Holland, the Queen is retired to this place. As soon as that news comes, she is to go to Kensington to open her Commission as Guardian and Regent of these Realms in Council.

There is no mortal here, but the Lady and Woman of the Bedchamber in waiting, so that my attendance on Her Majesty is (excepting three hours in the middle of the day) from 8 in the morning till 11 at night.

Were you not a little surprised to hear that Lord Cholmondeley[2] had quitted the Prince's service, and was made a Lord of the Treasury? I shall not comment or expatiate farther on this text, than by saying it put a stop to a scheme which I had a good deal at heart.

How the devil could you think it likely I should go with the King to Hanover? Your parts, poor Count, if this was a specimen of them, must be greatly impaired; but my comfort is, the rest of your letter shows this conjecture was not a specimen of your understanding, but a flaw in it.

You will certainly see Lady Hervey very soon with the Dss. of Richmond in France.[3] I am obliged to you for the offer you make me of bringing any thing I want from thence; but I have no trouble of that kind to give you. When do you bring your own sweet, vagrant person over? I go in 3 weeks to Redlynch, stay there 3 weeks, and then come back to Kensington for the rest of my life.

You have once for all a full discretionary power to show or give copies of any thing you ever received from me in writing,

[1] Holland House.

[2] George, 3rd Marquis (1703–70), to whom we have referred as Viscount Malpas on the occasion of his wife's death in 1731. (*See ante*, p. 132.) She was Mary, only daughter of Sir Robert Walpole. He succeeded to the titles in 1733.

Hervey was trying to get Stephen Fox made a Lord of the Treasury.

[3] They were staying at Aubigny, the Dss. of Portsmouth's former residence.

verse or prose, to whoever you have a mind ; a power I never gave to any other mortal, and one I would not give to you, but that I am sure it will never be abused by you nor repented by me.

Mr. Clayton is made an Irish Baron, by the title of Sundon. Ld. Lonsdale's quitting [1] surprised every body much more than Ld. Godolphin's succeeding him. You know, I suppose, that Ld. Robert Montagu [2] is my brother Vice-Chamberlain, and that he is married to Harriet Dunch. À propos the King made my brother Harry, a Captain, the day before His Majesty went, by giving him a company in Montagu's Regiment. What will Miss Harriet make Ld. Robert besides a husband, a father and a penitent ? There are few improvements his head will allow of ; but I dare say she knows his wants as well as her own so well, that all the improvement in her power will be amply bestowed. Adieu, my dear Count. Send me word when you are to come to England.

During the summer Henry Fox came back to England, much to his brother's relief; for besides the Hindon borough, where he now stepped into Stephen's shoes, and had thus at last become a full-blown member of Parliament, there were other complicated matters of business which could no longer await his problematic return. The session of Parliament, however, had come to its conclusion before his arrival ; so he could not take his seat till the following January when Parliament again met. We have no further letters to him until the autumn of 1736.

It is curious how few letters to Stephen are available at this period ; but as Hervey was staying for long periods at Redlynch, it seems clear that that friendship continued uninterrupted. We find one letter at Ickworth to Stephen of September 11, following on one to Horatio Walpole.

TO [3] HORATIO WALPOLE, AMBASSADOR AT THE HAGUE [3]

Kensington, September 9/20, 1735

. . . The natural and sensible account you give of your present situation in Holland, would certainly make me pity you in the

[1] Lord Lonsdale had held the Privy Seal since May 1733.

[2] Lord Robert Montagu (1710–62), son of 1st Duke of Manchester, became 3rd Duke in 1739. His wife was Harriet Dunch, daughter of Edward Dunch.

[3]–[3] In Hervey's writing. Ickworth.

midst of all the difficulties you have to struggle with, if I was not very well assured that the same honest and good sense, that have carried you through as intricate and delicate negotiations in former times, will not extricate you out of these with credit to yourself, satisfaction to your Master, pleasure to your friends, and benefit to your country.

I took the liberty to repeat to the Queen that part of your letter that related to her; for though to people I am indifferent to, I make it a general rule to repeat nothing they say or write to me, yet with those to whom I feel I mean friendly and wish well, I act differently: and always think there is a discretionary power lodged in me to make the use I think fit of what they communicate. If ever therefore I err in this way towards you, you may find fault with me perhaps for judging ill, but I am sure it will never be in your power to reproach me with not meaning well.

The Queen is so perfectly recovered that I never knew her in better humour, health and spirits, than she has been this morning. I wish some of those wise, sanguine people in the Opposition could have seen her, who affect such joy on the K—g's journey from Hanover being so long postponed, and give it out that a vacant apartment in St. James's is to be inhabited this winter by a new favourite. The joy this prospect gives them might perhaps be a little damped, when they found out apprehensions did not keep pace with their hopes, and that those, who are as nearly concerned and a little better informed, think as differently on the truth of this report, as they would feel to the consequences of it, if it were true.

It is no news to you I suppose that the Dss of Buckingham and her son are gone abroad again, any more than the particulars of the very extraordinary letter she wrote to your brother to notify her departure.[1]

[1] *See ante*, p. 99. The Duchess was an outspoken Jacobite. Her son, Edward Sheffield, 2nd Duke, died in Rome on October 30. At her death in 1743, she left Buckingham House to Lord Hervey for life, a few months before his own death. Her property passed to the 1st Duke's illegitimate son, by Frances, Mrs. Lambert (*Complete Peerage*), Charles Herbert. The latter took the name of Sheffield, and was created a Baronet in 1755. (*See also* p. 239, where Hervey spoke of Mr. Herbert as the Duke's *grandson*.)

The University of Oxford have lately paid my Lord Chancellor a great compliment by giving him his degree in person in the Theatre, which is a distinction never before shown to anybody but a Prince of the Blood. I remember formerly to have read in Cicero's *Epistles to Atticus*, that when the Senate of Rome conferred the Senatorial rank, by an extraordinary law, on young Octavius, Tully says this compliment was paid as much to mortify Anthony as to oblige Octavius. Whether the Bishop of London is the Anthony of this Oxford compliment I know not, but whatever the University and the Clergy meant by this act, it is thus the world and the laity interpret it; and, though the father's prudence is silent on this particular, the son's triumph as I am informed is less private.[1]

The Bishop of Winchester's [2] late book upon the Sacrament has made him many enemies, or at least has given occasion to many people to show themselves such. Those who censure him on this occasion say it is written to take off all reverence for the Sacrament; those who justify him say it is only to take off the horror; but those who are reasonable about it, I think should neither censure the doctrine nor justify the publication. Things are very well as they are. Why stir them? It is with many parts of policy, both in Government and Religion, as it is with some liquors. They will neither of them bear being shaken, nor going too near the bottom; for which reason, in both cases, it is very ill-judged to run the risk of spoiling all that is clear and good only, to squeeze a little more out of what is bad. When I reproached the Bishop of Winchester for publishing this book without ever saying one word to me about it beforehand, his answer was that he would not tell me of it, because he knew I should advise him against it, and he was determined to

[1] The reference is to the contest between the Bishop of London and the Lord Chancellor at the end of 1734 (*see ante*, p. 215), on the appointment of Dr. Rundle to the see of Gloucester. He was finally given that of Derry, a victory for the Bishop, and according to Hervey an unpopular one. "The two principals were very differently treated in these productions, for, whilst my Lord Chancellor's name was never mentioned but with decency, the Bishop of London was pelted with all the opprobrious language that envy and malice ever threw at eminence and power." (*Memoirs*, p. 401.)

[2] (*See ante*, p. 149.) Bishop Hoadly's book was entitled, *A plain Account of the nature and end of the Sacrament of the Lord's Supper.*

do it. Adieu. I have not room for a formal conclusion, but am without form most sincerely and affectionately

Yours, etc.

TO STEPHEN FOX *Kensington, September 11th, 1735*[1]

. . . I must now tell you that all your letters in general (but that of yesterday more than any) put me in mind of a Bill in Chancery. There are never above three words in a line, nor above three lines in a page;[2] but if you copy the Court of Chancery in the manner of filling your paper, I desire you would copy it too in the quantity, and then instead of a sheet in a month you will send me a quire every week. Do not excuse yourself by pleading nothing to say; whenever one thinks, one thinks in words, and whatever these words are, one may write them. Whenever you are awake therefore, you may certainly write. Villemain[3] has sent me two folios in an Elzevir letter, and as closely written as any Blue-Coat boy ever wrote the Lord's Prayer and the Belief in the compass of a sixpence. I laughed too twenty times in reading them, which is recommendation enough for any letter. I myself am at this moment proving to you that it is not necessary to have anything to write, in order to write; any more than it is necessary to be thirsty in order to drink. Provided one has liquor and ink, one can always write to one's friend and drink his health, if one has a mind to it.

The Duke of Richmond and his Caravan have left Paris. They are to stop some time at Chantilly, and to see places by the way; so that I believe they will hardly be in England this fortnight.

I hear to-day (but how true it is I know not), that the Duke of Buckingham (who was going to Italy for the recovery of his health) is dying at Dover. His title, I believe, will be extinct, which is all the loss he will be to the nobility or his country. His mother wrote a most extraordinary letter (even for her) to Sir Robert Walpole, to desire him to notify at Court her

[1] Ickworth. [2] Stephen Fox's handwriting was very large.

[3] Rev. Peter Willemin, vicar of Isey, near Cricklade, a living in Fox's gift. He appears in the group which appears as the frontispiece. Isey is said to be the church in the distance.

departure and her son's out of England. She said her son was going abroad for the recovery of his health, but as he was a *subject of this place*, as soon as that end was obtained, he would return hither.

I hear Lady Batemen has been very ill at Paris, that she accidentally happened to be lodged in the very room in which her brother died [1]; and some idiot officiously imparting this circumstance to her, her spirits that were before a good deal depressed by her indisposition, were so additionally disordered, that she fell into hysteric fits.

A piece of news was this day confirmed, that, when it comes to be publicly known, till the reason of it is made public too, will I fancy occasion great speculation. It is Prince Eugene's having left the army on the Rhine, and being gone to Vienna.[2] This whole war has been a suite of the oddest circumstances that ever were put together; it has been in my opinion a series of riddles and follies on all sides. I know you will except the conduct of Spain, but I do not; and if I had both inclination and time, of which I have neither, I think I could make it out.

Nobody knows yet for certain when the King comes. His staying where he is, and Prince Eugene's not staying where he was, will furnish the news-mongers with many paragraphs and the refiners with many conjectures.

Pray tell Winnington I love him mightily, and better this year than ever I did; and though affection does not always increase with the merit of those on whom it is bestowed, I really think he improves in the last, as much as I have done in the first. He is mightily mended in little things, on which you know I (from being a little genius perhaps) lay great stress. And his not wanting to be mended in great things made me always wish him mended in these. As for the Count, if he stays for a wet day to write to me, I desire he would not write at all; in the first place, because I do not care to be the *pis aller* to a partridge, and in the next, because a letter which his gloomy, philosophising head produces on a rainy day may perhaps infect me with his

[1] Robert, 4th Earl of Sunderland, died in 1729.

[2] The armistice on the Rhine was due to a secret negotiation between the Emperor and France.

spleen, but will I am sure give me no pleasure. Adieu, my dear Ste. I love you with all my heart and soul. You are used to my barbouillements, and on that I depend for your being able to read this letter. Once more, mon cher, & très cher & cherissime, Adieu.

On October 6, came a letter to Mrs. Digby, containing news of the untimely death of the young Duchess of Bedford. Hervey expatiated on her beauty, her character, and her religious views; but on the last subject his comments are too tinged by his personal beliefs (or rather non-beliefs) for publication.

TO MRS. DIGBY *Kensington, Oct. 6th, 1735* [1]

Dear Madam,

I have this moment received the favour of your letter, and though it is not post-day, knowing how little I can answer at any time for *my own to-morrow*, I have desired the D. of Richmond, in whose apartment I now am, to let me have writing implements to obey this minute the commands of one of the most agreeable correspondents and amiable companions in the world. I could not help being fine-gentleman and coxcomb enough on this occasion to brag and name you, and added what I have often told you, that I never knew La Bruyêre's receipt for an agreeable woman closer followed than in your composition; which receipt, lest you should not remember, I shall here transcribe, "Le plus charmant commerce qu'il y est au monde est celui d'une jolie femme qui a tous les agrèmens d'un honnête homme." But in order to execute your orders, I must make a transition to the memory of one, who though she had a great deal of the *jolie femme* had not the least grain of the *honnête homme.*[2] She was thoroughly a woman, which I do not mean as a silly sex-reflection; but as I should mean if I said any man was thoroughly human, that is that he had all the common passions of humanity unrestrained and all its vices uncorrected. She had beauty enough to make her person likeable, and wit enough to make her conversation entertaining, with coquetry enough to make anybody who liked the one miserable, and

[1] Ickworth.

[2] The Duchess of Bedford.

insincerity enough to make the other at least as dangerous in its consequences as it was agreeable in its possession. She was vain to a degree that exhausted flattery, more ambitious than any man, as dissatisfied and restless as any Spencer, and as avaricious and uncaring as any Churchill. You ask me if she was religious, [1] living, or only so dying ? [1] I think she was so in neither. . . . She asked to see Princess Emily, but that happening on the morning that the Sacrament operation was to be performed, she did not see her. The Duchess of Marlborough behaved like herself: that is, not barely unreasonably and tiresomely, but madly and brutally. She told the Duke of Bedford (who they say is really very much afflicted), that he had murdered his wife for want of common care ; and the moment his wife was dead, she sent to him for all the jewels she had given the Duchess of Bedford, pretending she had only lent them. This fact is hardly credible ; but I am told it is certainly true, and that the Duke of Bedford has yet sent no answer at all to this demand. Lord and Lady Bateman returned to England last Saturday, in hopes to find their sister still alive ; they are now at Old Windsor.

The yachts are at last ordered for the King. He has commanded them to be at Helvoetsluys the 19th ; the Princess Royal is to meet him there. Adieu. I have sent you all the news I know—perhaps unintelligibly ; for there is a quadrille table on one side of me, a cribbage table on the other, and a tea table noisier than both of them behind me.

TO MRS. DIGBY *St. James's House, November 13th, 1735* [2]

Nothing, dear Madam, but a very severe fit of one of my usual headaches, with which I almost lost the sense of seeing, and entirely the faculty of thinking, could have prevented me from thanking you by the last post for a letter, which, if it had been sent from any hand but yours, would have surprised me as much as it entertained me. I am very ready to acknowledge that no mathematician argues closer than you do ; but no political writer quotes more unfairly, and no Divine reasons from more *postulata* (to few women I would have made use of that word, at least

[1–1] In Hervey's writing. [2] Ickworth.

without explaining it). But to return to your letter, though I acknowledge you have not repeated one word for mine that I did not say, yet I must add too that you have taken bits of detached conversations, and have done by my prose, as people do by *les bouts rimées*, and filled them up so much *al vostro modo*, that the sense of the one so cemented is no more mine, than the verses can be said to be their's who give the other.

Now as to the temptation, and assisting the tempter, which you seem to accuse me of, in the affair you allude to, I acknowledge, upon thinking the he-person concerned in that transaction was a sort of body that would marry and wanted that domestic appurtenance to a married life called *a home to go to* (for everybody that has a home, has not a home to go to, any more than every body who has a home they *must* go to, have one they *would* go to). Thinking, I say, in short, that this body would marry, I own I was inclined to have them accept the offer you refer to; and when my opinion was asked (though I am always sorry on such occasions to have it asked), I gave it as I would to a favourite son, without disguise and without management, and am still of opinion that the first thing that ought to be considered by those who marry, merely because they choose a married life, is fortune. I never said, if one knew anything very bad of any woman's temper or morals, that money in one scale ought to be looked upon as a balance to any qualities you could put into the other (nor was that the case). But I did say, and continue to say, that the fortune may be a *certainty*; and that for the rest you must take your chance, for there is no getting a wife bespoke—you must take her ready-made. I know you will answer to this; that though one cannot have a wife made by a receipt, yet sure one would get one if one could that had the most of those ingredients in her composition, which one would put into a receipt if she were to be made by it. And you would be in the right; if things that one takes for some sort of ingredients had not, when one came to taste them, quite a different flavour than one expected. In short, conjugal happiness, like an agreeable countenance, is not always found where there are the most regular features. It is a pleasing result from the whole; and a casual, undefinable assemblage that constitutes both. I will grant you too that there are some qualities that will certainly prove a bar to happiness, though none are sure to procure it. And give me leave to say that this is granting a great deal, since there are very few bad qualities you can name that I have not seen in women whose husbands have been as fond of them as they could have been, if those wives had been made after your receipt or after your example. So much for the marriage chapter. Nor would I have ventured to everybody to say so much upon it, lest they should think I love money much better than I am sure I do, and that I have less regard to good and amiable qualities than the real esteem and friendship I have for you and your family make it plain I have.

But here in truth lies all the difference between your opinion and mine. We both think alike of the value of money, and the value of merit; but you imagine one may know the one as well before one marries as the other; whereas I think that in the fortune you may know to a farthing what your wife will be worth: and in her merit, as there is no touchstone for that ore but experience, you may marry pinchbeck for gold, wear it some time before you find out the cheat, and when you do find it out, be obliged to wear it on. Whilst all the world who see it at a distance only shall think you master of a most valuable treasure, which you, by a more familiar acquaintance, shall know to be nothing but a shining stink, that might for ever have deceived you had you never touched it, but that the oftener and the longer you touch it, the more plainly and disagreeably manifests the cheat. Adieu, dear Madam. I find, upon reading your letter for at least the tenth time, that I have not answered at most above the tenth part of it. However, I dare not fright you from my acquaintance by too long visits, for fear you should not return them. Pray tell Mrs. Horner [1] I wish her not only health but every other happiness; and, as I wish her some things she has not, so I wish too she had not some things she has.

TO STEPHEN FOX *Thursday, November 13th, 1735* [2]

. . . If I am to entertain you with matter of fact only, how can I hope to amuse you with the copy of things that tired

[1] Mrs. Strangways-Horner. [2] Ickworth.

me even in the original. Can you like to hear how many times a week I go to a Drawing Room, a Play, or an Opera; how many bows I make at the one, or how many times I yawn at them all? Can it be any diversion to you to hear things repeated from the lips of those who only open them because articulation is a compliment and study to say things that are indifferent, as much as Pope or Swift study to avoid it; and are as stiff consequently in trifles as the others are in refinements?

If I talk to you of the Peace, it must be only by repeating what I have said to you upon it already, for nobody mentions it that I meet with. I do not believe there ever was so material an occurrence that furnished so little conversation. There is one article of news from my own apartment that is so particular that I cannot help acquainting you with it, which is that in the very room I am now writing my Lord President[1] sat, not by accident but by appointment, an hour with me tête à tête; and for a more extraordinary piece of news, I was not tired of him. I was another hour with him and that ecclesiastical booby, the Bishop of Rochester,[2] in Westminster Abbey, but these two extraordinary meetings were at different times and on different occasions. Guess them if you can—it is as good a Christmas riddle as any you will find in the *Almanack*, the search just as amusing, and the solution just as profitable if you should find it. I must tell you one circumstance that diverted me after one of these interviews, which was that as soon as ever we got rid of the Bishop, the lay-blockhead began to talk to me of the extreme stupidity of the episcopal-blockhead, and asked me if I did not think the poor good man one of the dullest fellows I had ever met with. To which I answered, that notwithstanding

[1] Lord Wilmington.

[2] Dr. Joseph Wilcocks (1673–1756), Bishop of Gloucester 1721–31; Dean of Westminster; and Bishop of Rochester 1731–56. (*See ante*, p. 91.) Hervey's remarks to the King read as follows in the *Memoirs* (p. 500): "As soon as Lord Wilmington, Lord Chancellor and I had today discharged Your Majesty's Commission of proroguing Parliament, my Lord of Rochester carried us to Westminster Abbey to show us a pair of old brass gates to Henry VII's Chapel, which were formerly overrun with rust and turned quite black, but are now new-cleaned, as bright as when they were first made, and the finest things of the kind I ever saw in my life." The Bishop was clearly at least a good Antiquary!

he was my brother peer, I could not help owning that among my spiritual brethren I believed there was not a piece of more useless and contemptible, dignified dullness in our whole Senate; upon which his Lordship laughed very heartily, which flattered me extremely. For if my joke was so good a one as to afford all that mirth to one, who, by laughing at all, could understand it but by halves, what must it be to those (and consequently to you) who will comprehend the whole? I am in a great hurry and yet have nothing to do, which is perpetually my case; and yet I laugh at the D. of Newcastle for being like me. He is my Bishop of Rochester, and I his Lord Wilmington.

Remember to look for *Dion Cassius* and *Diodorus Siculus*.

In a succeeding letter, to Horatio Walpole, on November 18, Hervey adverted to the general situation on the Continent. The so-called "Triple Alliance" was fast breaking up. France was playing her own game secretly, so secretly that her Ambassador in London, Chavigny, was kept in complete ignorance of what was going on: and in October preliminaries for a Peace were signed between France and the Emperor. This was checkmate to Spain; for by it the Duke of Lorraine would obtain the reversion of Tuscany, and the hand in marriage of Maria Theresa, the eldest Archduchess. The third partner, Sardinia, fell between the two stools, and got the worst of a very bad deal. Hervey also shortly summed up the reasons for keeping England out of active participation in the war, Walpole's constant policy; which was often strenuously opposed by King George, encouraged at one moment by the offer by Kinski of the command of the Imperial army on the Rhine. This the British Monarch finally had the sense to refuse.

TO HORATIO WALPOLE (AT THE HAGUE)

St. James's, November 18/29, 1735[1]

. . . Between you and I, I cannot say, when F[rance] was to be detached from S[pain], or S. from F., that I should not have been more inclined to have broken the *Formidable Alliance* (as it was called) by *the marriage* that has been so often spoken of. I believe you were inclined that way too; but if the Emperor himself or the Princes of the Empire in general (not to mention

[1] Ickworth.

any particular Prince whom you and I should be obliged to consider more than the rest) were so averse to this marriage, that the obstacles to the breaking the *Formidable Alliance* that way were insurmountable, the breaking it all was your business, and though you could not break it the way perhaps you would, it was wise and prudent in you to break it the way you could. Nor do I indeed see that when you would not assist the Emperor in the war, that you could with any decency insist, or with any efficacy oppose his making peace the way he liked best. The short abstract, therefore, of the conduct of the English Administration I take to be this—a war broke out in Europe, in which you judged it not for the interest of England (if you could avoid it) to take part, knowing that England is always a great loser by a war whilst it lasts, and can never be a great gainer when it concludes. In the next place (as paradoxical as it may sound), I think it very evident that you were of greater use to those whom you must have joined had you gone into the war, by keeping your force in reserve, unimpaired and untried, than you would have been in exerting it; and that you have done the Emperor, as well as England, much more service by making peace *for* him, than you could have done by making war *with* him, not forgetting that you might by joining him have been left alone to finish what he alone began. In my opinion, let Patriots and Craftsmen say what they will, England never made so great a figure abroad, nor was ever in so flourishing a condition at home as in this reign; and nobody is ignorant where they owe their thanks for this situation, though they may be reluctant, knowing where they are owed, to pay them.

Your brother is still in Norfolk; the Duke of Newcastle returned yesterday. Thanks be to God, the Duke of Modena [1] is at last departed. Sure that is the most impenetrable piece of dignified dullness that ever any princely family produced. Most of the little conversation that used to be extorted from him consisted of inarticulate sounds, like *ah!* and *hah!*; and whenever he did deviate into articulation, his words were as bare of meaning as his noises generally were of words, whilst *si fait*,

[1] Rinaldo, Duke of Modena, who died in 1737.

nonne, celà se peut, and *peutêtre*, seemed to be all the furniture in his whole vocabulary. We have a female piece of foreign goods as extraordinary to the eye as the other was to the ear. I mean Madame Losse,[1] who is taller than any of the King of Prussia's grenadiers, and as slender as one of their muskets; and not more like a maypole in her shape and size than in her air and dress, being at least as stiff and adorned with as many faded flowers and dirty ribbons. Sure she must have some extraordinary occult qualities to be able to have made herself without beauty mistress to a King, and her husband without sense his first Minister. Adieu. I am too much ashamed of the length of this letter to own it by setting my name.

On November 25, Hervey wrote to Stephen and on the same day to Mrs. Digby: [2]

. . . You desire me to send you some news. Why don't you desire me to send a griffin's foot, a dragon's wing, a harpy's nose, or a phoenix's egg? I know no news. The Duke of Buckingham's dead, and his mother come to England. Mrs. Walpole has married a trooper. The present Lord Peterborough has but £500 a year left him by his grandfather. The Duke of Devonshire and Mr. Pelham are come back from Houghton. Mr. Edgecombe is then gone thither. Sir Robert Walpole stays there a week longer. Farinelli is recovered; and there is to be an Opera tonight for the first time. Lord Euston has got the smallpox at Turin. Tell me, if you call this news? And, if you do, I will transcribe two or three such paragraphs out the *Evening Post* or *Daily Journal* every time I write to you.

TO MRS. DIGBY *St. James's, November 25th, 1735* [2]

I know not, dear Madam, whether you will be returned to the Bath by the time this letter will arrive there; but, as a desire to show the readiness of my obedience to every command of yours is my single reason for writing, so that view being answered in all events, I cannot be very solicitous about the time you will receive what at no time I fear will be any great amusement to

[1] Baron Loss (or Loos) was Prussian Ambassador. [2] Ickworth.

you. For if the philosopher's rule be a true one, that *nothing can give that which it has not,* how can I hope to entertain *you,* when I live in a total privation of entertainment myself? I am this moment returned with the King from yawning four hours at the longest and dullest Opera that ever the ennobled ignorance of our present musical Governors ever inflicted on the ignorance of an English audience; who, generally speaking, are equally skilful in the language of the drama and the music it is set to, a degree of knowledge or ignorance (call it which you please) that on this occasion is no great misfortune to them, the drama being composed by an anonymous fool, and the music by one Veracini,[1] a madman, who to show his consummate skill in this Opera has, among half a dozen very bad parts, given Cuzzoni and Farinelli the two worst. The least bad part is Senesino's, who like Echo reversed, has lost all his voice, and retains nothing of his former self but his flesh; and St. Paul says, " Silver and gold have I none, but such as I have give I unto thee ", so poor Senesino for want of a throat presents us with his nose, which he blows upon the stage, whilst the trumpets and French horns are blowing in vain to drown his victorious nostrils in the orchestre. There is a new woman, who, if she would blow her nose, would, I dare say, sing much better; but, as it is, her voice is (begging your pardon) the snottiest, fattest, disagreeablest sound you ever heard. It is exactly in singing what Mr. Je—ys's is in speaking, when he says, " Dimults is trumps." The last air in the Opera has really some merit, besides the being the last; and I was extremely pleased with the wit of a footman (who has, I dare swear, ten times as much as his master) that called out at the conclusion of this air—" This song Ancora, and the rest no more-a." And to prove to you that the footman has more wit, or at least more judgment, than either Farinelli or the majority of the Directors, the song was [2] sung *no-more-a,*[2] and the Opera is to be on Saturday *ancora.*[2] Handel sat in great eminence and

[1] Francesco Maria Veracini (1685?–1750), a celebrated violinist, and composer. Actually the Opera *Adriano,* however, proved a great success, and was given 17 times. *Grove's Dictionary of Music* speaks of Veracini as a musician of remarkable originality and solid attainments.

[2–2] In Hervey's writing.

great pride in the middle of the pit, and seemed in silent triumph to insult this poor dying Opera in its agonies, without finding out that he was as great a fool for refusing to compose, as Veracini had shown himself by composing, nobody feeling their own folly, though they never overlook other people's, and having the eyes of a mole for the one, with those of a lynx for the other. That fellow having more sense, more skill, more judgment, and more expression in music than anybody, and being a greater fool in common articulation and in every action than Mrs. P—t or Bishop H—s, is what has astonished me a thousand times. And what his understanding must be, you may easily imagine, to be undone by a profession of which he is certainly the ablest professor, though supported by the Court : and in a country where his profession is better paid than in any other country in the world. His fortune in music is not unlike my Lord Bolingbroke's in politics. The one has tried both theatres, as the other has tried both Courts. They have shone in both, and been ruined in both ; whilst everyone owns their genius and sees their faults, though nobody either pities their fortune or takes their part.

You will see in the public prints that Lord Euston has the smallpox at Turin ; and that the Duke of Buckingham is dead at Rome. His mad mother returned to England. Between three and four thousand pounds a year of his estate devolves, I hear, to the Crown ; the rest of it goes to one Mr. Herbert, a natural son of the old Duke's natural daughter.[1] To this natural son (who is in the army) the old Duke, by a strange disposition of his affairs, left nothing but in case of this contingency : and an injunction if this estate came to him, to take the name of Sheffield ; which makes it very plain that he did not leave this estate to his son but to his name, and that he cared no more for the man than people do for the marble that makes the monument on which they order their silly name to be engraved, and which they leave two or three thousand pounds to erect and adorn. . . .

[1] *See ante*, p. 226.

TO HENRY FOX St. James's, December 2nd, 1735[1]

You desired a letter from me, my dear Count—*Eccola.* But unless I could flatter myself that barely writing, though I have nothing to tell you, would be agreeable unto you, as Princes barely speaking to you though they have nothing to say would still be reckoned a compliment, I cannot expect you should have any pleasure in the consequence of my obedience ; besides that of seeing that your commands without any other motive are sufficient to influence my conduct.

The return of all the company from Norfolk will, I hope, a little thicken our Levees and Drawing Rooms, which for this last month have seemed in the last stage of a consumption ; whilst I, like a good nurse, have attended them constantly day and night, the Duke of Grafton not being yet come to relieve me. I know but one thing I ever do, which is not in the round of the vieilleries of the Palace (all which you are as well acquainted with as I am), and that is playing at back-gammon of a night with the King in the Queen's apartment. Tout le reste va son train ordinaire.

As to politics, the Peace is so considerable an event, that if there was anybody in town to talk of it, to be sure one should hear that topic a good deal discussed. The questions that are asked by those who have a mind to depreciate it are : Will Spain come into it ? Is England to guarantee for the new disposition of Italy ? Is our fleet to come home ? Is our army to be reduced ? All which questions even I, who am neither in the secret of affairs nor a competent judge even of things which are no secrets, think I could answer without being much puzzled ; though I doubt not but those who have a mind to be witty on us Courtiers and Senators who are to support this measure and answer these questions, will say that our case is just the reverse of that mentioned thus by Livy, " Non defuit quid responderetur, quanquam deerat qui responsum daret ", [2] and that respondents will be easier found than responses.[2]

I hear your brother and you have looked in vain for a Latin translation of *Dion Cassius* and *Diodorus Siculus* at Redlynch. I

[1] Ickworth. [2–2] In Hervey's writing.

have got the first, but have in vain too sent to every bookseller in town for the last.[1] I know there is such a thing ; one Foggio, a Florentine, translated it into Latin by order of Pope Nicholas the fifth : but I could never hear of anybody that had it or had seen it. I believe therefore, as my Lady Wishfort says to Foible

[1] Hervey's frantic search for translations of these two Greek books, largely dealing with Rome and its history, is intriguing. There seem to be three possible explanations. The first and simplest is that he desired to further his knowledge on these subjects, in which he was always intensely interested. The second, that they might be useful to him in his vitriolic comparison between the Prince of Wales and Nero, which he set out in parallel columns with Latin quotations from Tacitus, Suetonius and Dion Cassius, given in the *Memoirs* (pp. 858, etc.). This is perhaps nearest to the truth ; but here Diodorus Siculus would have failed him, as he would in our final suggestion, for the last-named History closes long before the Neronian epoch. This brings us to a last possibility, but an unlikely one, owing to the lapse of nearly ten months since the publication of Pope's *Epistle to Dr. Arbuthnot* in 1735, after a long postponement caused by the illness and death of the Doctor. Included in this was Pope's coup-de-grâce, which once and for all disposed of Hervey and his puny attacks on the poet.

" P. Let Sporus tremble.
A. What that skein of silk ?
Sporus, that mere white curd of ass's milk.
Satire or sense, alas ! can Sporus feel ?
Which breaks a butterfly upon a wheel ?
P. Yet let me flap this bug with gilded wings,
This painted child of dirt that stinks and stings,
Whose buzz the witty and the fair annoys ;
Yet wit ne'er tastes and beauty ne'er enjoys. . . ."

And here then we come to our third query. Is it conceivable that Hervey did not know who Sporus was, and was straining every nerve to find out ?

To this outrageous lampoon which exceeds all bounds of decency, we find no direct reference by Hervey in the letters ; but the lines are important in the quarrel between the two men, and in the sequence of their various writings, so we cannot pass them over in silence. We feel bound therefore to explain the origin of the name *Sporus*, unpleasant as the story is, especially as Mr. Sedgwick has found the same necessity ; so that the filthy significance of the comparison may be understood. Dion Cassius seems to be solely responsible for the account, which appears in his work (*Loeb. trans.*, lxii). " Nero caused a boy of the freedmen, whom he used to call Sporus, to be castrated, because he resembled Poppœa Sabina [his favourite mistress, who had died recently], and used him in every way as a wife. . . . Indeed he formally ' married ' Sporus in Greece in the year 67." There are a number of other references to Sporus in Dion's text. This takes us to the root of the whole matter, and shows the depth of lewdness and malevolence to which on occasion Pope was prepared to descend.

and Lucy [1] when she can't get the ratafia, " A pox take you both ; fetch me the cherry brandy then." So I shall, with regard to the *Diodorus*, say to you two brothers, since you cannot get the Latin one,—" A pox take you both ; send me the Italian then."

We are to have two new peers (by that I mean newly come of age) this winter in the House, the Earls of Rockingham and Stanhope. The first they say will be with us, [2] the other against us.[2] My Lord Ch[esterfield], I hear, says that his kinsman [3] is too fond of Greek and Roman virtue to join the degenerate vices of the majority of a modern English Senate. He did not venture to say this before me ; he knew I should have laughed in his face, as much I should have done at that clever profligate Patrician, Claudius, [4] if I could have heard him in private say, when he turned [4] plebeian and got himself made Tribune of the People, that it was the love of his Country and not his enmity to Cicero that had made him take that step. There is really nothing I am so sick of hearing repeated from the lips of our modern Patriots, as the encomiums upon the wisdom of our ancestors and the virtue of the Romans. I would be glad to know for which age of our ancestors they would like to change the circumstances of the present ? Or if they would choose to have England resemble Rome in the time of what they must call that of it's great virtue—that is, when it was miserably poor, without any trade, involved in perpetual wars abroad, and torn by conflicting factions of the nobility and commonalty at home. For my own part I like extremely to read of those times, but to live in these : and think of such virtue as I do of his Lordship's understanding, that it makes an excellent figure in words, [4] though it is of very small use [4] in practice. And if it be a true maxim (as I have somewhere or other read, though I have forgot where) that,

> " Of wit and folly say the most you can,
> Who acts the wisest is the wisest man,"

[1] Characters in *The Way of the World* by Congreve, 1700.
[2–2] Added in Hervey's writing. [3] Lord Stanhope.
[4–4] Added in Hervey's writing.

what must one think of any man's wisdom who has worked himself out of a Court without making himself popular, ruined his fortune, and married a witch to redeem it;—and then behaved himself to that witch in such a manner as to frustrate all his hopes of having his fortune the better for it, and ruined his quiet without mending his circumstances. [1]When I write or speak to you, you know it is always quite naturally and just what I think; and I assure you there are few people to whom I should express myself so naturally on this subject, for fear of being thought to depreciate from envy, and not to comment from observation. Yet I can see and allow his good and agreeable qualities, as well as remark those which are not so. He has excellent what one calls *parts*, a great deal of wit, is extremely entertaining, very well-bred, much better natured than he is reckoned, and (his propensity to fable excepted) no petitesse about him. Adieu. I find myself what your brother calls very *chattish*, but writing (as usual) after the Opera, I am pressed (as usual) in time. Adieu.[1]

[1–1] In Hervey's writing.

CHAPTER X

1736

We quote a short extract from the only letter in the spring of 1735/36, that of February 14, addressed to one of the Foxes, probably Henry. It refers to Hervey's meeting with a son of Sir Robert Walpole. Was this the younger Horace, much later Earl of Orford? We have no real means of judging: but we print it, although his next brother, Edward, eleven years Horace's senior, would have been about the same age as the Fox brothers.

> . . . I dined the other day at Sir Robert Walpole's, where I told your story. His son joined with me in everything I said to your advantage. He seems to like and esteem you as much as you can wish: and for much better reasons than people of his age generally have for liking and esteeming anybody or anything.[1]

In the interval, the Prince of Wales's marriage to Princess Augusta of Saxe-Gotha, then seventeen years old, unable to speak any English, and with only a few words of French, was celebrated within a few days of her arrival in England, late in April. The King had announced the union, in a message to Parliament in February. Shortly after the ceremony the King left England for Hanover, reversing his usual practice of leaving three years to elapse between his visits, in his eagerness to get back to his new plaything, Madame Walmoden. She in the meanwhile, had had a son, who died at an early age.

The correspondence with Stephen during these months seems to have disappeared, if there was any. During the interval he married in March, Elizabeth Horner, Mrs. Strangways Horner's daughter, a child of thirteen. No mention of this occurs in the letters; so we do not enlarge further on the story, which is fully given in *Henry Fox, 1st Lord Holland* (i, 45, etc.). The marriage, or rather marriages, took place in the spring at Stephen Fox's house in Burlington Street, two ceremonies having succeeded one another in close succession. The girl then returned to her mother; and it was not till August 1739 that the young couple came together at Redlynch.

Before the regular series of letters starts in 1736, late in June or early July we find an isolated one, undated, and addressed, "To the Queen". In it Hervey imagined his own death, narrated the obsequies and the

[1] Ickworth. Horace Walpole was born in 1717.

ceremonies which followed, and gave a fantastic account of the wanderings of his spirit during the following week.

The letter was clearly based on a chance remark by Queen Caroline, asking what would happen at the Court if her Vice-Chamberlain was suddenly to be removed by the hand of death. "The Queen said what an alteration in the Palace Lord Hervey's death would make, how many people would mourn, and how many would rejoice; to which Lord Hervey replied, he believed he could guess just how it would be; and when pressed to tell, said he would do it in writing." (*Memoirs*, p. 575.)

He also wrote a short and rather dull play (*The death of Lord Hervey, or a Morning at Court. A Drama.*) on the subject, published in the *Memoirs*. A date, June 14, is mentioned in the letter, and from a contemporary reference in the play, the year is clearly 1736.

TO THE QUEEN [1] *[June or July 1736]*

Thoroughly sensible of all the gracious distinctions and innumerable favours with which Your Majesty honoured me when I was alive, I thought it my duty to give Your Majesty some notice of my death. On Saturday, the 14th June, about 5 minutes after eleven I died. Some malicious people perhaps may give out that I died drunk, for as I departed this life, just as I took leave of Your Majesty when you retired out of your Gallery, I cannot deny but that I expired with a drop in my eye. The next morning my corpse was carried down to Salisbury, where Bishop Sherlock of that diocese read the funeral service over me. From thence the body was carried to Mr. Fox's and there privately interred. It had not rested there above a week, when my poor carcass was taken up again, and conveyed to lie in state at the family seat of Lord Poulett.[2] My body was there exhibited to the view of all the country; and, according to the custom of Italy, in the same dress I wore when I was alive. My Lord Poulett himself was *the undertaker*, and the obsequies were performed (though far in the West) with all the pomp and magnificence of the East. The bed on which the body of the defunct was laid was velvet laced with gold, adorned with plumes of feathers; the staircase, by which all those who were admitted to see my body ascended, was vaulted with lapis-

[1] Ickworth. [2] Hinton St. George, in Somerset.

lazelly [*sic*]. They passed through five large rooms before they came to my mausoleum ; near thirty men in the same livery were perpetually watching the corpse ; and prayers were read over it regularly every night at nine a clock.

But whilst my body, Madam, was thus disposed of, my spirit (as when alive) was still hovering, though invisible, round Your Majesty, anxious for your welfare, and watching to do you any little services that lay within my power. On Monday, whilst you walked, *my shade* still turned on the side of the sun to guard you from its beams. On Tuesday morning at breakfast I brushed away a fly, that had escaped Teed's [1] observation and was just going to be the taster of your chocolate. On Wednesday, in the afternoon, I took off the chillness of some strawberry water Your Majesty was going to drink as you came in hot from walking ; and at night I hunted a bat out of your bedchamber, and shut a sash just as you fell asleep, which Your Majesty had a little indiscreetly ordered Mrs. Purcel [2] to leave open. On Thursday, in the Drawing Room, I took the forms and voices of several of my acquaintance, made strange faces, put myself into awkward postures, and talked a good deal of nonsense, whilst Your Majesty entertained me very gravely, *raccommoded* me very graciously, and laughed at me internally very heartily. On Friday (being post day), I proposed to get the best pen in t'other world for Your Majesty's use, and slip it invisibly into your standish just as Mr. Shaw [3] was bringing it into your Gallery for you to write. Accordingly I went to *Voiture*,[4] and desired him to lend me his pen ; but when I told him for whom it was designed, he only laughed at me for a blockhead, and asked me if I had been at Court for four years to so little purpose as not to know that Your Majesty had a much better of your own. On Saturday, I went on the shaft of Your Majesty's chaise to Richmond. As you walked there, I went before you, and with an invisible wand I brushed the dew and the worms out of your path all

[1] "The Queen's chocolate maker." (Lord Hervey's note, *Memoirs*, ed. Sedgwick, p. 575.)

[2] "The King's laundress, that was always about the Queen in a morning to bring her breakfast. A pert, silly woman." (*Ibid.*)

[3] One of the Queen's Pages of the Backstairs. (*Ibid.*)

[4] One of the household, who evidently had recently died.

the way, and several times *un-crumpled* Your Majesty's stocking. This very day, at Chapel, I did your Majesty some service by tearing six leaves out of the Parson's sermon, and shortening his discourse six minutes. Your Majesty sees how ready I am to boast of the small services I am capable of doing you; but little geniuses must submit to little occupations, and those who wish to do you any services, if they are not able to do you all they would, must at least perform all they can. And if Your Majesty thinks after this purgatory I have gone through, I deserve any reward, do but pronounce my Sentence and say, "Je vous laisse vivre". My resurrection will immediately ensue, and the heaven of your presence again enjoyed by, Madam, etc.

Letters recommence in August from a new source, a series written to Count Algarotti, the friend of Voltaire and Frederick the Great.[1] Twenty-five of these have recently come to light among Sir John Murray's manuscripts. These, extending from 1736 to 1742, he is very kindly allowing us to use. We have spoken of them in our Preface.

We make a short extract from the first, on August 14, as it speaks of a growing friendship:

. . . En tout cas, si vous restez ou si vous partez, ne m'oubliez pas, mon cher, car je vous n'oublierai de ma vie. Je me souviendrois toujours quand je vois le gens qui m'amusent, ou ceux que j'admire, ou ceux que j'estime, que je profite en détail seulement de ces qualités dont je ne suis joui dans un seul objet pendant que ie vous possedois. . . .

TO HENRY FOX *Kensington, September 4, 1736*[2]

I can not write to you without thanking you again for all that air of real kindness, that seemed to me to run through the whole letter I received from you the post after my arrival here; and believe me, dear Count, the reluctance I know you must have to giving advice on most occasions (from your being sensible

[1] Francesco Algarotti (1712–64) born in Venice. He was in Paris in 1723; and published a book there in 1733. Lady Mary Wortley-Montagu was a friend; and much later he became intimate with Frederick the Great, King of Prussia, who appointed him his Chamberlain.

[2] Holland House.

how ill it is generally received), makes me think it no common favour for you to have got over the double obstacle of doing violence to yourself, and risking the being disagreeable to another. In return, I must inform you that, though I hate receiving advice full as much as you can hate giving it, or as most people hate taking it, yet for the sake of the physician, I have smelt several times at your physic, though I have not swallowed a drop of it ; and have found, like smelling at hartshorn, that it raised my spirits whilst the bottle was at my nose, though none of it went down my throat. In short, dear Count, I have studied my own nasty constitution, my worse temper, my odd body and odder mind so long, that whether I understand it better than any body else or not, at least the oddness of thinking I do, being yet uncured, I shall act on as if I did. All you say about diet, physic, bills of fare, feeding upon chemical extracted quintessences, and taking them in postures that should make them long in travelling through one's body, instead of hurrying them through, post, upon Ward's pills : the cradle and the tricilinium you bring in, and all the animated manner in which you seemingly jumble, and really connect the whole, shows great ingenuity ; and I shall certainly say of your letters and your company, as I have formerly done of other physicians, "Write to me upon any subject but your trade, and whenever I am not too sick to be entertained with anything, pray let me see you."

I was glad on my first coming to town to find myself so much easier than I expected to be, and said, like Anthony, "Gods, I thank you. I formed the danger greater than it was, and now 'tis near, 'tis vanished." I am proud of this, and if I was not ashamed of what followed, I would relate it. I know you say now of me in your heart what I said in black and white on another body, *Idem manebat neque idem decebat.* Tis true.

But what avails our own defects to find ?
If impotent to cure, 'twere better we were blind. . . .

The more ludicrous, dramatic performance I finished in my first two days of jollity and spirits, and seasoned it so strong, that I had some apprehensions about showing it. But I am extremely glad they did not prevail ; for it succeeded to admiration. Sometimes you advise me against studying, but you are in the wrong,—reading and writing do me more good, when I can force myself to apply to them, than any other employment; and *no* employment hurts me beyond what you can imagine. When my thoughts take their own course for an hour, I return from the audience I have given them, leaner, paler, and more worn than any mathematician from studying Sir Isaac Newton's *Principles* all night by a college lamp.

Algarotti goes away on Monday, which I am extremely sorry for, for he amuses me exceedingly. Dear Count, adieu; and depend upon it, how contrary soever I may act to my own advantage, or how much soever I may neglect it, that whatever is in my power to do for you or your brother that may either promote your interest or conduce to your pleasure, those things shall never be neglected. I am too old to make new friendships, and I hope too honest to neglect old ones, as well as too sensible to part with such as are equally creditable, pleasurable and valuable. . . .

TO COUNT ALGAROTTI *Septembre 9/20, 1736. de Kensington*[1]

Vous m'avez prié de vous écrire en Anglais; et savez-vous la sotte raison pourquoi je ne le fais pas. C'est parceque je ne me suis pas accoutumé de vous entretenir dans cette langue; et je ne veux pas me détromper par une preuve de plus, de l'agréable illusion de croire que je vous parle quand je vous écris. Je suis, mon cher, dans une veritable affliction de ne vous voir plus; et il faut bien que vous souffrez l'ennui de l'entendre dire une fois, puisque vous ne le faites sentir mille fois par jour. Tout le monde me trouve d'une humeur exécrable, et me le dit tout net; pendant que je leur reponds avec la mème sincerité, avouant que c'est vrai, et que c'est le départ de Monsr. Algarotti qui en est la cause. . . .

Vous allez me dire encore que je pense en vers. Il est sur que quant je vous écris je pense sur le papier; et que si c'est des vers, de la prose, du françois, de l'Anglais, du Latin ou l'Italien, que j'ai au moment en tête, je vous donne les *rough diamonds* justement

[1] Sir John Murray's MS.

comme je les puise, sans attendre de les tailler et les raffiner en brilliants. . . .

TO HENRY FOX *Kensington, September 16, 1736*[1]

My dear Count, I love your letters extremely, and I love you still much better than them. If I was to say I love you better than myself, it might sound like a nauseous, *outré* compliment; but it would in reality be no compliment at all. For at this moment I know nobody I am so angry with, or despise or hate so much. I do not believe there ever was so contemptible or absurd a composition: and have so much benevolence, as well as deference for the rest of mankind, that I hope there is none so disagreeably made, as well as firmly believe there is none so weakly put together. Without any one external alteration, I found so great an internal change in myself last Friday, that from being quite easy, I grew what I can not describe any otherways than by telling you it was the reverse of what I have last described —I mean easy. I was a little better for bleeding on Saturday; and since that have continued much as you saw me at Redlynch. I am to go to-morrow morning for 24 hours to Sundon, where Lady Hervey has been this fortnight. Celà sera deux jours de relâche. Perhaps not; and I shall find, like the man described by Boileau,

"—En vain de lui-même il s'enfuit,
Le chagrin monte en croupe et galoppe avec lui."

Parlons d'autre chose. I will get *Agrippina*[2] copied, and send it to you as soon as I return. I desire you will send me your remarks upon it, and your corrections. If you do not; when I am fitter to correct my own faults than I find myself at present, I will correct it myself.

Algarotti has been gone this fortnight, which was really a very

[1] Holland House.

[2] This is referred to in the *Dict. Nat. Biog.*, as a "Tragedy in Rhyme", in manuscript. It does not appear to be amongst the Ickworth Manuscripts. Another set of verses "Aceronia" is mentioned several times at this period; but no copy of it seems to be preserved there.

great loss to me; for I saw him often, and was always amused when I saw him, either by conversing with him or reading to him. I am now generally in this house (triste séjour), and generally seeing or thinking of the same thing. Adieu. I write like a fool, think like a fool, talk like a fool, act like a fool; and have everything of a fool but the content of one. This is no news to you; and if there is anything stirring that would be so I know it not, or can not recollect it. I would not send this letter if I had time to write another, but I had rather you should think anything of me than that I neglect or forget you. Pray burn it as soon as you have read it, and pray allow it the only merit it pretends to, which is being a piece of my silly heart that I would trust to few eyes and few hands but your own. Once more. Adieu.

TO HENRY FOX *Kensington, October 6, 1736*[1]

. . . All the commotions expected on the commencement of the Gin Act[2] have been so well guarded against by the care of the Government, that there has not been the least disturbance. I can tell you nothing of the King's return, any more that it is generally said by people who know no more of it than I do, though they give themselves greater latitude in conjecturing, that he will certainly not be here by the Birthday. The Duke & Duchess of Richmond set out for Holland tomorrow. She has been in waiting this fortnight, during which time she has been very often here, & I much with them both. I never knew the rage of moving preside so in any composition as his. For my part I had as lief be the master of a packet-boat, or a post-boy, or drive a stage-coach like my Lord Salisbury, as lead his life. Yet I acknowledge this life in him to be an exception to that philosophical axiom of *all motion proceeding from disquiet*: for I think I never saw more true marks of a Chevalier sans Souci

[1] Holland House.

[2] In order to curb the growing evil of general taste for strong liquors, an Act was brought in to curb sale in the streets, and altered in 1733 with further measures to limit the sale in houses. The 1736 Act placed a duty of 20*s.* per gallon on spirits, and £50 for a license to sale. This came into force at the end of September.

in any character in my life than in his, & I am quite at a loss to comprehend how so much indolence & agitation could ever meet.[1]

The Queen is to have all the new singers with her this afternoon. You will not envy me my share in that entertainment, any more than I do the Duke of Richmond his journeys. You have as little notion of musical, as I of itinerant pleasures.

I am as indifferent as it is possible for any one to be to any thing, to what is printed in the *Grub Street Journal* : & so much so, that I have never given myself the least trouble to inquire any thing about it.[2] As to what you mean about violent remedies in another case I can not comprehend, unless you would have me put out my eyes & stuff cotton in my ears. I have had thoughts of going to the Bath this season for a month, but do not know whether I can make it practicable with ease. But if I am not better by the Birthday, with or without ease, I am determined to do it.

The 20th of this month I shall hope to see you in town with

[1] "Indolence and agitation." Duke and Duchess of Richmond. [Note in Horace, Earl of Orford's writing.]

[2] *The Grub Street Journal*, a semi-political, semi-literary, weekly periodical, first made its appearance in 1730, lasting until 1737. Pope had a definite connection with it in its first years, but few contributions from his pen can be traced in its later period ; and it became quite independent of him. The *Journal* paid little attention to Hervey until the end of 1733, after the latter's *Letter to a Doctor of Divinity*. From then onwards there were occasional attacks. In September 1736 we find two insulting epigrams, one "To the Earl of B." (which Mr. J. J. Hillhouse in his work, *The Grub Street Journal*, connects on one page with Lord Burlington, on another with Lord Bathurst, pp. 77, 339). One of these reads, in answer to certain verses said to be by Hervey :—

"You wonder who this thing has writ,
So full of fibs, so void of wit?
Lord! never ask who thus could serve ye,
Who can it be but fibster H——."

Some partisan of Hervey's replied ; and later in the month came the following, an answer to someone who admired a bust of Hervey :—

"The Sculptor praised, and praising laughed,
A pretty figure I profess,
This is Lord Fanny's head I guess.
How happy Rysbrack are thy pains!
In life, by G—d, it has no brains."

your brother. I invited Hamilton [1] yesterday to meet you that day at dinner at my lodgings. Adieu.

Amongst the Ickworth papers, we find a long letter to Algarotti, written on October 30. The original is in Sir John Murray's series. Part of it is devoted to a dissertation by Hervey on the respective values and qualities of the English seventeenth-century poets.

TO MONSIEUR ALGAROTTI *St. James's, October 30th, 1736*

. . . As to the task you have assigned me of transcribing the most shining passages out of the most shining of our English poets, I hope I need not tell you that the trouble of executing such a task would never deter me from undertaking it, if I had any hopes of succeeding in it; but there are ten thousand reasons for my declining this commission. In the first place, you know all our best authors as well as I do; you understand them as well, and can judge of them better, from having more skill, a juster taste and less prejudice. In the next place, I am generally speaking an enemy to particular quotations for the proof of general assertions with regard to the merit of authors. I hardly ever know them answer the end; for so much depends on the introduction, the connection and accompaniment of those sort of things, that they always lose most of their grace, if not all, when they come to be detached; and preserve no more of the merit they have in the original, than a lip, a nose or an eyebrow would do taken out of a face, and separated from the rest of those concomitants that make that harmony of countenance and symmetry of beauty, which strike us in the result of the whole and will no more admit of separation than definition.

However, that I may in some degree comply with your request, I will give you my opinion in a crude, indigested manner of our best poets, without attempting to back it with any examples. I think *Dryden* much the easiest and finest versifier, as well as the most classical poet that ever wrote in the English language. *Waller* had smoothed and softened our language a little before Dryden wrote, and is surpassed by nobody in ingenuity and

[1] Hamilton. Charles Hamilton, brother of D. Abercorn. [Note in Horace, Earl of Orford's writing.]

urbanity. (Don't venture that word, for it is not English; it is only *Herveyish.*) Cowley has wit, but much more false than true: his thoughts are often puerile: his turns glare, but there is not much light in them when examined, and his flights are like those of swallows, very quick, but frequently very near the ground. There is infinite wit in Lord Rochester's and Lord Dorset's Satires; but the finest, the keenest and the correctest Satire we have is *Dryden's Absalom and Achitophel*, on King Charles the 2d's Court. You have heard so much on *Milton* and *Shakespear's* Chapter, that I need say nothing with regard to them, any further than that you esteem the first much less, and many people the latter much more than I do. *Prior* in my opinion excelled in more different sorts of writing than any of the authors I have named: the tender, the heroic, the burlesque, the epistolary, the elegy, the tale, and the ode. He has attempted everything but satire, and I think succeeded in everything but epigrams. His epigrams are indeed infamous, and show how low drink, age, infirmity and bad company, may bring the most elevated geniuses.

Were I to curse my foe, I'd have him live,
Himself, his friends, and credit to survive:
Into contempt from reputation hurl'd,
His own defamer to the scoffing world.

But I forget myself, and instead of giving you a good opinion of other people's verses, I am giving you a bad one of my own. But as my thoughts without any affectation fall some days so naturally into rhyme, that I am forced to think twice to put them into prose, and as I never constrain my nature when I write or speak to you, forgive the inconveniency of my sincerity for the sake of that affection which occasions it. . . .

When I tell you that today is the King's Birthday: that I have been obliged all the morning to hear Bishops make spiritual, and the Courtiers temporal compliments to the Queen: that Sir Robt. (who goes tomorrow into Norfolk) dined with me: and that I am obliged to go up at nine a clock to take out a parcel of bad dancers to expose themselves one after another at the Ball, you will perhaps wonder how I have found time to persecute you with this infinite letter. . . . I told Sir Robt. Walpole that I had just received a letter from you, in which he was mentioned. This gave occasion to *his* saying many many just and obliging things of you. Adieu.

The clock strikes nine.

I forgot in speaking of the English poets to mention *Pope*; but you know my opinion of him is that when other people think for him nobody writes better, and few people worse when he thinks for himself.

My Lady Hervey has charged me with a thousand compliments to you, which I have not time to particularise.

I desire you to write in French.

TO HENRY FOX *November 13, 1736*[1]

I am just returned with the Queen from a long dull Opera, and a cold, empty House: and have only time to reproach you with having broken your word; for you promised to write to me as soon as you got into the country, and I have not received a single line from your fair hands. However, being a good Christian, and consequently determine to return good for evil, as I thought you seemed rather to wish I would write to the Bishop of Salisbury, though you would not ask me directly to do it, I sent him a letter, to which I received the enclosed in answer.

What do you do with your selves in the country? Where are you? Who is with you? When do you return? Ld Cholmondeley and the D. of Kingston[2] came together from France, and are to set out tomorrow together to Houghton. There are various reports and opinions concerning his Grace's returning to France. He has been lodged in Ld Cholmondeley's house ever since he came over. Adieu. The clock strikes eleven.

TO HENRY FOX *Kensington, November 25, 1736*[3]

I am confined to my room by a great cold, a sore throat, and a slight fever, for which I have been this morning blooded. But

[1] Holland House.

[2] Evelyn Pierrepont, 2nd Duke (1711–73), who had succeeded his grandfather.

[3] Holland House.

a letter from you is so uncommon a favour that it is impossible for me to defer my acknowledgments another post; lest you should think me as unworthy of such favours after you have bestowed them, as I conclude you do beforehand by conferring them so seldom.

The orders are at last arrived for the yachts to sail for Holland. The courier that brought them came the day before yesterday at noon, and the King is to leave Hanover the 7th of next month.

The Duke of Kingston is not to go back to France. France[1] is come to him, and lodges in St. James's Street. France's flight makes some talk here, but much more noise at Paris. Her husband pursued her, but concluding she was gone to Calais, miss'd her; she having taken the Flanders road, and embarked at Ostend.

I have spoken to ——[2] about the American Governments the day after he return'd to London. He says there will be no removals. I shall commit no more particulars of our conversation to black and white.

I do not send any other news, because if there is any, I do not know it. I am obliged to be so much here, have so few avocations to London, and the roads are so infamously bad, that since you went out of town, I have been less in it than ever, and am consequently au fait of nothing but the quotidian vieilleries of this almost depopulated Palace.

My service to Mrs. Horner and Mrs. Fox,[3] and tell the former when I go next to Redlynch I will endeavour to obey her commands: and when she comes to town will entertain her (or endeavour it at least) with some other little things, which I do not send to you, because I can only say—"tu *solebas* meas esse aliquid putare nugas".

[1] "France" was a certain Madame de la Touche, the natural daughter of a Paris banker, M. Bernard. "The young Duke fled with her to England; and a prosecution for the abduction was commenced before the Parliament of Paris in 1737. The French King put a stop to the proceedings" (*Lady Mary Wortley-Montagu's Letters*, ii, 195). The Duke lived with the lady for many years. Lord Bathurst writing to Dean Swift, in December, said, "I want no foreign commodities. My neighbour, the Duke of Kingston, has imported one; but I do not think it worth the carriage."

[2] Name missing.

[3] Stephen Fox's child-wife.

After many messages and some appointments that proved abortive, I have at last seen Mrs. Horner. I found her in good health, good humour and good spirits : and as I like her mightily, and that she seems quite easy with me, I propose seeing her very often.[1]

A messenger arrived today at four a clock from Holland, that brought the news of the Princess Royal's having brought to bed last Wednesday. She was so ill in labour that the midwife was forced to squeeze the child extremely to deliver her, which kill'd it. The Princess of Orange wrote the Queen word that the Princess was asleep, and out of all danger. The Queen, however, has been extremely fluttered and disordered on this news, but is now better. They are letting her blood in the next room to that where I am now writing. As soon as that operation is over I am to return to her, but snatched this opportunity to give you this account. Adieu.

Saturday night. 7 a oclock.

The first letter in 1736 from Hervey to Stephen Fox is in December. But this demonstrates quite plainly that their friendship remained constant.

TO STEPHEN FOX *Kensington, Dec. 4, 1736*[2]

If it were possible for me to write to you, my dear Ste., with the same security that I speak to you, and that I was sure what I write would be as safe in it's way to you, as I am very certain it would be when it got there, you should have no opportunity

[1] He did see her very often about four or five years after this, when he had become intimate with the Dss of Manch[ester], whom he has abused so much in former letters, and betrayed to Mrs. Horner Mr. Fox's passion for that Duchess. [Note in Horace, Earl of Orford's writing.]

Presumably Walpole was referring to the 2nd Duchess, Lady Isabella Montagu, a grand-daughter of 1st Duke of Marlborough. Hervey mentioned her earlier in these letters ; and Hanbury-Williams spoke of her later, and got into trouble when she married Edward Hussey and he wrote verses on her. One of the offending passages read :

"How slight the difference is between
The Duchess and the Hussey."

[2] Melbury.

to complain of my silence. As it is you have no reason to complain, since you know this to be the only cause of it, and that if I did write frequently it must either be with a freedom that would be dangerous to me, or in a constraint that would be tiresome both to you and me. However I have one comfort, even in being debarred the pleasure of entertaining you with any little pieces of secret history by letter, and that is the being better able by the number of things I have by these means in store, to make our tête à têtes when we meet less tiresome to you, when I prolong the pleasure of them to myself. And when you seem in a hurry to be gone ; it is with no small degree of satisfaction that I recollect some new story, which I throw out to your curiosity (as Hippomenes did the gold apples), to stop you in your flight.

It is incredible the bustle Madame de la Touche's adventure makes at Paris. One should have imagined the Duke of Kingston, by the manner the French people speak of this affair, had seduced a Vestal from her sacred Fire, rather than only suffered a forsaken mistress of the Duc de la Trémouille's to follow him to England. The style in which old Bernard talks of this affair they say is admirable. You know she is his natural daughter, and when first he heard of her elopement, he went to her mother, and told her, if it had not been for her, he had long ago put the D. of Kingston to death, and then, il n'auroit pas été dans son pouvoir de deshonorer publiquement nôtre famille par ce dernier coup. "Pour moi (dit-il), je ne crois pas qu'il y'a au monde un homme qu'un Anglois qui est capable d'avoir fait un pas si indigne d'un honnête homme. Quand j'étois en Allemagne tout le monde sait qu'il y avoit plusieurs Princesses qui avoient envie de s'enfuir de leurs maris avec moi pour venir en France, et que jamais je n'ai été assez scélérat pour les encourager ; mais au contraire que je leur ai déclaré qu'elles avoient beau faire, et que je ne voulois point les reçevoir. Voilà la différence entre l'honnête procédé d'un françois, et la coquinerie d'un Anglois."

I hear the Duke of Marlborough is ruining himself at play at the Bath, though he won 4600 upon one card at basset. The Queen goes to settle in London on Tuesday, which is the same day the King is to leave Hanover. The Parliament is not to meet till the 21st of January. It was put off one day later, and to a Friday ; because the Thursday and the 20th is the Prince's Birth-Day. Adieu. They say London is still very empty. I know little of it, for I hardly ever go out of these walls, which, by the identity of faces they enclose, one should imagine belonged rather to a Turkish Seraglio than an English Palace.

Tell the Count I will write to him very soon.

TO HENRY FOX *St. James's, Dec. 14, 1736*[1]

. . . I am obliged to you for the verses you enclosed, and will not chide you for your abominable conduct at the Bath, not because you do not deserve to be chid, but because I find you are incorrigible. The epigram I had seen before ; but the mere puns on Sestos and Abydos were not what I should have thought would have hit your taste. I know why you sent me Mr. Hammond's verses, but I never commended him out of prose.

There came another express to-day from the Hague which has set the Queen's mind quite at ease about her daughter. She says, " Grâce à Dieu ma fille se porte bien, et pour la sienne, je ne m'en soucie point ". The same messenger brought word that the King has been waiting ever since Saturday at Helvoetsluys for a wind ; all the letters say he is in good health, but not a word of his humour. This puts me in mind of old Johnson,[2] who told a certain person that every body commended his justice, but no body ever mentioned his generosity.

There is at present in my manner of living no difference from that at Kensington, but the houses. I see the same people, and do the same things I did there every day of my life ; but as Amurat says, *Tout dans le palais va changer de face*. I question much whether I shall like the change,[3] or whether if I do not, I shall be able to seem to do so.

[1] Holland House.

[2] James Johnston (1635–1737), known as Secretary Johnston. Old Johnson, Secretary of State of Scotland under King William. [Note in Horace, Earl of Orford's writing.]

[3] " The Change." The King's return. He was better with the Queen. (*Ibid.*)

TO HENRY FOX *St. James's, December 16, 1736*[1]

I was forced to leave the Queen an hour earlier than ordinary this morning, to execute this commission,[2] which I assure you was making no small sacrifice. She would know what business I could have to pin me down to so much punctuality. I told her it was yours, and not my own, upon which she dismissed me with a benediction of, " Allez vous en, vous et vos stocks, et vos amis, tous au grand Diable ". We know nothing for certain of the King. The wind was fair yesterday ; and is contrary today. Some say he is at sea, and others that he has not yet embarked ; but both these opinions are mere conjecture. The Prince gives a dinner tomorrow, at his house in Pall Mall, to my Lord Mayor and a thousand citizens, who are to bring him the Freedom of the City tomorrow morning in form. I make no comments. Adieu.

TO HENRY FOX *St. James's, December 21, 1736*[3]

A thousand thanks to you, my dear Count, for your long, agreeable, miscellaneous letter. I hope that the same letter that carry'd it to Bruton, brought back one from me to tell you that yr commands were obeyed, your annuities sold, and the money lodged at Mr. Hoare's.

I dined yesterday with Mrs. Horner in her dressing-room, and we were both in excellent health, good humour, and not bad spirits. She thinks much better of me than I deserve ; but my amour-propre will not let me have the pleasure of thinking I deserve all she professes, and I believe thinks. Yet it is so ingenious a chemist that it will extract some food out of every thing. And whilst I confess her prejudiced, my amour-propre still tells me she has imbibed those prejudices from you and your brother ; and in the things she says *to* me, I am continually reflecting what she you must have said *of* me : pleased still with considering the impressions you must have given of me when I

[1] Holland House.

[2] A small private financial transaction for Henry Fox.

[3] Holland House.

A. Pond, pinxit

MRS. STRANGWAYS-HORNER (pastel), 1737

was absent, though I feel the mortification of not being able to maintain them when I am present.

Mrs Horner had shown me the verses you sent me last, before I received them from you, and I liked them so well that I had begged a copy. I do not guess by your style whose they are, for I know no one who writes with so much thought and such strong, close meaning. C'est un style cramponné que j'aime fort, qui frappe d'abord, et plait même quand on l'examine.

The King is still at Helvoetsluys ; and it is reported not alone, *ma non lo credo* . . .

I am but just come from the Opera, and am going upstairs to play cribbage as usual with her Royal Highness : [1] and am consequently as usual in a great hurry. Adieu donc. When do you come to town ? My service to Ste., who owes me a long letter.

TO HENRY FOX [*Postmark : December 23, 1736*] [2]

The King is safe, thank God, at Helvoetsluys. I send you the enclosed, in return for the Latin verses you sent me.

The English ones you sent me on Henley I had read but once when I wrote last. I do not like them as well on a second reading ; though, I think a little mending might make them good.

I wish I could give you an account of a conversation I had to day ; but you know I often write *for* you, when I do not write *to* you.[3]

[1] Princess Caroline. [Note in Horace, Earl of Orford's writing.] Hervey was always reputed to be on specially friendly terms with this Princess. Certainly he goes out of his way on all occasions to praise her. " Princess Caroline was just the reverse [of her sister Princess Emily]. She was extremely sensible, and not remarkably lively. . . . She had the finest complexion, and the finest bright brown hair that could be seen. She had very pretty limbs too ; but her person was rather too fat. She had affability without meanness, prudence without falsehood. She spent her whole time in reading and drawing ; was a favourite neither with her mother nor her father . . ." (*Memoirs*, p. 276.)

[2] Holland House.

[3] " Often write *for* you," means his *Memoirs*. [Note in Horace, Earl of Orford's writing.] Hervey also used this expression earlier in the letters.

CHAPTER XI

1737–1738

The only letter in the early part of 1737 is one to Count Algarotti in the Ickworth series, in January. It is full of long dissertations on verses and other literary productions of no special interest: but a few extracts on Court subjects may be quoted. It does not occur in Sir John Murray's series.

TO COUNT ALGAROTTI *St. James's, January 16/27, 1737*[1]

. . . I am glad to hear you divert yourself so ill at Venice, as I hope it will make you seek that which every body seeks elsewhere. If you could make every place as agreeable to yourself as you must make it to every other body, I should despair of seeing you again; since the consequence of that would be your desiring to change your company as little as your companions desire you should.

A cold winter, without fire, at Venice, perhaps may enable you to bear damp summers without sun in England. Make haste hither then, before the season comes for the renewal of your acquaintance with that planet, and do not let it intercept the revolution of the comet that appeared last year in our Western world. . . .

As often as we talked of the *Caesar, of Voltaire*,[2] how came you never to tell me of your letter to the Abbé Franquini [*sic*] on that subject? Why did you suffer me to owe[3] the pleasure of reading that piece of criticism to chance, and not to your friendship? Why were you not the canal as well as the source? And why did you let me feel myself obliged to the agreeable author only as one of the public, when you know I always wish to feel myself obliged to him as one of his friends? . . .

We have at last got the King back to England, in spite of contrary winds that kept him five weeks at Helvoetsluys. He

[1] Ickworth.

[2] No doubt the reference is to Voltaire's *Mort de César* (publ. 1735).

[3] Corrected in Hervey's writing.

arrived here last Saturday. I need not tell you how near he was to being drowned in a tempest a fortnight ago, that drove him back to the coast of Holland. All the public Gazettes were full of this incident, and for once did not exaggerate ; but the true reason was because they could not. All England for 24 hours thought him lost. . . .

I make your court to the D. and Dss of Richmond, to Lady Albemarle and Sir Robert Walpole, as often as you could wish ; and I never name you to any of them without receiving this answer : "I am very much obliged to him, I like your friend extremely. Pray when will he come to England again ?"

We find a letter to Stephen Fox on June 11. The speech made by Henry Fox, to which Hervey refers, was on June 9, shortly before the termination of the Session, on the second reading of a Bill of Pains and Penalties against the Provost and City of Edinburgh—the result of the Porteous riots, in which Captain Porteous had been lynched by the mob, for his action in ordering his men to fire into the crowd.

Earlier in the year, indeed shortly after the last letter, Hervey had been instrumental in defeating a secret attempt by the Prince to get his allowance again referred to Parliament. Hervey took this opportunity of trying anew to obtain for Stephen a peerage or some small office, especially as the latter had refused a promise of future advancement from one of the Prince's entourage. But Walpole was, as ever, unhelpful in such matters ; and it was not until 1739 that a junior seat on the Treasury Board was forthcoming, followed in 1741 by a Barony. Hervey's efforts on behalf of Henry Fox, a far more live wire and likely to become of great use to Walpole, were at once effectual ; and he received the Surveyorship of the King's Works, with a salary attached of over £1,100. He took up the duties of this office late in June. Letters to both brothers follow.

TO STEPHEN FOX *Ickworth, June 11, 1737*[1]

I am obliged to you, my dear Ste, for your letter : but should have been much more so if you would have added a postscript to let me know if the Count spoke, and whether well, ill or indifferent ; and what the numbers were on the division for the Commitment of the Bill.

I have passed many hours since I came here alone, and many in Lord Bristol's room when he was too much out of order to

[1] Melbury.

converse (he is now better), but, as you know I hate being idle when I could neither talk nor read. Pray tell Mrs. Horner I was employed in the task she set me, which goes on tolerably fast.

When I shall return to London I know not, and in another week I believe I shall not much care: for when once I am in a track, you know I can plod on for ever. My Lord's indisposition keeps neighbours aloof; and if one mouth in the house I could name was gagged, I should like this relaxation very well. . . . But that orifice is so like that of Mount Vesuvius, that every thing that comes out of it that is not fire is rubbish, and every thing within the reach of it's disagreeable influence the worse for it. Adieu. Mount Vesuvius is this moment roaring for my letters, because the man that carries them is to bring my Lord's pills.

TO HENRY FOX *Ickworth, June 13, 1737*[1]

I have heard of your speaking from two hands besides your own, and from neither of them with less commendation than you say (adding modestly the epithet of *undeserved*) you received on that occasion from many of your auditors; so that your vanity, which, as you are human, I suppose has not a blunter appetite than other people's, may feed on these *hors d'œuvres*, as well as those dishes that were immediately served up for it's own eating. You need not fear my checking your vanity on any occasion for two reasons; in the first place, because I would never check you in any pleasure, much less in the most sensible as well as the most durable of all the pleasures; and in the next, because it is generally a proof of a quality I would have predominant in your intercourse with me on all occasions, which is sincerity.

I entreat you to write to me often, and to give me credit for these literary debts till we invert our situations, and that I am in the scene of business in town and you in that of inaction in the country; from whence I know and feel it is impossible to be always spinning, like a spider, out of one's own bowels, or, if one could, like a spider, one should catch nothing but flies. I will therefore take a form of a note for a play-debt of the late

[1] Holland House.

Duchess of Bolton's, for the model of my answers to your letters: and only say like her, "I own I owe to the bearer of this, etc.——which I promise to pay when I am able." [1]

I wish you had not stayed for our meeting (which I know not when will happen), to tell me why your opinion of my friend, Lord Ilay, is not alter'd in his favour. I dare say the Bill [2] at last will pass in no form: and think, as I always did think, and have often said, that some people's meddling with this prosecution by way of Bill, is not better policy than Pulteney's not meddling with it at all.

You know long ago my opinion about the displacing Lord A.; [3] that I think it right in no light, and wonder where you see *du pour*, as well as *the other considerations* you hint at, that make you wish this measure had not been taken. You see how dull I am grown by a week's rustication. I can comprehend nothing by intimation. Therefore for the future leave my sagacity nothing to conclude; but if you have occasion to tell me what 3 and 2 make, for fear of mistakes be so good to add the word *five*, or I shall certainly guess 4 or 6.

Lord Bristol is much better. Adieu. Make my compliments to Mrs. Horner, whom I love and like.

[1] Dss of Bolton. Natural daughter of the Duke of Monmouth. She was a cunning fool, who diverted George II and Queen Caroline with affected blunders and étourderie. She told the former she came from the play of "La dernière *Chemise* de l'Amour". Another time she told the Queen she had been at Whiston's, who had frightened her out of her senses. He had told her the world would be burnt in two years; and to be sure she was determined to go to China. [Note in Horace, Earl of Orford's writing.]

This was the 3rd wife of Charles, 2nd Duke of Bolton, not the well-known actress, Lavinia Fenton, mistress, and later wife, of the 3rd Duke. Rev. William Whiston was a scientist and celebrated lecturer.

[2] On Porteous riots.

[3] Lord Archibald Hamilton (1673?–1754), brother of 4th Duke of Hamilton. His 3rd wife was Jane, daughter of 6th Earl of Abercorn. He had been absent from a division supporting the Prince of Wales's allowance; and was the only one who was not turned out, although the King and Queen were most anxious to dispense with his services as a Lord of the Admiralty. He was finally dismissed late in 1737. Hervey wrote of him, and of his wife, reputed to be the Prince's mistress, "Lady Archibald was not young, had never been very pretty, and had lost as least as much of the small share of beauty she once possessed, as it is usual for women to do at 35. . . . Her husband was of so quiet, so secure and contented temper, that he seemed cut out to play the passive character his wife and the Prince graciously allotted him. . . ." (*Memoirs*, p. 475.)

TO STEPHEN FOX *Ickworth Park, June 25, 1737*[1]

You can not imagine, my dear Ste, how sorry I am to hear you are so much, and so disagreeably out of order ; but I would not for the world in your present circumstances, you should take a journey, and in this heat, on my account ; and for that reason will not tell you what day I shall be in town, though I have fixed it, and shall write to Lady Hervey to forbid her telling you. . . .

I am glad Mrs. Horner was sorry I huffed her. I would have her a little angry too, rather than quite easy ; for I feel, by recent examples, how thorough a contempt one must have for any body whose huffs can neither give one sorrow nor anger ; and have too great a real value and esteem for her not to wish that even a mock-huff should have some effect upon her, and that she should be at least half as much afraid of my taking any thing ill of her, as I shall ever be of doing any thing she might take ill of me.

I really feel so settled and so easy here, that I begin to think I am fitter to live in the country than I thought I was. Not that I think of the common pleasures of a country at all differently from the manner in which I used to think of them :

Not that in dogs or horses I delight ;
 That country sports or business I pursue ;
That lawns or woods or waters feast my sight,
 Or landscape, fair as Claud Lorain e'er drew.

I own, my Friend, my only pleasures lie
 In human creatures, and in black and white :
Whilst in my conduct still I only try,
 To reconcile what's pleasant with what's right.

Nor need I blush, whilst in these paths I tread,
 Since (as in Xenophon's grave page you read)
These paths great Socrates himself once led,
 And by this rule his ev'ry action weigh'd.

N.B.—The remainder of this letter is badly torn and undecipherable.

[1] Melbury. Fox was at Burlington Street.

The accouchement of the Princess had taken place at St. James's on July 31, where there were no preparations whatsoever, and whither her husband had removed her at the risk of her life from Hampton Court, after she had been taken ill and the symptoms of labour had already commenced. The Royal family were playing cards, and went to bed at 11, no word having reached them of the Prince's indiscretion.[1] The Queen, however, on hearing what was happening, at once rushed up to St. James's in the dead of night. Subsequently letters from the Prince reached both the King and the Queen, offering explanations; but the King refused to see him on his return to Hampton Court. The Prince next sent a further letter which is here mentioned.

TO HENRY FOX *Friday [August 5] 1737*[2]

Yesterday's letter was to desire earnestly to be re-admitted into the King's presence, protesting the uprightness of his intentions, and not owning himself in the wrong in any one step. Not a word *of* or *to* the Queen. The K's answer to Lord Carnarvon[3] was, that, as the purport of this letter was the same as that which Lord Jersey brought the night before, it required no other answer than what had been given to that. Lord Carnarvon desired an answer in writing. Lord Essex told him he could only give his Lordship the answer as he had received it. Lord Carnarvon persisted, and would not stir, Ld. Essex persisted too; and at last Ld. C. wrote it down, and asked Ld. E. if that was right. I am tired to death of hearing nothing but this sort of stuff over and over again; it *ennuies* me to a degree that is inconceivable. I shall see you to-morrow, and I suppose you, not being so tired of the subject as I am, will make me talk it all over again.

TO HENRY FOX *St. James's Palace, August 30, 1737*[4]

Dear Count,

You know I have a most laudable and insurmountable aversion to writing *Evening Posts* and *Daily Journals*; and therefore it is

[1] *Memoirs*, p. 757 etc. [2] Holland House.
[3] Lord Carnarvon, the Duke of Chandos's eldest son, one of the Prince's equerries, arrived while the King was dining in public.
[4] Holland House. Fox was at Redlynch.

utterly impossible for me to relate anything about last night's christening farther than that there was one.[1] For all the names of gossips and proxies, the descriptions of cradles, canopies, gallons, embroidery, basons, white satin quilts, velvet mantles, jewels, laced pillows, etc., etc., etc.—I refer you to print. How the Archbishop [2] grunted, the D. of Grafton stammered, Lady Burlington glouted,[3] my Lady Torrington grinned and my Lady Archibald smiled, are particulars I fear you will not find in print, and are circumstances so very interesting that I am infinitely sorry I was not present at the ceremony, to give you an exact account of such material occurences.

The Prince, I hear, hating all German innovations on our old English customs and Constitution, has ordered everybody not to call his daughter the Princess, but the Lady Augusta. I wish I knew how hieroglyphically to write through my nose,[4] and I would then without naming names insinuate to you, who I imagine it was put this popular stroke of deep politics into his R.Hs's head. For the rest of his R.Hs's late steps and proceeding, I hear Lord Chesterfield publickly purges himself of having had any hand in them; and says, "Carteret is our adviser at present; and I am too just to rob him of the honour of such able counsel by pretending to have any share in it."

What will you say I wonder when I tell you the D. of Montagu has quitted his Troop, and retaken the Band of Pensioners? [5] Homo stabilis et rationalis. You will hear other things soon, I believe, that will surprise you, unless your motto is *nil admirari*. You fancy you guess about what; but you guess wrong. Adieu, I am in a great hurry going back to Hampton Court with the D. of Richmond, who stays for me. Adieu. Je suis charmé que votre frère se porte si bien.

The date of the next letter is uncertain. It is certainly in the latter part of the year 1737. It speaks for itself. Henry Fox by this time, as we have seen, was at the head of the King's Works.

[1] That of the Prince and Princess's daughter. (*See Memoirs*, p. 805.)

[2] John Potter (1674–1747) had succeeded Archbishop Wake, who died at the end of 1736.

[3] Looked sulky.

[4] "Thro' my nose", I believe, means George Lyttelton. [Note in Horace, Earl of Orford's writing.]

[5] The *Dict. Nat. Biog.* states that he was removed.

TO HENRY FOX[1] *St. James's, Thursday night, 1737*

Which of the devils in Hell prompted you to tell the Queen that everything in her Library was ready for the putting up of her books ?—Thou abominable new broom, that so far from sweeping clean, has not removed one grain of dirt and rubbish. Come to me to-morrow morning to take the rest of your scolding ; and go with me to scold all your odious, dilatory subalterns. Bad night.

TO STEPHEN FOX *Hampton Court, September 10, 1737*[2]

I took the advantage of a hunting-day (the only mornings I have at my own disposal) to walk to Richmond today to breakfast with Mrs. Horner, and found her all alone ; for Mrs. Fox[3] and my Cousin Ayliffe, not loving home so well as she does, and loving hunting much better than I do, were gone to the rendezvous. Mrs. Horner and I talk'd a *duetto* for about two hours without any intermission : it put me more out of breath than my walk. I am just this moment return'd, and though I have very little time left to get dressed for dinner, I had rather be too late in any thing than my acknowledgments to you and your brother for your letters. And to show my modesty and my humility, though you always prefer a dog and a partridge to me, I am thankful for your preferring me at least to the Parson of the Parish, and giving to me the time Co. Fen and Fly sigh for your not giving to your salvation. There was a Cabinet-Council here yesterday. Can you guess about what—when I tell you that one of the Cabinet-Counsellors was asked if a great many people had been condemned ? And he answer'd, " No, there is nobody to be hanged, and only one ordered for transportation ". I think it an excellent bon-mot : and you are very dull, if it does not inform you as well as make you laugh.

[1] Holland House. Addressed : " Henry Fox Esq.
Neglector of his Majesty's Works."

[2] Melbury.

[3] Stephen Fox's child-wife was living with her mother. Hervey's " cousin " Ayliffe was doubtless Judith, youngest daughter of George Ayliffe of Grittenham and his wife Judith, daughter of Col. Giles Strangways. Miss Ayliffe died in 1747.

I must now tell you a *mauvais-mot* of the D. of Newcastle's. Sir Robt Walpole and he and the Archbishop, and some more of the *grosses-têtes*, and a good many ladies, were invited to dine at the Duchess of Richmond's (who is in Waiting here); and just after they were sat down, his Grace said to Sir Robert in his shrill Cock-pit voice cross the table, "Well, Sir Robert, I desire you would not talk in your usual strain to these ladies, but remember the Archbishop is here." Sir Robert answered very gravely, "I am not conscious of ever having presumed to say any thing to these ladies any Bishop might not hear". And with much ado, his Grace, after being teazed about an hour for this pretty speech, began to find out he had ingeniously in these few words told Sir R. that he never knew how to behave himself, intimated to the Archbishop that the D^ss of Richmond and the ladies of the Court were accustomed to hear such bawdy as must shock episcopal ears; and that his Grace's presence put a constraint upon the whole company. Was there ever such an animal? The D^ss of R^d. sends to say she stays dinner for me. Adieu.

Following upon two letters of thanks sent by the Prince to the King and Queen on the day after the christening, in neither of which the words, "Your Majesty", were used, an omission repeated from former occasions, with other studied insults, the King decided to remove the Prince and his Court from St. James's. Consequently, Sir Robert was told to draw up a letter to this effect. Walpole asked Lord Hervey to write a draft, on which the final letter, with certain improvements, was based, after it had been shown to the Lord Chancellor and the Duke of Newcastle. It is printed in the *Memoirs* (p. 814). Sir Robert, who was seemingly becoming jealous of Hervey's influence with Queen Caroline, forbade the former to say one word of his hand in the letter to her: whilst the Queen spoke to Hervey about it, and placed him in a difficult position, by taking the same line, in forbidding him to mention the subject to Walpole! The letter was then shown to the Cabinet, and was passed, with some reluctance on the part of certain courtier members, who would have preferred a compromise. The letter was despatched on September 10; and its results were shortly related in the next letter to Henry Fox on the 13th.

TO HENRY FOX[1] *Hampton Court, September 13, 1737*

Dear Count, The enclosed is the message sent last Saturday in the evening from the K. to the P. It is so well drawn and explains itself so well, that I need not add any comments upon it. The order to forbid any body that goes to the P. coming to the K. followed the message the very next day; and the P. with his whole family removed yesterday to Kew. Where they are to be at their return to London, I know not.—Ld. Delaware[2] kissed the King's hand on Sunday for the D. of Montagu's troop of Horse Guards. I am glad poor Del. is saved from his disagreeable exile to the West Indies. I have obtained of the D. of Newcastle a promise for Mr. Jackson to succeed to the Consulship of Genoa. The present incumbent (as the parsons say) cannot possibly live a month; so I shall write to-night to Leghorn to tell Mr. Jackson he is secure. Pray do you write too, for fear my letter should miscarry. I think of you often, but have lately had occasion to think much more than I would do of some things you said to me a little before you went into the country. When I said you would be surprised soon, don't think I was fool enough to mean this message; and what I then thought would surprise you, perhaps will never happen. You shall know what it was when we meet. I am not concerned in it any way. I know you think that's a lie; but it is not.

A further letter to Count Algarotti follows, much of which is omitted, as is a copy of verses to Lady Mary Wortley-Montagu in it.

TO COUNT ALGAROTTI

Hampton Court, September 17/28, 1737[3]

. . . Not that my giving you this preference to the rest of my acquaintance in everything that is most agreeable should make you vain. For when I say I think Matchiavel the greatest politician, or Horace the politest author, or Monsr. Algarotti the best companion I ever met with, I have not such an opinion

[1] At Redlynch. Holland House.

[2] John West, 1st Earl Delawarr (1693–1766).

[3] Ickworth. This letter is not in the Murray series.

of the inequality of the gifts of Providence as to imagine there is a real superiority in any one man to all the rest of the world. There may, for ought I know, be now a Mandarin at Pekin, who regulates the Emperor of China's affairs with as much ability as Matchiavel could have done ; as polite an author in the Court of Thamus Kouli-Can [*sic*] as Horace ; and as good a companion as you at this moment toasting his black mistress in Mequinez, and laughing at the fools who venture their lives and fortunes to feed the ambition or satiate the revenge of Muley Abdalla or his brother. All I mean when I commend anybody is by comparison, within the little circle of my own knowledge, and leave the bigotry of commendation of those who, like Monsr. Montesquieu, worship their own little idols as he does Caesar, when he says, "J'ai de la peine à croire qu'en quelque état qu'il auroit pu naître, il ne s'en seroit point rendu le Maître.[1] . . ."

You talk to me of my being taken up with the publication of the Peace ; but you mistake my occupations extremely if you think foreign Peace has half so great share in them as domestic wars. The two Courts of the K. and the P., over which a cloud has hung for some time, are at last quite separated by a storm that has broken out upon the lying-in of the Princess. The details of this rupture would be little interesting to you, improper for me, and tedious for both.

> In these wise trifles and important joys,
> Your busy'd friend his useless hours employs.

You say nothing to me in your last letter of your *Newtonian Dialogues.*[2] Are they published, or are they forgot ? The last is a question which will never be asked after they are published. . . .

As you love verses, I will transcribe some written to Lady M. W. about three months ago, in answer to some of her's on the death of Mr. Hedges,[3] a friend of mine, who was Treasurer to the Prince, one you have often seen at Court, and often heard

[1] From his *Considérations*, etc.

[2] The name of the book was *Newtonianismo per le dame*.

[3] Winnington wrote to Henry Fox in January 1728–9, when the Prince of Wales was arriving in England, and an establishment was being set up for him. "You will see by the prints your friend Mr. Hedges is Treasurer to the Prince." John Hedges was M.P. for Bossiney, Cornwall, for many years.

me speak of. I have not the copy of Lady Mary's at Hampton Court, or I would send you those too. . . .

I have lately received a letter and a vast packet of verses from Voltaire, without any date, or anything that makes me guess where he is, or where I can send him any answer. Adio, Carissimo.

TO HENRY FOX *Hampton Court, Sept. 24, 1737*[1]

You have much more curiosity about the thing I said would surprise you than it deserves ; and I begin to think it will never happen. However when we meet, you shall know what it was.

Lord Delaware is to give no money. Lord Hertford is to be made Governor of Minorca, and Lord Albemarle of Jamaica ; but this not being yet known. Don't talk of it.

The order for the separation of the Courts was not to oblige any body to quit who had places in both ;[2] and Jemmy Pelham goes to both. However Ly. Torrington and Ly. Effingham have quitted without being obliged. Ly. Irwin[3] stays. The other two, it is said, are to be succeeded by Ly. Charlotte Edwin and Lady Mary *Fooly*[4] (you know who I mean). The P. has taken the D. of Norfolk's house in St. James's Square, and is to take Cliveden. Mr. Lumley, I conclude, will quit nothing.

[1] Holland House.

[2] Compare *Memoirs* (p. 838), where Hervey wrote that many left the Prince's service, but no one the King's. James Pelham, the Prince's Secretary, was teased by his Master later into leaving His Majesty. He was an M.P. and died in 1761. The Duchess of Norfolk consulted the Queen as to her views, before the Duke decided to let Norfolk House to the Prince. Edward, 9th Duke (1686–1777), had succeeded his brother in December 1732. Less than a month later the new Duke and his wife made a declaration to the King and Queen of their loyalty to them. (*Carlisle*, p. 96.)

[3] Lady Anne Howard, daughter of 3rd Earl of Carlisle, married 5th Viscount Irvine. She was the first Lady of the Bedchamber appointed to the Princess, and had always shown a strong bias in her letters to her father towards the Prince and his Court. (*See Carlisle* MSS.)

[4] "Lady Mary Fooly." Lady Mary Cooley, Lady Archibald's sister. She was not made Lady of the Bedchamber. [Note in Horace, Earl of Orford's writing.] Daughter of 3rd Earl of Abercorn. She married Henry Colley, M.P. in 1719, brother of 1st Lord Mornington. He died in 1723.

I have always had a better opinion of the D. of M.'s [1] understanding than anybody I converse with, yourself excepted ; and have a thousand times wondered with so little knowledge how it came to be a good one, and with so little utterance how one came to know it. Adieu. I have seen Mrs. Horner often, and was to have seen her to-day ; but that my health is not good and the weather abominable.

TO STEPHEN FOX *Hampton Court, Oct. 15, 1737* [2]

How very ill, my dearest of all friends ! must I have expressed myself, for you to imagine by my last letter that I ever suspected you of forgetting or neglecting me. I deserve too well of you (that is, as far as loving you is deserving well), and have too good an opinion of your penetration to doubt of your knowing it well enough to secure me from either of those misfortunes. And whenever I see in you, what I should in any other body construe marks of forgetfulness or neglect, I should certainly impute them to chance, inadvertency or laziness. I have loved you ever since I knew you, which is now many years, so much better than most people are capable of loving any thing, that for your own sake at least you would not nor could not, I am sure—there is so great a pleasure in being so well beloved—be insensible of it, and consequently not desire to preserve it. This seems to be giving myself great merit towards you ; but I am too fair to pretend there is any merit in it. You have no more obligation to me for choosing to live and converse with you preferably to the rest of my acquaintances than Tacitus or Matchiavel have ; for choosing to take them up preferably to any other books in my library, it is for my own sake, not their's, and I recur to them and to you from other amusements merely because they are more agreeable to me than any other. I only wish it was in my power to show you how well I love you, that all your pleasures and wishes depended on me only ; and if they did, you would find

[1] "D. of M.", Montagu. [Note in Horace, Earl of Orford's writing.] Sarah, Duchess of Marlborough spoke of him in 1740, in her *Opinions* (Lord Hailes), p. 58, as addicted to practical jokes, more worthy of a child of 15, than of a man of 52.

[2] Melbury.

yourself never deprived of the one or disappointed of the other. There is an air of melancholy rather to be collected from the whole of your letter than fix'd on any particular passage, which gives me great uneasiness. Why do you only hint it? Tell me what it is. Take my advice, and take my assistance; and believe the first will always be as faithful though not perhaps so able as you could wish it, and the last as willing though not as effectual. Adieu. I had the letter you fear'd was lost, and I shall expect an answer to this with great impatience.

A little more than a month after this letter was written, Queen Caroline was dead. This whole painful episode was fully related in the *Memoirs*, and we have no direct account of it in Hervey's letters at the time. But one from Henry Fox to Stephen on November 22, 1737, tells of their friend's grief. (Melbury.) "Lord Hervey is as calm as ever I saw him, but afflicted to the greatest degree, and will not soon forget it, or, I fear, cease to look upon it, as he at present does, as the greatest misfortune that could befall him, and the loss of so much of the pleasure of his life as makes the rest not worth thinking of. I see him every morning till 10 or 11, and dine with him every day, which, except his half hour's walking, is every moment he is below stairs. He is in health so-so, not so ill as you might expect; but I greatly fear less likely to mend than grow worse."

A note in some correspondence between the 3rd Lord Holland and Mr. John Murray in 1821 (Holland House MSS.), is worth quoting: "Mr. (Henry) Fox was in the room with Sir R. W. when he heard the Queen was dying. He walked about the room very much disturbed, and said to himself, 'My God, My God, why hast thou forsaken me?' This might be his first reflection; but he soon grew pleased at finding that he governed the King alone. He did not love her particularly, for having promoted the quarrel between him and Ld Townshend, in order to make them both dependent on herself." (Compare *Memoirs*, p. 904.)

Some weeks after the Queen's death, Hervey wrote two epitaphs, one in Latin, and one in English. The first reference to the Latin one appears in a letter from his father (*Lord Bristol's Letterbook*, publ. 1898, iii, 196), dated Ickworth, Jan. 7, 1737/38. "Dear Son, quite charmed with the finished beauty of the epitaph you sent me, I could not forbear saying to myself almost at every line,

Cedite, Romani scriptores, cedite, Graii;

for I do not remember to have read anything of its kind that ever equalled or came near it. If any of the phrases seem not to carry the same strength of colouring you have painted all her other great and good qualities with, will not that of—sine levitate pulchra—be reckoned of that sort? But this said with all submission to better judgments. As I conclude the whole performance will be published, and that you will be known to be the author of it, I would not have any article of it liable to be questioned. But whether (I ask pardon of her Manes if I am in the wrong, for I mean well to the honour of her memory)—Christianam religionem sincere sancteque coluit—is an attribute that will be allowed her by many of your readers, is a problem I shall not enter into the discussion of, but leave it to be so well tempered by your prudence, that it may meet with as little incredulity, as I sincerely think every other branch of her character deserves. . . ." [1]

Next Hervey mentioned the epitaph to Algarotti on January 15/26, (Murray series); and to Mrs. Digby six weeks later he spoke of both the Latin and English versions. Both are mentioned by Croker (i, xlix, ed. 1848). The letters follow.

TO DR. MIDDLETON [2] *St. James's, February 4, 1738*

I can say, Dear Sir, with great truth that I never receive a letter from you without being both pleased and instructed. All you say in your last is perfectly just; except that part of it where you make me the Lucullus of the Epitaph I sent you, since his faults, according to your own account, in the Greek tongue were voluntary, and I confess mine whatever they are in the Latin are absolutely the effect of ignorance. However that you may not think me more to blame than I really am, I will come to you as my Father Confessor, tho' not with auricular, with this ocular confession and tell you the whole naked history about this epitaph. There was one on Card. Mazarin, soon after the Queen's death, printed in one of the weekly journals, and some part of it, most cruelly, unjustly and infamously, by the usual method of Italics, applied to her. The K., with great truth, said she deserved one of a greatly different kind. I took the hint, and a few days after brought him this. His eyes were the first after

[1] This letter is mentioned in the 1884 ed. of Croker (iii, 334). The Editor added: "Lord Hervey, however, adhered to the statement and translated it in his own English version, 'The Christian religion she firmly believed and strictly practised.' The truth, I suppose is, that she read and argued herself into a very low and cold species of Christianity."

[2] Ickworth. In a separate volume of letters to Dr. Middleton.

my own that saw it; but upon his liking it, from a partiality to the subject and not the depravity of his taste, I desired before he showed it to anybody that he would let me submit it to Dr. Friend.[1] I did so. Dr. Friend kept it five days, and sent it me back, with some corrections merely verbal, some of which I took, and some I rejected . . . Thus corrected, the K. had a copy and the Duke another. The Duke gave some copies; and from one of those I suppose it got into print. The copy from which it was printed was not quite a perfect one, but had I corrected it when I sent it to you, it would have discovered what till I had your opinion of it I wished to conceal. That it is not in what the critics call in a lapidary style, I am very sensible; but what I meant was rather to write her character under the name of an Epitaph, than to write what should have all the privileges of style to be called an Epitaph. It was written to please a fond husband, not an uninterested reader. It succeeded in that design; and in what I did not design, I assure you I am very indifferent whether it succeeds or no. But if you would oblige me, send me your criticisms, just as you would have criticised it had it been Doctor Friend's. So much for the Epitaph. . . .

The Latin Epitaph is clearly that printed by T. Cooper, 1738, as *Epitaphium Reginæ Carolinæ*. It is in folio, 3 pages, and is in the *British Museum*. No attribution to Lord Hervey is given, either on the printed copy or in the General Index; but it compares exactly with the words quoted in the subsequent letter to Dr. Middleton.

The English Epitaph mentioned in the letter to Mrs. Digby must be the one which was printed in *Gentleman's Magazine*, 1737, p. 759. "Written ex tempore by Lord H—— ; on the melancholy News of her Majesty's Death.

While ev'ry heart bemoans the widow'd land,
And George, in sympathy, our tears demand,

. . . .

Here lies inclos'd—Tremble, ye great and high!
As much of human greatness as could die:
Yet think not, mournful reader, aught amiss,
She's gone to heavenly joys and endless bliss;
She's gone from care and pain to peace above,
From George, that's first below, to him that's first above."

[1] Dr. Robert Freind. (*See ante*, p. 161.)

TO DR. MIDDLETON *St. James's, February 14, 1737/38*[1]

The King has kept me above tonight so much later than ordinary, that I have only time to obey your commands in sending the enclosed, and to tell you that with regard to the *Principissa* and *Regina Consors*, that my Epitaph till *Orta Splendida* is a verbal copy of the inscription which by order of Council is engraved on the Queen's coffin[2]; and that a majority of that respectable body should not write the most classical Latin is not extraordinary. I hope their elegance and accuracy in English makes up for that defect. . . .

TO COUNT ALGAROTTI

St. James's, Jan. 15/26, 1737/38[3]

The letter I received from you, my dear Friend, from Milan about three weeks ago, found me in such real affliction for the death of the Queen, that I could not think of giving you sooner the trouble of my thanks; and though real affliction be a term as often lightly made use of, and as often prostituted as that of a real friendship or real love, yet I assure you what I felt for her gave me a full right to express myself in those words. I know too the ridicule that generally attends an affectation of personal friendship for crowned heads; but you are so well acquainted with the manner in which I lived with her, that, if she had personal merit, you are sensible I must have had opportunities of finding it out; and if so, it would be a very hard fate indeed upon princes, if from those with whom they lived in the same familiarity as if they had been private persons, they might not expect the same warmth of gratitude, which if they had been

[1] Ickworth.

[2] In *Gentleman's Magazine*, 1737 (p. 766) appears, "The Inscription on the Plate of her late Majesties' coffin, on silver washed with gold". This, however, does not tally in any way with Lord Hervey's Epitaph, which, if the order of the Council was carried out, should also be on the Queen's coffin. Both the present Dean of Westminster and Mr. Laurence Tanner, Librarian of the Abbey, the only two survivors of those who were present when the vault was last opened in January 1943, inform me that they had no recollection or note of any inscription on the marble sarcophagus.

[3] Murray series.

private persons they might have claimed in return. Upon my word, if I knew her, she was a thorough great, wise, good and agreeable woman ; and the distinctions with which she always honoured me, joined to the satisfaction I had in her company, makes me look upon her death to be as great a loss to my interest as to my pleasure, and makes my heart regret the loss of her as much as my vanity or my ambition.

I can at present talk to you on no other subject, and for that reason I send you a Latin epitaph upon her, which the King has honoured with great approbation. As it is written by one I love, and upon one I love, so perhaps I may be partial in thinking it worth transcribing and sending so far. Give me your opinion of it freely. If the character is as well drawn as it is just, and that the things it contains are as well said as truly said, I am sure you will approve it. Adieu.

TO MRS. DIGBY *St. James's, March 4th, 1737/38*[1]

Whether, my dear Cousin, you thought the epitaph mine because you liked it, or whether you liked it because you thought it mine, I am either way pleased, and either way obliged to you. I sent it to you without telling you I was the author, that I might know your real thoughts, and am glad to find them what they are. The Latin cost me great pains, but the English none ; for Truth furnished the thoughts, and my heart felt too much for words not to flow from me on that occasion as naturally and as plentifully as my tears.[2] Grief and anger have that one quality in common with one another, that they can make people eloquent who are so in no other situation. I do not wonder you can have no idea of her manner of passing her last twelve days.

[1] Ickworth.

[2] In a letter to Count Algarotti of March 6/17, 1738, Hervey wrote : " As to the Epitaph I sent you, I am so unused to writing Latin, that it is no wonder I should not write it correctly ; and if you ask me then why I attempted writing it at all, my answer is, I was put down to it by one whom I neither ought nor desire to refuse. And for the length, my design was to draw a character of the Queen, and not merely to fit the size of a stone or confine myself to the lapidary style. . . ."

It is not only inconceivable, but incredible to anybody who had not ocular proof of it. I myself who knew her well, who knew her temper, her strength and greatness of mind, her patience, her resignation, her mildness, and her indifference to life, could yet have had no conception of her firmness in bodily pain and such acute sufferings as she showed; knowing the whole time she must die, preserving her senses to the last moment, and behaving to the last as if she had nothing to regret in the place she was leaving, and nothing to apprehend in that she was going to. Let those who used to call her affability, falseness, to say her piety was grimace, and her easiness in all situations put on, now blush, if shame can enter into such compositions, for all their rancorous insinuations and malicious lies on the best and greatest, not only woman, but human creature that ever was created. If anything could give me an exalted idea of that dignity of our species which I so often hear of, it would be having known this excellent Queen. But as I know none of the species equal to her, and so few anything like her, it only gives me a greater contempt for the odious herd; when by reflecting on what she was, I see what they might be, and by considering them, reflect on what they are. The words of Solomon might be justly written on her tomb, and should be engraved on adamant, to tell posterity in indelible characters: "Tho many daughters may have done virtuously, yet she excelled them all." And, *if they shall prosper that loved her*, I am sure I can never know a misfortune after the loss of her, any more than I can ever know one equal to it.

The silly story you have heard about the King's fancying he saw her, is quite without foundation. What you have often heard me say about her daughter, the Princess Caroline, is strictly true; and her whole behaviour on this, as well as every other occasion, shows her nature does not degenerate from that of her mother, and that her head and her heart are capable of valuing and following the great and amiable example which nobody can value enough or follow too closely.

I am too much taken up with the subject of this letter to care much for any other, and shall therefore refer you to the newspapers for what is called the great affairs and occurrences of the world ; and from them you will learn the Parliament is deliberating about Peace or War with Spain ; that the Duke of Bolton is come back to St. James's, that Lord Archibald Hamilton is turned out of the Admiralty, that to-morrow Sir Robert Walpole owns his marriage with Mrs. Skeritt, and on Monday is to bring her to Court. Adieu.

TO STEPHEN FOX *Kensington, Aug. 10, 1738*[1]

You see by the date of this letter with what punctuality I obey your commands ; and, if you could see my heart, you would as plainly perceive how much I regret the never having it in my power to show how much I wish to please or serve you but in such worthless trifles. As to the rest of your orders, sending news, etc.—I am absolutely impotent. That the Dukes of St. Albans and Marlborough, Lord Rochford and Lord Falconbridge are to kiss hands to day for the Bedchamber is only news to you as to the day, for the fact sine die you knew before you left London. Peace and War are at present the topics of all conversation both public and private, both of the high and the low, the rich and the poor ; and it is generally believed that Peace will at last be the result of all our consultations, armaments and negociations ; though none but the inhabitants of the Sanctum Sanctorum of politics, the Cabinet-Priests, who eat the shew-bread of Counsel, are yet acquainted with the particulars. The Duke of Richmond, you know, was sent for up to assist at these Mysteries, and so was every other Cabinet Counsellor in what part soever of England he was resident or itinerant. The D. of Grafton was called from dispensing fate to partridges and heath-poults, to fix that of Spain and England ; but will, I fancy, be more merciful by sea than by land. I dare indulge myself no farther on this subject, for fear of saying more than I either should or would.

You will see a very remarkable story in the *Prints* of a highwayman who was pursued two days ago and finding himself so beset that he could not escape, alighted off his horse just by

[1] Melbury.

Fulham, swore he would shoot the first of about thirty people who should advance to lay hold of him, and then clapped both his pistols at once to his own head, fired them, and died on the spot. They say he was a distiller, who had formerly lived in a thriving, creditable way, till ruin'd by the Gin Act. He took to this method of robbing to maintain himself and his family. There is no country in the world but England, where so many clowns are heroes, and so many men of quality clowns.

FINIS

APPENDIX A

Verses from Lord Hervey to Lady Hervey, in England.

These verses, written in 1729, commence on p. 35; and the final lines finish on the following page. Only the portion which deals with Hervey's relations with his wife, to whom they are addressed, are there printed, showing also his facility for writing in prose and especially in verse. The remainder are placed here, and recount the adventures of Hervey and Stephen Fox on their return from Florence to Lyons.

Persuant then to my design,
From Florence, fam'd for silks and wine,
To Pisa first we bend our course,
And vile the inn, tho' I've found worse.
Our beds were musty, coarse our fare,
And gnats extremely busy there.
A Gothic church, and leaning tow'r,
Are all the sights in Pisa's store.
Thence to Leghorn, so prosp'rous made
By strangers, industry and trade,
A fair of bus'ness here you see,
As if they boasted liberty,
And, like their port, themselves were free.
Throughout all Italy beside,
What does one find but want and pride?
Farces of superstitious folly,
Decay, distress and melancholy,
The havoc of despotic pow'r,
A county rich, its' owners poor,
Unpeopled towns, and lands untill'd,
Bodies uncloath'd, and mouths unfill'd.
The nobles miserably great,
In painted domes, and empty state,
Too proud to work, too poor to eat.
No arts the meaner sort employ,
They nought improve, nor ought enjoy.
Each clown from mis'ry grows a Saint,
He prays from idleness, and fasts from want.

Finding the fickle wind averse,
The vessels bad, the weather worse;
And quite impatient to pursue
My way to England, and to you;
After consulting dearest Ste.,
To stay no longer both agree;
So back by land o'er Pisa's plain,
In thunder, lightning, and in rain,
(Just like the witches in Macbeth,
Or good old Lear on the wide heath)
To Lerici we take our road:
But there we made no long abode;
We supp'd, and then to bed we went,
Not for our rest, but punishment,
For fleas and bugs kept such a rout,
That Pisa's gnats were nothing to't.
We scratch'd, and toss'd, and burn'd all night;
And sleepless saw revolving light,
Which at the earliest peep of day,
Into the Chamber where we lay,
Found an unintercepted way,
For door or window there was none,
To keep out either wind or sun.
We rose, embark'd, and with fair gale,
Clear sky, and a smooth sea set sail.
But soon, as we had clear'd the bay,
And got a league or two to sea,
The weather chang'd, the wind grew high,
The sea grew rough and dark the sky.
And now began, through all the crew,
Each head to turn, each mouth to ——,
(You know the rhyme, and 'tis more clean
To let you guess at what I mean.)
But to revenge th' affront, the sea,
Pour'd such a torrent back on me,
That from my foot up to my head,
I had not one unwetted thread.
My cloaths were changing, when old John
Cry'd, " Speak, or else, by G—d, we're gone;
" Pray look, nay 'tis no laughing matter!
" Her very sails are under water.

"Make 'em, my Ld., get nearer shore,
"Furl all the sails, and ply the oar.
"Damn their feluccas; such a boat
"In such a sea a'n't worth a groat."
I took his counsel; and in short,
At Genoa got safe in port.
And as sick drunkard and —— rake,
Swear (whilst they're suff'ring) that they'll take
A bottle and a w—— no more,
So Ste. and I, our fright not o'er,
And seeming still on billows tos't,
Resolve no more to quit the coast,
But sleep on dry land, in a sure inn,
And go to Lyons round by Turin.
As soon as each had fill'd his belly,
With heart'ning soup and vermicelli;
Still giddy, jaded and half-dead,
For want of rest, we hast to bed,
Nor wanted rocking, for we soon
Slept, and ne'er wak'd 'till next day noon.
When Genoa three days we'd been in,
To rest our bones and wash our linen;
Tho' much contented with our lodging,
We grew impatient to be jogging.
With ortolans the Consul fed us,
And ev'ry day to sights he led us.
He did the honours of the town,
As well as all had been his own.
And of all countries I have cross'd,
A fairer city none can boast,
By streets of marble beauteous made,
By situation apt for trade.

Oh! Freedom! Benefactress fair!
How happy who thy blessings share!
These barren hills, these rocky shores,
Cheer'd by thy smiles, produce such stores;
That plenty flows in ev'ry place,
And gladness sits on ev'ry face;
Whilst Milan's sons, oppress'd by pow'r,
Their fate in Paradise deplore,

Ah ! what avail her fertile plains,
Her olives, vines, and swelling grains ?
A foreign Prince her wealth demands,
Her vintage press'd by foreign hands,
A foreign hand her harvest spoils ;
Vienna fattens on her toils.
Digression this, perhaps you call,
But since I'm in for't, take it all.—
  Our journey hence I need not tell,
'Twas nothing bad, nor nothing well.
  With Coleman [1] and his pretty wife
(Who seems to dread a Florence life),
Behold us then at Turin prating,
We questioning, and they relating
Factions and Parliaments and Court,
What news, what scandal, and what sport !
Treaties and commerce, Peace and War,
Seem'd my friend Ste.'s peculiar care ;
Whilst to your love and merit true,
My sole enquiry was of you.
This joy was mine one day alone,
For lo ! tomorrow Coleman's flown ;
'Twas right. His Embassy asks haste,
For Florence says her Duke cant last.[2]
And if the English dont take care,
Don Carlos [3] shall succeed him there ;
Our peace perhaps may turn to war,
The face of things again may alter,
And Spain once more besiege Gibraltar.
  We, one day more at Turin stay'd,
Whilst to her King,[4] my court I pay'd ;
On whose unkingly, Royal head,
Pallas such partial gifts has shed.
Himself the weight of rule sustains,
He's lov'd by those o'er whom he reigns,
And wears a Crown, yet dont want brains.
By method now I come at last,

[1] Francis Colman, British Minister. *See ante*, p. 89.
[2] Gian Gastone, 7th and last of the Medici Grand-Dukes. He died in 1737.
[3] For Don Carlos, son of Philip V of Spain, *see ante*, pp. 7 8–9.
[4] Victor Amadeus II, King of Sardinia.

To tell you how the Alps we pass'd:
A dreadful journey. I remember,
Twas hardly worse ev'n last November.
Imagine, child! our piteous plight,
No food by day, no rest by night.
How wet, how comfortless, how cold,
We pass'd Mount Sinis [Cenis ?], can't be told.
Impervious to a chaise, we rode
In chairs, eight human creatures load,
Twelve miles beneath our weight they groan,
Five up, five plain-way, and two down.
To name each village where we lay
Is needless sure; but ev'ry day,
Before Aurora op'd the East,
To let out Thetis' nightly guest,
We're haul'd out of our beds to stray
O'er rocks and hills, a tedious way.
Such hills in fabled fights, we're told,
The Giants threw at Gods of old,
Tho' so enormous ev'ry one,
That each a country seems alone
These in full bulk conspicuous rise;
Those lose their summits in the skies:
Whilst this it's form so oddly shrouds,
Its head's in snow, its foot in clouds.
The whole, what scenes romantick crown!
A grove in air, a pendant town.
Here barrenness and plenty join,
For snows surround the rip'ning vine,
Cascades and rivers, flocks and fields,
Each vary'd view promiscuous yields.
Sometimes, o'ertaken by the night,
We climb, by Cynthia's doubtful light,
O'er precipices, such a height,
So steep their sides, the way so straight,
That if Achilles self were there,
Achilles might confess a fear,
But sick or well, where'er I move,
In ev'ry hardship that I prove,
Fidus Achates still is near,
And makes my welfare all his care. . . .

APPENDIX B[1]

Sarah, Duchess of Marlborough's letters on the inheritances of Lord Sunderland and his brother John Spencer

SARAH, DUCHESS OF MARLBOROUGH TO MRS. STRANGWAYS-HORNER, AT THE SPAW [*sic*] *July 14, 1732, Scarborough*[2]

. . . What you heard concerning my Lord Sunderland's marriage is true. I think it a very improper match for a man that might have had any body, without being at all in love with the person, to marry a woman whose father is a mighty ridiculous man,[3] a family of beggars, and all very odd people. The woman herself (as they say, for I have never seen her) has been bred in a very low way and dont know how to behave herself upon any occasion ; not at all pretty, and has a mean, ordinary look. As to the behaviour, if she has any sense, that may mend. But they say she has very bad teeth, which I think is an objection alone in a wife, and they will be sure to grow worse with time.

I am sure 'twill be natural for you to wonder how this could happen, since my Lord Sunderland declared to several of his friends that he was not in love with her. But the truth is, he is a very weak man and is entirely governed by his sister Bateman, who some people say has great talents. But as you have known people, I am confident, whose wit runs away with them, she was so eager for what she imagined was her interest, as not to see that she could have made this match in a more decent way, by letting me be acquainted with it before 'twas quite settled. But as nobody of common sense could think it a proper match for her brother, she ordered it in the most foolish and brutal manner. For had I been acquainted with it, as I ought to have been, I could have only represented against it, and must have seemed satisfied if my Lord Sunderland had insisted upon it; though it could never have been my choice.

My Lady Bateman is an extreme interested woman, and of very ill principles. And though I have done her a great deal of good,

[1] *See ante*, p. 133.

[2] Holland House. The Duchess was taking the waters at Scarborough. Henry Richard, 3rd Lord Holland's remarks on this correspondence may be worth noting. "Very entertaining and characteristic of that violent and spiteful woman."

[3] Thomas, 2nd Lord Trevor. (*See ante*, p. 134.)

as she was my grand-child, and never mentioned any of her faults till she made it impossible for me ever to have any more to do with her, I will tell you now the truth of her character. She is very false and very covetous, and has made this match purely to be her brother's First Minister, and to manage his finances; by which she has got a great deal and hopes to get a good deal more. But that sooner or later may fail, and I am apt to think that she and the wife in some time may fall out about the government of my Lord Sunderland, who, some people will tell you, has sense, generosity, and many good qualities. But this comes chiefly from low flatterers who get by him, and others who are cautious what they say of a man who has so great an estate in prospect. I believe there are a good many that may be deceived from his being very reserved and speaking very little. But his behaviour to me, and his proceeding in this whole matter, shows that he has not sense enough to know what a principle is. He is extremely like his father, violent and ill-natured. But his understanding is infinitely worse; and yet his was far from a good one. But from a great deal of pride and vanity, and weakness in letting himself be cheated by everybody, the present Lord Sunderland is called by many a mighty generous man. And he is so much pleased with that character, that even when I am dead, his debts will be so much increased by his extravagance of all sorts, that till his aunt dies, who may live these thirty years, he will be always taking up money upon hard terms, being only tenant for life in my Lord Marlborough's estate; and his own is but a small one with mortgages upon it.

In replying to earlier letters from the Duchess, with whom Henry Fox was always on good terms, he held out against her abuse of his friend Sunderland, and frankly disagreed with her. The following long letter is her reply.

SARAH, DUCHESS OF MARLBOROUGH TO HENRY FOX

November 23, 1732

. . . You seem to think I have not given a true character [of Lord Sunderland], and therefore I will, in as short a manner as such a thing is capable of being done, set down some facts which all the world know to be true. That for more than thirty years, I have been labouring to serve every one of his family. I begun with his own grandfather,[1] for whom I got £2000 a year pension of Queen Anne,

[1] Robert, 2nd Earl of Sunderland, died in September 1702, a few months after Queen Anne's accession. The pension must have been given earlier.

and paid it to him as long as he lived, myself privately. For he was in such circumstances, that without it he could not support himself even at Althrop. What I did for his father,[1] and what I suffered from his madness, I wont dwell upon, that being most notoriously known. But I will say that I gave great sums to my daughter for her's and his support; and the truth of this was known to all my Lord Sunderland's family by a letter that my dear daughter left at her death to her Lord, naming how much he had had of the money her mother gave her, desiring that my Lord Sunderland would only give the interest of that sum yearly to her eldest son.[2] After my Lady Sunderland's death,[3] I took care of all her children with the same tenderness as if they had been my own. I got a portion and a settlement for that vile woman, my Lady Bateman, which could not have been done without me. Nor was there any hopes of getting so much as justice of her father, when he made that ridiculous match,[4] and had nothing but debts at that time, and an expectation of a house full of children. And I took that occasion to settle all the furniture of Althrop upon the heirs, if there happened to be no debts, that it might not be gutted for the use of a new family. This was lucky, for it happened to save all that was in that house; for my Lord Sunderland had no debts, and that settlement could not be broke into to pay legacies that were more than his effects.

I will say nothing of my care and kindness to Di. Spencer; which most elder brothers that have any honour would have taken very kindly. I looked after the two younger brothers, now living, in sickness and in health. For their father was so unnatural that when they had the small-pox he would not see them, though his face was one entire mark. And some of the children in that sad condition lay beside my bedside. The Duke of Marlborough, who was only their mother's father, had not the same obligation as if a great estate had come down by descent from my Lord Sunderland's ancestors to settle upon that family, and only settled his estate upon the title where it should happen to fall, without making any provision more than as younger children for any of the branches. But thinking it unreasonable that there should be nothing given out of so great an estate to the elder son of any daughter that possessed it, I prevailed with the Duke of Marlborough to give every son as they succeeded a rent

[1] Charles, 3rd Earl (1674–1722). The Duchess's daughter, Anne, was his second wife.

[2] Robert, 4th Earl (1701–29).

[3] In 1716.

[4] Charles, 3rd Earl, married, as his third wife, Judith, daughter of Benjamin Tichborne, in 1717.

charge of £8000 a year, clear of all taxes; and when I died they were to have £20,000 in the same manner. And *this* Lord Sunderland knows; that if it had not been for me, he could have had nothing, but as a younger brother, till the Duchess of Marlborough's death.

You are a judge yourself, who have passed some hours in my company with them, whether my manner with them was uneasy. Other people that have been witnesses of it, I believe, will say, that I courted them as much as if I had been to have been supported by them; and though I can't brag of any comforts they endeavoured to give me, I was resolved to make the best of it, and always treated my Lord Sunderland with great civility and kindness. And as one instance of my manner with him, I beg leave to relate the very last conversation I had with him.

One day he made me a visit, which he was very sparing of; and I took the opportunity of talking to him on marriage, saying that I was very glad he was not so averse to it as he us'd to be, that I had been thinking round the town and country to find a wife for him, but I could not see any that I could recommend. What I wish'd him was a woman with good sense, good humour and good education, of a creditable family, not a flaming beauty, nor an Assembly lady: but she should be genteel and healthy, and for money, 'twas no matter whether she had any thing or nothing. I believe most people wou'd have made some obliging expression in answer to such a conversation from a grandmother. But his good Lordship only reply'd with a stiff air and disagreeable voice, "*I won't marry without telling you.*" And having never heard a word of Lady Bateman's design, I was so stupid not to think that he designed it; but that 'twas only his disagreeable manner. So I dropped that discourse, talked of other things; and we parted very civilly.

After this I saw him no more. For he came one day when I had a violent fever upon me, had been blood'd and blistered, and could see nobody. And upon my sending an excuse to him and the Duchess of Manchester, who were in the next room, that I was in so much pain that I could not see them; without expressing the least concern for my illness, his Lordship was so reasonable and good as to take that opportunity of acquainting me that he was determined to marry Mrs. Trevor: that he had got her consent and her father's; and that he was going the next morning to his sister Bateman's at Totteridge, concerning the business of his marriage. As odd as this may seem to some people, 'tis literally true that he sent me this message exactly as I tell it.

After this, finding by several that he had declared he was not in love with this woman, I writ to him as soon as I was able, to show him how improper a match it was for him ; and it was such a letter that I don't care if it was printed. 'Tis what I show to everybody ; likewise his answer to me, and my reply upon his monstrous letter to me. But they are too long for the post ; and therefore I will only transcribe two paragraphs, the conclusions of my Lord Sunderland's letter to me, and mine to him upon it :—

Copied out of my Lord Sunderland's letter.

"I have nothing more to add, but to assure your Grace that this is the last time I shall ever trouble you by letter or conversation. I am, your Grace's grandson,

Sunderland."

The whole letter was of a piece with that.

My answer to that paragraph :—

"You end that you are my grandson, which is indeed a very melancholy truth, but very lucky for you. For all the world except yourself is sensible that had you not been my grandson, you would have been in as bad a condition as you deserve to be.

S. Marlborough."

After this, having no mind to live ill with John Spencer,[1] I sent for him, read his brother's letter and my own to him, and gave him an account of all that had passed. But I could not get him so much as in a look to find the least fault with his brother's monstrous behaviour to me. I showed him at the same time what I had settled upon him, which amounted to more than £300,000. Then I asked him if I had not been mighty kind to him, which he acknowledged to be true : adding, that if he expected to be my heir, he must live with me as my son, which I own did imply that he was not to correspond with his brother. Andwe parted without more anger than my telling him I wished him very happy, and that I was very glad that he had a better fortune of his own than any younger brother. He was then in so ill a state of health that he could not walk cross a room easily. However his sister Bateman persuaded him to go a

[1] John Spencer (1708–46), father of 1st Viscount and Earl Spencer. This brotherly attitude is corroborated by Lord Perceval (*Egmont*, i, 279), who wrote that he thereby gained great reputation. "No sum," said Spencer, "would make him desert his brother and break his friendship."

journey, in contempt of all I had said, to celebrate that great wedding;[1] and she took great pains to make my Lady Russell[2] go; but that failed, which I was glad of for her sake more than my own, when I heard of it, for I never spoke a word to my Lady Russell about it.

Since the beginning of the business, I have writ several letters to John Spencer, and have explained that matter concerning the seeing his brother, giving up that point, and showing him he was lucky to have his interest and his honour go together, as to his behaviour towards me. But he is governed by the worst woman that ever was born; and I have been forced to strike him quite out of my will.

I know 'twill be natural for you to ask on this account, what could possibly make my Lady Bateman bring so much mischief upon her family, when she might have made her brother do the same thing in a decent manner. For had he said he liked her so much that his happiness depended on the match, I must have complied with it, as I did in the case of my Lord Blandford,[3] though I could never have made it my choice to have married a grandson into a mean, ridiculous family; the father of the woman, between a madman and a fool, and the grandfather, one of the most violent prosecutors that ever my Lord Sunderland's grandfather had, who left him such an estate.

I believe there are yet several people in the world that have honour enough not to have made such an alliance without the excuse of being in love; which was the only thing he could have said for it. But he took frequent occasions of declaring he was not at all in love; and though I detest as much as anyone living any falsehood, yet I think upon that occasion I would have lied. But the truth is, Lady Bateman governs him as much as the Duchess of Cleveland does her husband; and she certainly had money for making this match. And though she is far from being a fool, she could not see the best way of doing it, from the fears she had of a disappointment, if it were known before she had made it sure.

This is a very exact account of this whole matter, without the least flourish on my own account or aggravation of their crimes. And I desire to be blessed or punished at my last hour, as I have given a true relation of it.

I never yet met with any of my Lord Sunderland's acquaintance that are not ashamed for him. But you have said he is neither foolish nor worthless. And yet I am confident if I should send you such

[1] The wedding took place at East Barnet, on May 23, 1732.

[2] Lady John Russell (Lady Di. Spencer).

[3] (*See ante*, p. 79.)

a account of anybody without naming them, you would start with horror; and indeed the best excuse I can make for him is, that he is so simple that he don't know what a principle is.

SARAH, DUCHESS OF MARLBOROUGH TO MRS. STRANGWAYS-HORNER

March 1 1732[/*33*]

Madam, . . .

The Duchess of Bedford [1] is married with the greatest prospect of happiness that can be in all respects. She is now extremely well in her health; and the loss of her child is no more than what one calls a miscarriage, and occasioned only from want of experience, which makes young people think they can do anything. And the cause of that misfortune proceeded from being thrown out of a chaise she was driving herself, when she was about 6 months gone with child; which accident made it impossible for the child to live, though it was born alive. . . . But thank God, she is now as well as ever she was in her life; and I daresay, when she is next with child, will be as careful, as she was at first otherwise. . . .

. . . I gave you formerly an account of the indecent manner of my grandson's behaviour to me on his marriage. Since that, it appears that he was sold by his sister, Lady Bateman, and her husband: and they prevailed with him to make settlements on his marriage, more infamous than anything I ever heard of. His wife, Mrs. Trevor's real portion was £25,000, £10,000 of which is quite sunk; which, to be sure, is divided amongst those that were useful in making this match. For, without self-interest, his own sister could have no interest to serve Mrs. Trevor. And the portion she has is only £15,000, of which not one shilling is to be paid, or the interest for it, till after my Lord Trevor's death, who I believe can't be above forty years old, except the interest of £1300 Bank Stock, which amounts to about £80 a year. That great sum, my Lord Sunderland is to receive while he lives; but that, and the whole fortune before mentioned, when the father dies, is settled upon Mrs. Trevor's younger children; and my Lord Sunderland can never have a shilling of it, unless his wife dies and leaves no children at all. For this they have tied my Lord Sunderland not to have the power of one shilling of his own estate; and have settled, by cutting off entails, all the Sunderland estate and Althrop, to pay Mrs Trevor £2,000 a year, free of

[1] Lady John Russell had become Duchess of Bedford in October 1732.

Parliamentary taxes and deductions whatsoever; which, with the prior settlements of former marriages, takes up the whole estate. But her jointure is to be released, if my Lord Sunderland lives longer than his aunt Marlborough (which he may very well happen not to do). But if he does, he is tied to give her £4,000 a year, in the same manner he has settled £2,000. And if he should die and leave sons, all the Marlborough estate will go to them, and the Sunderland estate likewise, which the Duke of Marlborough gave to John Spencer, the younger brother, and which really was no more in proportion than what younger brothers usually have, considering the vast estate which he gave to the elder brother. This is being very ungrateful and dishonourable to his grandfather, who provided for him so greatly. But it will certainly be the case, if that happens which may happen; for the Duchess of Marlborough's life, I think, is as good as Lord Sunderland's from some reasons that I know, though she may be about 23 years older than he. Besides this, they have settled £600 a year pin-money at present; and £800, if my Lord Sunderland lives to be Duke of Marlborough. But what is yet more extraordinary in this account is, that my Lord Sunderland declared to several of his friends before he made this match, that she was nothing like handsome and that he was not in love with her, which, I think, would have been the best excuse he could have made for marrying into a contemptible family, the chief of which cheated his grandfather by a false mortgage of £10,000; and by all his actions in the public did what he could to show that he would have murdered that grandfather, who has made my Lord Sunderland what he is. Notwithstanding this relation, which I solemnly protest to you that I know to be all true, Mr Fox will tell you that my Lord Sunderland has a very good understanding and is a man of the most nice honour. . . .

APPENDIX C

Sets of verses sent to Henry Fox, on Feb. 8, 1734, by Lord Hervey.[1]

(*a*) THE LORD H-R—Y'S FIRST SPEECH IN THE HOUSE OF LORDS [2]

My Lords,
Tho' when I stand upright,
You take me for a skein of silk;
And think me with a face so white,
A perfect curd of ass's milk.

Yet from the rosie gates of breath,
When painted prose more quaint than song
Breaks through this thin-set hedge of teeth,
I shall delight you all day long.

As of old Rome's Imperial dames,
Whoever was the boldest ramp,
The Army grac'd with sounding names,
And styl'd her *Mother* of the *Camp*.

So I, the softest, prettiest thing,
This honourable House affords,
Come here by order of the King,
Created *Lady* of the *Lords*.

To teach hereditary fools,
And the rude race of elder brothers,
To dress and vote by newer rules,
And make you gentle as your mothers.

Then for this Speech (our Gracious K——'s),
I move (as in my sphere it lies),
To say the best-bred, sweetest things,
That in my soul I can devise.

[1] *See ante*, p. 191. All these are in Holland House MSS.

[2] Lord Hervey was called up to the House of Lords in 1733. Apparently this is unknown elsewhere. It is not discoverable in the Bodleian Library and we have been unable to find it in the British Museum. There may, however, be copies at Ickworth of all three sets.

"HORACE TO BARINE", IMITATED

As ev'ry one my talents knows,
  Observe my Lords how I shall serve you,
I'll turn Swift's satire into prose,
  It shall be praise from my Lord H——.

(*b*) HORACE TO BARINE, IMITATED TO LD. HERVEY. BOOK 2. ODE 8 [1]

If for thy breach of sense and truth
Thou should'st but lose another tooth,
  Or spots thy finger stain;
Tho' for thy rhymes I've often paid,
Been often bauk'd as often read,
  Perhaps I'd read again.

But thou'rt successful in thy crimes
Unpunish'd, spun so many times
  False verse from thy John-Trot-head,
You issue forth the publick care
Of pamphlet-shop and bookseller,
  So very much your noted.

It well becomes thee for Fame's sake,
Thy elder brother's urn to take,
  With keenest irony;
And then revile in gallant words,
The starry sphere of noble Lords,
  Whose honours never die.

Sapho who might have answer'd thee,
But smiles at all thy ribaldry,
  Centlivre, Haywood [2] laugh:

[1] Title in Hervey's writing. A copy of this is in the Bodleian. We have been unable to find it in the British Museum.

[2] Well-known literary ladies of doubtful reputation. Suzanna Centlivre (1667–1723) dramatist and actress under the name of S. Carroll, married Queen Anne's cook, Joseph Centlivre, and wrote many comedies. It is a coincidence to find, in the notice on her in *Dict. Nat. Biog.*, a suggestion that she married early in life a nephew of Sir Stephen Fox, the father of the Fox brothers. Later in the article we find another note stating that her father was "one Rawkins". Now Rawkins was the name of Sir Stephen's maternal uncle, so there may be more in the story of some relationship with the Foxes than appears on the surface.

Mrs. Eliza Haywood (1693–1756, née Fowler), novelist and actress, was satirised in Pope's *Dunciad.*

And ev'n from Swift's all-cutting pen,
(Ne'er whetted on his desk in vain)
Perfidious boy, you're safe.

To thee, false fair-one of the Court,
It's fools, both young and old, resort,
And praise thy pretty face.
Of thee the bridegroom jealous grows,
The brided virgin breaks her vows,
For thy perfum'd embrace.

(*c*) AN APOLOGY FOR PRINTING "THE NOBLEMAN'S EPISTLE"[1]

As in the gay circle Lord Fanny recited,
The nymphs and the swains of the Court were delighted.
He audibly read 'em his late famous letter,
Which he, to dear Doctor, had sent for a better.
The well-judging hearers, full quick of discerning,
Approve his smooth metre, brisk wit and nice learning,
His words so well chosen, his proverbs so pat in,
His laudable hate and neglect of old Latin;
So poignant his rallies, so keen the ill-nature
That shines thro' the turns of his delicate satire:
The whole so compleat—to his Lordship they hinted,
A poem so sprightly deserv'd to be printed.
O thou! whate'er title best please thee, Lord Fanny,
Or Hebe, or Iris, Narcissus, or Ganny,
Or fragrant Adonis, or Fair Maid of Dian,
Who cans't rouse the proud Patriot, or chase the fierce Lion.
Hail, victor in satire! hail, hero in rhymes!
Sworn foe to all dullness, and scourge of the times!
Avenger of insults from dull pamphleteers,
Devourer of critics, and poets, and p—rs!
How vast is that mind, unassisted by art,
Such treasures of learning, like thine, to impart:
No study pedantic has tainted thy knowledge,
Nor strong of the lamp didst thou e'er smell at College,

[1] Title in Hervey's writing. A copy of this is in the Bodleian. We have not been able to discover it in the British Museum. "The Nobleman's Epistle" was Lord Hervey's copy of verses to "a Doctor of Divinity, Dr. Sherwin. (*See ante*, p. 177.)

Thy learning and wit shine with unborrow'd grace,
And thy verse is thy own, like the bloom on thy face.
When you woman first knew—if e'er woman you knew;
When your beard first appear'd—if your beard ever grew;
As Achilles rough Chiron's, you shook off friend's tramel,
And, a female in beauty, were counted a female.
Mid the chaste Maids of Honour, a sister-maid acted,
And all the grave precepts of Chiron neglected,
Till the dangers that threaten'd thy Country, call'd forth
Thy vigour, and courage, and masculine worth.
O! then, high-inspir'd, what assistance you brought her,
How great thy revenge! Oh! what terrible slaughter!
While beneath thy white hand groan'd the wide spreading plain,
And Thames, more than Simo'is, ran red with it's slain.
But now, with Death sated, you quit the grim field,
And the hero confess'd to the critic you yield.
With replies and smart comments you sting every word,
Nor your pen's less tremendous and sharp than your sword.
By thee, we have fairly discover'd a cheat,
That Pope has not learning, nor judgment, nor wit;
For well hast thou prov'd it, that all he hath wrote
In Homer translating, was what Homer thought.
Thus Mars, by stout Diomed's lancet, was wounded:
Thus triumph'd the mortal, thus the God was confounded.
So Midas impartially judg'd from Apollo
The prize in dispute—so this pattern you follow;
And doubtless of Pope, thus, a judgment you make well,
Since Phœbus and he are in singing but equal:
O! Had I the skill of each sage in the law,
In the grant made to Cibber, to find out a flaw,[1]
As grander thy merit and juster thy claim,
I'd amend the great fiat, and put in thy name.

[1] Cibber had been appointed Poet Laureate in 1730.

APPENDIX D

Tit for Tat[1]

Hervey wrote (*see ante*, p. 195): " I sent you enclosed *Tit for Tat*, which is suppressed on account of the eight lines on the Queen, and reprinted without them. This copy is therefore precious ; keep it."

The portion of this version which has been altered (on p. 4 of this first edition) runs as below. There are also small changes in a number of the lines throughout the broadsheet. Four obscene lines in the 8th and last page, referring to Hervey and Voltaire, are omitted altogether. We print the two versions side by side.

Unexpurgated version	*Expurgated version*
See, Sir, these staring things in Ermin,	See, Sir, these staring things in E——,
That huff and strut to frighten Vermin.	That huff and strut to frighten Vermin ;
This Lady fair,[2] with Harpy's Claws, Who all things to her centre draws ; And sways with universal Rule, Yet keeps the Secret from the Fool.[3]	*Omitted.*
This M—r that cant indite,	A S——n great that can't indite,
These Sec—ries, that can't write :	Those S—— that can't write :
These B—ps pawning Votes and Souls,	Some people pawning V—s and Souls
These men, made great, because they're Fools ;	Some men made great, because they're Fools ;
These tearing military Blades,	*Those* tearing military Blades,
Whose Courage lies in their Cockades ;	Whose Courage lies in their Cockades ;
(Or a Court Paradox by urging)	(Or a new Paradox by urging)
These Maidens six,[4] without one Virgin.	*The* maidens six, without one V——.

[1] Holland House. The expurgated edition is clearly intended to soften down all references to the Court and to public figures.

[2] Queen Caroline.

[3] King George II.

[4] The six Maids of Honour. Some lines entitled *Six Maidens* have been recently printed by the late Mr. Norman Ault, in his *New Light on Pope*. The manuscript is in the Portland Papers, at Longleat ; and Lord Bath has given us leave to quote from them. Mr. Ault wrote that it probably dated from 1732, and that it is certainly from Pope's pen. He said : " The poem is, without

Unexpurgated version	*Expurgated version*
Or told him, how you fool away In Show or Nonsense, Night and Day ;	Or told him, how you fool away In Show and Nonsense, Night an Day ;
One noisy, silly Scene of chatt'ring, Lying, swearing, cringing, flatt'ring ; The same dull Round you each day prance, Like Poet *Bayes'* grand jumbling Dance ; Where Atheists, B—ps, J—es, Knaves, Make one continued Group of Slaves : . . .	*Omitted.*

the slightest doubt, a squib on Frederick, Prince of Wales and his supposed intrigues with the six Maids of Honour to his mother Queen Caroline."

" A Tower[a] there is, where six Maidens do dwell,
This Tow'r it belongs to the Dev'l in Hell ;
. . . .
. . . .
There Mordaunt, Fitzwilliams, etc. remain ;
(I promised I never would mention Miss Vane).[b]
Ev'n Carteret and Meadows, so free from desires,
Are lumped with ye rest of these charming Hell-fires.

O ! sure to King George, 'tis a dismal disaster,
To see his own maids serve a new Lord and Master.
Yet this, like their old one, for nothing will spare,
And treateth them all, like a Prince of the Air."

a Windsor Castle.
b The Vane intrigue was then at its height.

INDEX

THE usual abbreviations are used. Where the name is mentioned both in the text and in the notes, *and n* is employed; if the name only appears in the notes the numeral is in italics. Members of the peerage follow one another in chronological rotation, irrespective of their Christian names. A wife always appears next to her husband's name. Square brackets are used for explanations; round brackets to denote alternative spellings, as used by Lord Hervey, and change of name.

A

B

C

D

G

H

I

J

K

Q

R

Y

HIGHGATE
INSTITUTION
LITERARY & SCIENTIFIC